MEDIEVAL AND RENAISSANCE CLOTHING AND TEXTILES

TEXTILES OF THE VIKING NORTH ATLANTIC

MEDIEVAL AND RENAISSANCE
CLOTHING AND TEXTILES

ISSN 2044–351X

Series Editors
Robin Netherton
Gale R. Owen-Crocker

This series focuses on the study and interpretation of dress and textiles throughout England and Europe, from the early medieval period to the sixteenth century. It seeks to bring together research from a wide variety of disciplines, including language, literature, art history, social history, economics, archaeology, and artifact studies. The editors welcome submissions that combine the expertise of academics working in this area with the more practically based experience of re-enactors and re-creators, offering fresh approaches to the subject.

The series is associated with the annual journal
Medieval Clothing and Textiles.

Proposals or queries should be sent in the first instance to the editors or to the publisher, at the addresses given below; all submissions will receive prompt and informed consideration.

Ms. Robin Netherton, robin@netherton.net

Professor Gale R. Owen-Crocker, gale.owencrocker@ntlworld.com

Boydell & Brewer Limited, PO Box 9, Woodbridge, Suffolk

Previous volumes in this series are listed at the back of this volume

TEXTILES OF THE VIKING NORTH ATLANTIC

ANALYSIS, INTERPRETATION, RE-CREATION

Edited by
ALEXANDRA LESTER-MAKIN *and*
GALE R. OWEN-CROCKER

THE BOYDELL PRESS

© Contributors 2024

All Rights Reserved. Except as permitted under current legislation
no part of this work may be photocopied, stored in a retrieval system,
published, performed in public, adapted, broadcast,
transmitted, recorded or reproduced in any form or by any means,
without the prior permission of the copyright owner

First published 2024
The Boydell Press, Woodbridge

ISBN 978-1-83765-013-2

The Boydell Press is an imprint of Boydell & Brewer Ltd
PO Box 9, Woodbridge, Suffolk IP12 3DF, UK
and of Boydell & Brewer Inc.
668 Mt Hope Avenue, Rochester, NY 14620-2731, USA
website: www.boydellandbrewer.com

A CIP catalogue record for this book is available
from the British Library

The publisher has no responsibility for the continued existence or accuracy of URLs for external
or third-party internet websites referred to in this book, and does not guarantee that any content
on such websites is, or will remain, accurate or appropriate

To my parents, James and Rowena, who gave me a love of history, textiles and embroidery, and taught me the enjoyment and power of learning.

A L-M

For my granddaughter, Eleanor Rose Crocker, born 10 August 2023.

GRO-C

Contents

List of Illustrations	ix
List of Contributors	xii
Preface	xv
Introduction	1
Note on Old Norse Characters	9

PART I: TEXTILES AND THEIR INTERPRETATION

1. Sheep, Wool, and Fleece Processing: Where It All Began   13
   Carol Christiansen

2. Potential Insights on Archaeological Textiles: The Nature of Preservation and the Conservator's Eye   30
   Elizabeth E. Peacock

3. King Harald's Grey Cloak: *Vararfeldir* and the Trade in Shaggy Pile Weave Cloaks between Iceland and Norway in the Late Viking and Early Middle Ages   51
   Michèle Hayeur Smith

4. Re-clothing the Inhabitants of Tenth-century Dublin based on Archaeological Evidence   74
   Frances Pritchard

5. The Sensory Archaeology of Early Medieval Fabrics from the North Atlantic   91
   Alexandra Lester-Makin

6. The Function of Written Textiles in the *Íslendingasögur*   109
   Rachel Balchin

7. The Medieval Mantles of Hibernia: Functional Markers of Ethnic Identity   126
   Dolores Kearney

viii CONTENTS

PART II: UNDERSTANDING THROUGH REPLICATING

8. Making the Best of It: Planning Decisions for Reproduction Fabrics   147
   Ruth Gilbert

9. The Value of Intangible Knowledge: How Living History Can Aid
   Experimental Archaeology in Exploring the Past; Iron Age Scandinavian
   Tablet Weaving and *Nalbinding*   157
   Ann Asplund

10. Collaborative Working Practices: Creating and Theorising Sprang   178
    Carol James

11. From Wool to Mitten: When History Comes to Life in Your Hands   199
    Liselotte Öhrling and Anna Josefsson

Glossary   216
Index   219

Illustrations

MAP

Geographical location of sites. © Peter Lorimer — xvi

FIGURES

1.1 Shetland ewe with primitive traits. © Carol Christiansen — 14

1.2 A year in the life of a ewe, recorded in her fleece. © Carol Christiansen — 20

1.3 Fleece staple separation. © Carol Christiansen — 25

1.4 Shetland nineteenth-century woolcombs. © Carol Christiansen — 26

3.1 Diagram of the method for inserting the pile into a textile. From Else Guðjónsson's own drawing in *Forn röggvarvefnaður*, p. 20 — 55

3.2 Two textile fragments sewn together from Heynes. Photograph: Michèle Hayeur Smith, courtesy of the National Museum of Iceland — 59

3.3 Pile-woven cloth from Stóraborg, Iceland, 1987-369. Photograph: Michèle Hayeur Smith, courtesy of the National Museum of Iceland — 60

3.4 Pile-woven cloth from Borgund Kaupang, Norway. Photograph: Michèle Hayeur Smith, courtesy of the Bryggen Museum, Bergen — 64

3.5 $^{87}Sr/^{86}Sr$ ratios for analysed textiles from the site of Borgund Kaupang. © Michèle Hayeur Smith — 66

4.1 Tabby woven wool cloth with pile from tenth-century Dublin. © Frances Pritchard. Photograph: Michael Pollard — 78

4.2 Seamed fragments of a wool 2 x 2 broken diamond twill bound with a band in 2 x 2 warp chevron twill. ©Frances Pritchard. Photograph: Michael Pollard — 81

4.3 Fine quality wool 2 x 1 diamond twill. © Frances Pritchard. Photograph: Jon Bailey — 82

4.4 Gold-brocaded silk tablet-woven band. © National Museum of Ireland. Photograph: Valerie Dowling — 86

4.5 Detail of a wool 2 x 2 warp chevron twill band. © Frances Pritchard. Photograph: Jon Bailey — 87

ILLUSTRATIONS

4.6   Reconstruction of a woman's clothing in tenth-century Dublin. © Christina Unwin.   88

4.7   Reconstruction of a man's clothing in tenth-century Dublin. © Christina Unwin.   89

7.1   Irish chieftain wearing a calf-length, smooth mantle. *The Image of Irelande*, by John Derrick (London, 1581 Plates)   131

7.2   Group of people wearing shaggy 'Waterford rugg' mantle. *The Image of Irelande*, by John Derrick (London, 1581 Plates)   131

7.3   Mixed English/Hibernian dress. *The Image of Irelande*, by John Derrick (London, 1581 Plates)   132

8.1   Diagram showing the *chaîne opératoire* for length of cloth. © Ruth Gilbert   150

8.2   Two replica cloths based on a 2 x 2 diamond twill textile. Photograph: Ruth Gilbert   155

9.1   First reconstruction attempt of the *nalbound* sock. © Ann Asplund   164

9.2   Second reconstruction attempt of the *nalbound* sock. © Ann Asplund   164

10.1   Interlinking, interlacing and intertwining structures produced when making sprang. Photograph: Carol James   179

10.2   Detail of sprang textile missing its selvedge. Photograph: Carol James   180

10.3   Diagram: loom-woven twill textile and a sprang twill. © Carol James   180

10.4   Krefeld 15204 bonnet and author's replica. Photograph: Carol James   186

10.5   Author's replica of bonnet Krefeld 15204. Photograph: Carol James   187

10.6   Krefeld 15203 pattern. Photograph: Carol James   189

10.7   Author's replica samples of bonnet Krefeld 15203. Photograph: Carol James   189

10.8   Author's re-creation of the Arizona Openwork Shirt. Photograph: Carol James   192

10.9   Working order of Arizona Openwork Shirt motifs. Photograph: Carol James   194

11.1   Inscribed tool from Lödöse, Sweden. Photograph: Liselotte Öhrling   200

11.2   *Nalbound* mitten from Lödöse, Sweden. Photograph: Ian Schemper for Lödöse museum   201

11.3   Spindles and whorls from Lödöse, Sweden. Photograph: David Jeffrey   206

11.4   Amber spindle whorl from Lödöse, Sweden. Photograph: Liselotte Öhrling   210

11.5   *Nalbinding* needle from Lödöse, Sweden. Photograph: Liselotte Öhrling   210

11.6   Pair of mittens made by a course participant. Photograph: Liselotte Öhrling   212

11.7   Anna Josefsson and Liselotte Öhrling, happy *nalbinders*. Photograph: Jessica Randén   213

ILLUSTRATIONS

TABLES

0.1   Timeline of Viking contact and settlement across the North Atlantic.
© Alexandra Lester-Makin   2

3.1   Possible pile-woven textiles from Icelandic and Greenlandic
archaeological sites. Data and table © Michèle Hayeur Smith   57

3.2   Weave types used for producing pile-woven fabrics at Borgund Kaupang,
Norway. Data and table © Michèle Hayeur Smith   63

3.3 ^{87}Sr/^{86}Sr strontium ratios from Borgund Kaupang's pile-woven textiles.
Data and table © Michèle Hayeur Smith.   65

3.4   Selection of possible pile-woven textiles from Folkebibliotek, Trondheim,
Norway. Data and table © Michèle Hayeur Smith   68

7.1   Technical details of St Brigid's mantle, 1866. Compiled by Dolores Kearney   136

7.2   Technical details of St Brigid's mantle, 1935. Compiled by Dolores Kearney   137

7.3   Technical details of the Cloonshannagh mantle. Compiled by Dolores
Kearney   141

The editors, contributors and publisher are grateful to all the institutions and persons
listed for permission to reproduce the materials in which they hold copyright. Every
effort has been made to trace the copyright holders; apologies are offered for any omission, and the publisher will be pleased to add any necessary acknowledgement in subsequent editions.

Contributors

ANN ASPLUND is a Swede currently residing in the United States of America. She has a Master's degree in science and more than two decades' experience of living history re-enactment from both sides of the Atlantic. She teaches historical textile techniques, and runs a Facebook group for Medieval Makers.

RACHEL BALCHIN was a PhD student at the University of Leicester, where she also completed her MA in English Studies, and BA in English Literature. Her PhD thesis is concerned with the function of written textiles in medieval literature with a particular focus on the Old Norse *Íslendingasögur*. It explores the function and significance of written textiles in the *Íslendingasögur* and a selection of poems from *The Poetic Edda*.

CAROL CHRISTIANSEN is a Curator at Shetland Museum and Archives and oversees the Museum's nationally recognised Textile Collections. She received her doctorate from the University of Manchester, specialising in textile archaeology, in 2003. She has worked with colleagues in Britain and Scandinavia on numerous projects related to hand methods of textile production using wools from indigenous breeds of the North Atlantic area and Scottish knitting history. She is the author of *Taatit Rugs: The Pile Bedcovers of Shetland* (2015) and is currently finishing a publication on design development of the Shetland fine knitted lace tradition.

RUTH GILBERT is a handweaver, who studied for an M.A. in the History of Textiles and Dress at Winchester School of Art and subsequently an M.Phil. at the Textile Conservation Centre (University of Southampton). She began to research appropriate techniques and cloth types and to weave replica cloths, having become involved in historical re-enactment. The focus of her research is on how skills were learned, remembered and taught, and whether evidence for this can be deduced from surviving textiles. She has for many years been the resident weaver at Kentwell Hall's sixteenth-century re-creations.

MICHÈLE HAYEUR SMITH is an independent researcher and anthropological archaeologist with research interests in gender, textiles, dress, adornment and material culture studies. She is largely known for her work on the North Atlantic and Iceland regions and has been working on research projects focused on gender and the production and circulation of textiles from the Viking Age to the early nineteenth century. Bringing Norse women and their labour to the forefront of research, she has helped establish the foundation for a gendered archaeology of the North Atlantic. Her monograph, *The Valkyries' Loom and Archaeology of Cloth Production and Female Power in the North Atlantic*, was published in 2020.

CAROL JAMES is a self-taught textile artist and independent researcher, exploring ancient and low-tech methods for the production of fingerweaving and sprang cloth. She has worked for numerous international clients and has made modern wearables for exhibition. She has taught across Canada, the US, New Zealand and Europe. She is the author of four books: *Fingerweaving Untangled* (2008); *Sprang Unsprung* (2011); and two books of Sprang Lace Patterns; as well as numerous articles and two DVDs.

ANNA JOSEFSSON teaches science and textile crafts as a public education teacher at Billstromska folkhogskolan, Sweden. In her science classes she spends a lot of time outdoors with her students, helping them learn about ecology and ecological resources. Her textile classes cover many techniques working with wool and are held as public summer courses, and with resident students in the winter. She also runs a small craft company, 'Vinterverkstan', supplying craft materials and training courses in *nalbinding*, spinning and other crafts.

DOLORES KEARNEY is currently studying for her PhD at the Centre for Experimental Archaeology and Material Culture, University College Dublin. Her topic is the use of archaeological, historical and experimental archaeological evidence to explore the materiality of women's lives in early medieval Ireland.

ALEXANDRA LESTER-MAKIN (Editor) is the Post-Doctoral Researcher for textiles on 'Unwrapping the Galloway Hoard', an Arts and Humanities Research Council-funded project jointly run by the National Museum of Scotland and the University of Glasgow. She is a textile archaeologist specialising in early medieval embroidery and textiles. Her most recent publications include *The Lost Art of the Anglo-Saxon World: The Sacred and Secular Power of Embroidery* (2019); 'Embroidery and Its Early Medieval Audience: A Case Study of Sensory Engagement', https://doi.org/10.1080/00438243.20 20.1835530 (2021); and 'The Embroidered Fragments from the Tomb of Bishop William of St Calais, Durham: An Analysis and Biography,' in *Art and Worship in Anglo-Saxon England: Papers in Honour of Elizabeth Coatsworth*, ed. Maren Clegg Hyer and Gale R. Owen-Crocker (2021).

LISELOTTE ÖHRLING holds a Master's degree in Archaeology from the University of Gothenburg. She works as a museum teacher at Lödöse Museum, a medieval museum on the west coast of Sweden, teaching medieval arts such as dancing, spinning and *nalbinding*.

GALE R. OWEN-CROCKER (Editor) is Professor Emerita of the University of Manchester, where she was previously Professor of Anglo-Saxon Culture and Director of the Manchester Centre for Anglo-Saxon Studies. She has published extensively on medieval literature and culture, including *Dress in Anglo-Saxon England* (revised edn 2004), *The Bayeux Tapestry: Collected Papers* (2012), and the co-edited *Textiles of Medieval Iberia* (2022). She co-founded the journal *Medieval Clothing and Textiles*, directed the

Manchester Lexis of Cloth and Clothing Project (http://lexisproject.arts.manchester.ac.uk) and is Chief Editor of the *Encyclopedia of Medieval Dress and Textiles of the British Isles c. 450–1450* (2012).

ELIZABETH E. PEACOCK is a research conservator and Professor (Emerita) of Conservation at the University Museum, Norwegian University of Science and Technology (NTNU), Trondheim, Norway and previously, the University of Gothenburg, Sweden. Her research interests encompass conservation, taphonomy and diagenesis of organic archaeological materials; conservation pedagogy and education; textile and leather science; collections care; and preservation and management of archaeological sites. She has extensive experience as a practising conservator, teaches and lectures widely in conservation practice with a research focus, and has hosted numerous conservation interns.

FRANCES PRITCHARD is an Honorary Research Fellow of the University of Manchester. As a museum professional her career encompassed sixteen years in the Department of Urban Archaeology, Museum of London, and twenty-three years as Curator (Textiles) at the Whitworth Art Gallery, Manchester. She has acted as a consultant on textiles to the British Museum, National Museum of Ireland and English Heritage. Most of her many publications have focused on textiles from excavations in London, Dublin and Egypt. She recently edited *Crafting Textiles. Tablet Weaving, Sprang, Lace and Other Techniques from the Bronze Age to the Early 17th Century* (2021).

Preface

The genesis of this volume was a conference strand that took place at the *IONA: Early Medieval Studies on the Islands of the North Atlantic* conference, held at Simon Fraser University, Vancouver, Canada, in 2019. 'From Fibres to Decorated Textiles in the Early North Atlantic: Making, Methods, Meanings' brought together scholars, practitioners and other professionals specialising in different aspects of textile study and production from the Viking North Atlantic (800–1000 CE). The aim of the interdisciplinary strand was to explore how scholars and makers interpret and understand early medieval textiles and, as a result, the people and cultures that inhabited the early North Atlantic region.

The strand combined taster workshops and seminars that ran across the three days of the conference. The workshops gave attendees opportunities to experience weaving on a warp-weighted loom, tablet weaving, sprang, *nalbinding*[1] and preparing fish skin for use as leather. The first seminar focused on theoretical approaches to studying surviving textiles and their meaning and use within society. The final session brought together both practical and theoretical strands with presentations demonstrating how both approaches can work together to give people who would not normally consider themselves interested in history opportunities to explore and enjoy both craft and the distant past. The success of these sessions could be measured by the buzz and positive atmosphere that pervaded them and it was through the resulting discussions that the idea for an edited volume was first conceived.

This book is the culmination of that project. Many of the original contributors to the conference strand have written chapters for the book. These have been supplemented with chapters by other emerging and leading scholars and practitioners of research on textiles from the early North Atlantic. The editors hope that the work it contains will enthuse those who already work in the field and engage others who are new to it: that it will show that many different approaches can be used to generate knowledge and understanding of the people and cultures that inhabited the North Atlantic lands in the Viking period and that by engaging in interdisciplinary approaches to the study of textiles, we can develop a more nuanced and holistic knowledge and understanding not only of these now-fragile objects but also of the worlds in which they were made, used, treasured, buried and discarded.

---

[1] Technical terms are explained in the Glossary, p. 216.

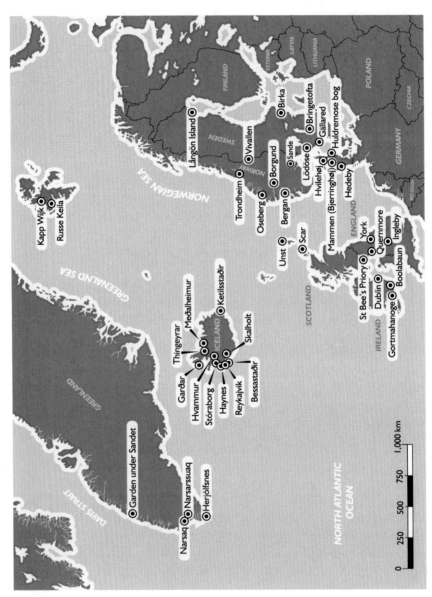

Geographical location of sites. © Peter Lorimer

Introduction

Alexandra Lester-Makin and Gale R. Owen Crocker

THE NORTH ATLANTIC IN THE VIKING AGE

The term North Atlantic describes the geographical area situated between modern Scandinavia in the east and the east coast of North America in the west; and from Greenland in the north to the south coast of England (see Map, p. xvi). This is the area that people from Scandinavia explored, raided, traded with and settled between *c.* 750 and 1050 CE. The Norse people who engaged in these expeditions are now called Vikings, and sometimes thought of as sea pirates. However, the word Viking is of uncertain origins. It has been linked to two Old Norse words *vikingr* (m.) and *viking* (f.), which refer to an individual who is away from home engaged in group activities, and a group endeavour also taking place away from home, respectively. In turn, these two words may have derived from *Vik*, The Oslofjord, *Viken*, The Bay, and/or *vik*, bay, which could indicate that a *vikingr* was originally an individual associated with one of these places, either a local or a sea pirate.[1] The etymology of all these words is part of a complex and ongoing debate that has only been touched upon here.[2] The term Viking has become synonymous with a whole society that flourished first in Norway, Sweden and Denmark and, later, in parts of the British archipelago, Ireland, the Faroe Islands, Iceland, Greenland and possibly as far west as the coast of North America.[3] To the east, this society or culture spread into Finland, the Baltic and Russia and had trade networks that extended into the Byzantine Empire (the capital of which, Byzantium, is present-day Istanbul, Turkey), and along the

---

Alexandra Lester-Makin: ORCiD: 0000-0002-6871-5745; Gale R. Owen-Crocker ORCiD: 0000-0002-3123-346X

[1] Jayne Carroll, Stephen H. Harrison and Gareth Williams, *The Vikings in Britain and Ireland* (London: British Museum Press, 2014), p. 6; Judith Jesch, *The Viking Diaspora* (London: Routledge, 2015), pp. 4–8.

[2] Jesch, *The Viking Diaspora*, pp. 4–8.

[3] There is still much debate around the subject of Viking contact and settlement in North America. For an excellent discussion see Gordon Campbell, *The Story of a Founding Myth: Norse America* (Oxford: University Press, 2021).

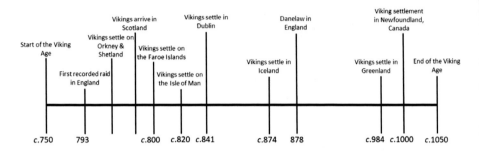

Table 0.1   Timeline of Viking contact and settlement across the North Atlantic. © Alexandra Lester-Makin.

silk route, possibly as far as China, although this is still debated. To the south, the Norse penetrated as far as the Iberian Peninsula in the Mediterranean and the north coast of Africa, setting up winter camps and raiding there between c. 859 and 862.[4] Viking Age society was complex and it is not the aim of this volume to unpack what others have already done, and continue to do so well.[5] For many cultures, including those of Scandinavia, the British Isles and Ireland, this period of history is now called the Viking Age.

As Viking/Norse culture spread within Scandinavia it encountered the nomadic Sámi who also inhabited Norway, Sweden and Finland, and still inhabit northern parts of these countries. As the Vikings/Norse migrated out from their traditional homelands, they encountered other cultures with whom they eventually co-occupied lands, through enslavement, intermarriage and political means. As recent DNA research has shown, 'Viking' settlements in Iceland were actually groups of people from different places, including the British Isles, living and working together.[6] These scientific results throw positive light on evidence found in the Icelandic sagas (stories), the authenticity of which had been questioned because they follow literary conventions and were verbally passed from generation to generation before being written down at some point after 1150 CE.[7] It also confirms newly emerging archaeological evidence in, for example, the form of Viking dress, discovered during the excavation of a burial at Ketilsstaðir in north-eastern Iceland. This evidence pointed towards the deceased woman having links with, if not

---

[4]   Neil Price, *The Children of Ash and Elm: A History of the Vikings* (London: Allen Lane, 2020), pp. xiii, 372–76.

[5]   See, for example, Stefan Brink in collaboration with Neil Price (ed.), *The Viking World* (London: Routledge, 2008); Carroll, Harrison and Williams, *The Vikings in Britain and Ireland*; Jesch, *The Viking Diaspora*; Marika Mägi, *The Viking Eastern Baltic* (Leeds: Arc Humanities Press, 2019); Price, *The Children of Ash and Elm*.

[6]   See Agnar Helgason, Eileen Hickey, Sara Goodacre, Vidar Bosnes, Kári Stefánsson, Ryk Ward and Bryan Sykes, 'mtDNA and the islands of the North Atlantic: estimating the proportions of Norse and Gaelic ancestry', *American Journal of Human Genetics* 68 (2001), 723–37.

[7]   See Lars Lönnroth, 'The Icelandic sagas', in *The Viking World*, ed. by Stefan Brink in collaboration with Neil Price (London: Routledge, 2008), pp. 304–10.

INTRODUCTION

originally migrating from, the British Isles.[8] This, then, was an area and time of complex interactions which current research is revealing.

The focus of this volume is textiles; specifically, the analysis and interpretation of textiles from the North Atlantic lands during the Viking Age (Map, p. xvi). Most recovered textiles from these areas are archaeological finds, variously from graves, excavations of farms and other inhabited sites, or from medieval towns. Archaeological textiles are often fragments, delicate and easily damaged. For maximum preservation and study, it is necessary that the textile is treated with the same respect as the metalwork to which it may adhere, or the built structure in which it has, perhaps unexpectedly, been found. It must be cleaned and conserved before study.

Some ground-breaking studies of textiles in our period were concerned only with one site, such as Agnes Geijer's publication of the textiles from the Viking Age cemetery at Birka, Sweden,[9] and Penelope Walton Rogers' studies of excavated material from 16–22 Coppergate, York, England, a site occupied from Roman times until the sixteenth century, but in Viking times divided into four tenements which proved rich in evidence for textile production as well as textile remains.[10] Other published studies are confined to individual graves, such as that from Ketilsstaðir, Iceland mentioned above, some of which, like a boat burial from Scar, Orkney, Scotland[11] and three burials from western Norway,[12] contained not only textiles but tools with which they were made.

Urban contexts, particularly damp areas such as Anglo-Viking York and the harbour area of Bryggen, Bergen, Norway, can preserve enormous quantities of organic material which may have to be stored for years before it can all be analysed and published – if and when economic constraints allow it and when the textiles have to take their place in a queue for publication of many significant discoveries and artefacts. Textiles excavated from Dublin number over 2,000; selected items have been published, many as articles in specialist volumes.[13] Yet other publications have focused on the type of fabric, for

---

[8]   Michèle Hayeur Smith, Kevin P. Smith and Karin M. Frei, '"Tangled up in blue": the death, dress and identity of an early Viking-Age female settler from Ketilsstaðir, Iceland', *Medieval Archaeology* 63.1 (2019), 95–127.

[9]   Agnes Geijer, *Birka III; die Textilfunde aus den Gräbern* (Uppsala: Kungl. Vitterhets, historie och antikvitets akademien, 1938).

[10]   Penelope Walton, *Textiles, Cordage and Raw Fibre from 16–22 Coppergate*, The Archaeology of York, The Small Finds 17/5 ((London, York Archaeological Trust/Council for British Archaeology, 1989); Penelope Walton Rogers, *Textile Production at 16–22 Coppergate*, The Archaeology of York, The Small Finds 17/11 (York: York Archaeological Trust/Council for British Archaeology, 1997).

[11]   Thea Gabra-Sanders, contributions on textiles and textile tools in *Scar: A Viking Boat Burial on Sanday, Orkney*, ed. by Olwyn Owen and Magnar Dalland (East Linton: Tuckwell Press/ Historic Scotland 1999), pp. 67, 93, 99, 198–200, 133–35.

[12]   Ingvild Øye, 'Production, quality and social status in Viking Age dress: three cases from Western Norway', *Medieval Clothing and Textiles* 11 (2015), 1–27.

[13]   For example, Frances Pritchard, 'Silk braids and textiles of the Viking Age from Dublin', in *Archaeological Textiles, NESAT II Symposium 1–4 May 1984*, ed. by Lise Bender Jørgensen, Bente Magnus and Elisabeth Munksgaard (Copenhagen: Archæologisk Institut, Københavns

instance, silk textiles, which were always imports into the Viking world, both as prestigious cloths for religious use and as secular dress trimmings.[14] Michèle Hayeur Smith's recent book, *The Valkyries' Loom: The Archaeology of Cloth Production and Female Power in the North Atlantic*, investigates wool cloth, 'the everyday cloth used by the masses'.[15] Her work focuses on homespun textiles produced and used across the North Atlantic from the Viking Age to the early modern period. Bringing together many examples, both previously published and those languishing in collections and storage, Hayeur Smith draws out the stories of the cloth and its evolution from simple textile to legitimate currency and the roles played by North Atlantic female textile makers down the centuries.

As these few examples demonstrate, previous work on Viking Age textiles has been sporadic and isolated, a point emphasised by Michèle Hayeur Smith in her overview of the state of archaeological textile research, particularly within the Viking North Atlantic, in the introduction to *The Valkyries' Loom*.[16] She goes on to argue that none of this work has used the objects to unlock the social dynamics of Viking societies within the North Atlantic *through* textiles,[17] something that her book demonstrates it is possible to do. This is also a theme that has been highlighted more broadly in Julie Lund and Søren M. Sindbæk's recent review of the state of Viking archaeology studies.[18]

Universitet, 1988), pp. 149–61; Frances Pritchard, 'Missing threads from medieval textiles in north west Europe', in *Archaeological Textiles. Occasional Papers No. 10*, ed. by Sonia A. O'Connor and Mary M. Brooks (London: United Kingdom Institute for Conservation, 1990), pp. 15–17; Frances Pritchard, 'Aspects of the wool textiles from Viking Age Dublin', in *Archaeological Textiles in Northern Europe, NESAT IV Symposium 1–5 May in Copenhagen*, ed. by Lise Bender Jørgensen and Elisabeth Munksgaard (Copenhagen: Konservatorskolen det Kongelige Danske Kunstakademi, 1992), pp. 93–104; Frances Pritchard, 'Textiles from Dublin', in *Kvinner i Vikingtid*, ed. by Nancy L. Coleman and Nanna Løkka (Oslo: Scandinavian Academic Press, 2014), pp. 224–40; Frances Pritchard, 'Twill weaves from Viking-age Dublin', in *Archaeological Textiles – Links between Past and Present, NESAT XIII*, ed. by Milena Bravermanová, Helena Březinová and Jane Malcolm-Davies (Liberec and Prague: Technical University of Liberec, Faculty of Engineering/Institute of Archaeology of the CAS, Prague, 2017), pp. 115–23; Frances Pritchard, 'Evidence of tablet weaving from Viking-Age Dublin', in *Crafting Textiles: Tablet Weaving, Sprang, Lace and Other Techniques from the Bronze Age to the Early 17th Century*, ed. by Frances Pritchard (Oxford and Philadelphia: Oxbow, 2021), pp. 37–52; Elizabeth Wincott Heckett, *Viking Age Headcoverings from Dublin*, Medieval Dublin Excavations 1962–81, Ser. B, vol. 6 (Dublin: Royal Irish Academy for the National Museum of Ireland, 2003).

[14] Anne Hedeager Krag, *Ornetæppet og andre silkefunde fra Knud den Helliges helgenskrin i Odense Domkirke/The Eagle Silk and other silks in the shrine of St. Canute in Odense Cathedral* (Herning: Poul Kristensens, 2010); Anne Hedeager Krag, 'Byzantine and oriental silks in Denmark 800–1200', *Medieval Clothing and Textiles* 14 (2018), 37–60; Marianne Vedeler, *Silk for the Vikings* (Oxford and Philadelphia: Oxbow, 2014).

[15] Michèle Hayeur Smith, *The Valkyries' Loom: The Archaeology of Cloth Production and Female Power in the North Atlantic* (Gainesville: University of Florida Press, 2020), p. 10.

[16] Hayeur Smith, *The Valkyries' Loom*, p. 2.

[17] Hayeur Smith, *The Valkyries' Loom*, pp. 2–3.

[18] Julie Lund and Søren M. Sindbæk, 'Crossing the maelstrom: new departures in Viking archaeology', *Journal of Archaeological Research* 30 (2022), 169–229.

INTRODUCTION

However, there have been new developments. Although reproductions of clothing and other historical textiles have been presented in the past as educational aids in museums and for re-enactment, the acts of precise re-creation have come to prominence in recent decades as 'Experimental Archaeology'. Notable practitioners include textile specialists Eva Andersson Strand (University of Copenhagen) and Ulla Mannering (The National Museum of Denmark), who have undertaken major experimental archaeology projects that explore the making processes involved in producing yarn, making textiles such as ships' sails and the funerary costumes of a high-status man (d. 970–971 CE) buried at Bjerringhøj, Mammen, Denmark, and an elite woman (d. late 900s) interred at Hvilehøj, also Denmark.[19] The value of experimental making with regard to small textile accessories is also shown in several of the chapters in Frances Pritchard's recent edited volume *Crafting Textiles*.[20]

Another productive recent development, as Lund and Sindbæk have pointed out, is the move towards the use of object biography, socio-anthropological and interpretive and cognitive frameworks that bring together different ways of thinking about and approaching research within this field. The example they use to show the possibilities of such combined approaches focuses on the work of textile archaeologist Lise Bender Jørgensen. She calculated the number of sheep needed to produce enough wool to make a sail for a large Viking ship and some of the wider implications. Lund and Sindbæk suggest that an integrated, meshwork approach to this work would also enable the environmental factors of farming such large numbers of sheep (200 according to Bender Jørgensen) within the landscape.[21] Hopefully, this points towards a move towards more holistic approaches to the study of textiles across the North Atlantic as well.

The aim of this volume is to expand our thinking about and understanding of Viking Age textiles, not only their uses and meanings but also their social impact in their respective societies. It is the first book to bring together experts from such a wide vari-

---

[19] For examples see, Eva Andersson, *The Common Thread: Textile Production during the Late Iron Age–Viking Age* (Lund: KFS, 1999); Eva Andersson Strand, 'Tools and textiles – production and organisation in Birka and Hedeby', in *Viking Settlements and Viking Society: Papers from the Proceedings of the Sixteenth Viking Congress*, ed. by Svavar Sigmundsson (Reykjavik: Hið Íslenzka Fornleifafélag and University of Iceland Press, 2011), pp. 1–17; Eva Andersson Strand, Stefan Lindgren and Carolina Larsson, 'Motion capture and textile experimental archaeology, a possible combination', *Origini* 40 (2017), 129–40; Ulla Mannering, 'Fashioning the Viking Age', *Archaeological Textiles Review* 60 (2018), 114–17; Ulla Mannering, 'Fashioning the Viking Age: status after the first three years', *Archaeological Textiles Review* 63 (2021), 139–44.

[20] See note 13. This volume is wide ranging both geographically and historically, but does include studies of both tablet weaving and sprang, which feature in the present volume. Pritchard's book is dedicated to the memory of textile specialist Peter Collingwood, and it is pointed out in the Introduction (p. vii) that his *The Techniques of Tablet Weaving* (London: Faber and Faber 1982) was inspirational in promoting the making and re-creating of tablet-woven textiles.

[21] Lund and Søren, 'Crossing the maelstrom', p. 201; also see, Lise Bender Jørgensen, 'The Introduction of sails to Scandinavia: raw materials, labour and land', in *N-TAG TEN Proceedings of the 10th Nordic TAG Conference at Stiklestad, Norway*, ed. by Ragnild Berge, Marek E. Jasinki and Kalle Sognnes, BAR International Series 2399 (Oxford: Archeopress, 2012), pp. 173–81.

ety of specialisms – archaeology, history, literary studies and the processes of learning and practising traditional making skills – to the study of textiles from the early North Atlantic. While experts trained in the painstaking process of textiles analysis are few,[22] re-enactors and enthusiasts for textile craft work exist in considerable numbers. Some of the experimental archaeological activities described in the present volume make use of the enthusiasm and varied life experiences of such non-professional contributors to historical research. This book demonstrates that collaboration between specialisms and methods can develop more nuanced understandings of textiles and the world(s) of which they were an integrated part. This is an innovative approach to researching textiles from this period and geographical area. The volume aims to push beyond what has become the research norm to raise questions about methods of manufacture, use and meaning across broader cultural territories. Original scientific analysis is combined with experimental archaeology, historical reviews and new theoretical approaches to give us unprecedented access into the minds of the people who inhabited the Viking North Atlantic, through their textiles. Through their work the contributors have unlocked new ways for us to explore and understand the worlds of the Norse and the cultures they encountered, through their textiles.

The book does this in two parts. The first, 'Textiles and their Interpretation', focuses on surviving textiles, and literary and art sources. In Chapter 1, 'Sheep, Wool and Fleece Processing: Where It All Began', Carol Christiansen gives a detailed consideration of sheep's wool, the most important fibre for cloth making in the Viking Age. She discusses in detail the animal husbandry of the period, different types of wool – a versatile fibre – and the processes which went into making cloth from it, including the tools employed. In Chapter 2 Elizabeth E. Peacock then examines the approaches employed by conservators who analyse and stabilise archaeological textiles. After explaining how archaeological textiles survive within the North Atlantic region, she moves on to give a detailed account of how conservators investigate them and the wide-ranging knowledge and skill sets they have. In doing so, the author shows how conservators can add to our developing understanding of archaeological textiles, illustrating her discussion throughout with case studies.

The book then moves from developing understanding of the most important fibre in the Norse world and how we 'read' and understand it in extant archaeological textiles, to surviving evidence and use. Firstly, in Chapter 3, 'King Harald's Grey Cloak: *Vararfeldir* and the Trade in Shaggy Pile Weave Cloaks between Iceland and Norway in the Late Viking and Early Middle Ages', Michèle Hayeur Smith leads the reader into a wide-ranging consideration of the evidence for shaggy, pile-woven cloaks and the trading of them across the North Atlantic. She includes her own scientific examination of the relatively few material remains of pile-woven cloth from Iceland and Greenland and preliminary results from her strontium isotope analysis of finds from western Norway, which

---

[22] And regrettably, as Michèle Hayeur Smith has recently noted, some have died leaving work incomplete and collections unstudied, including Thea Gabra-Sanders (d. 1998), Else Guðjónsson (d. 2003), Nicolina Jense (d. 2016) and Else Østergård (d. 2018); see Hayeur Smith, *The Valkyries' Loom*, pp. 2–3.

INTRODUCTION

suggest the Norwegian cloaks were a local product, not imports as previously thought. In Chapter 6, 'The Function of Written Textiles in the *Íslendingasögur*', Rachel Balchin examines the Old Norse vestimentary code behind the descriptions of textile processes and clothing in three Icelandic sagas from the collection of medieval tales known as *Íslendingasögur*. She shows that simple translations of the words fail to convey the cultural, semiotic, symbolic, even metonymic significance of the items in their contexts. Garments may assume the identity of a former wearer or wearers, to various effects from the emotion of grief to the action of murder.

The focus now moves from Greenland, Iceland and Norway to Ireland. In Chapter 4, 'Re-clothing the Inhabitants of Tenth-century Dublin Based on Archaeological Evidence', Frances Pritchard draws together her analysis of recovered textiles from tenth-century Dublin to give the first archaeologically accurate description of both male and female dress. She demonstrates, also for the first time, that clothing was regional, not part of a standardised form of Norse/Viking attire and that it changed over time. Staying in Ireland but moving back to the shaggy, pile cloak, in Chapter 7 Dolores Kearney traces the meaning and use of this emblematic garment from the literary evidence for its use in pre-Norse Ireland through to the sixteenth century when the English exploited it, suggesting it identified otherness in those who wore it. In doing so the author compares surviving examples of the mantles from the Viking world, investigating their complex shared similarities in design and collected, cultural meanings that outstripped the functional and aesthetic qualities of these garments.

Finally, in Chapter 5, 'The Sensory Archaeology of Early Medieval Fabrics from the North Atlantic', Alexandra Lester-Makin approaches the study of textiles from the Norse and Sámi worlds through sensory archaeology. After outlining the development and aims of this theoretical approach, particularly in relation to the study of archaeological textiles and the early medieval world, the author goes on to draw together a wide range of archaeological, historical, literary and experimental evidence for how the Norse and Sámi understood textiles and clothing through their own sensoria. The chapter demonstrates that both societies had diverse understandings of textiles through their cultures' sensory perceptions. It also highlights how interactions between the Norse and Sámi brought about new sensory experiences and a development of textile cultures within both societies.

The second part of the book, 'Understanding through Replicating', brings together four practical case studies. Ruth Gilbert's Chapter 8, 'Making the Best of It: Planning Decisions for Reproduction Fabrics', considers some outstanding pioneer work in reconstructing medieval cloth from the mid-twentieth and present centuries and discusses the different standards of re-creation appropriate for different purposes today. Some costume reconstructions may be purely speculative, others based on surviving cloth, more or less well understood. The availability of suitable materials and the skill of the maker – who might, in some cases, be making a cloth type for the first time, though skilled in similar techniques – are among the crucial criteria. In the second case study, Chapter 9, 'The Value of Intangible Knowledge: How Living History Can Aid Experimental Archaeology in Exploring the Past; Iron Age Scandinavian Tablet Weaving and *Nalbinding*', Ann

Asplund discusses the different motivations for re-creating historical textiles, the institutions that use such re-creations, from museums to re-enactment societies, and the different levels of accuracy that are sought, for reasons varying from deadlines, to budget, to availability of materials. With focus on two specific exemplars, a sock in *nalbinding* from Coppergate, York, UK, and a tablet-woven band from Birka, Sweden, the author examines what can be learned from such experimental archaeology, from teaching the crafts and from the utilisation of the re-created textiles in living history contexts.

In Chapter 10, 'Collaborative Working Practices: Creating and Theorising Sprang', Carol James explores how the act of reconstructing sprang garments can reveal otherwise invisible aspects of the textile's production and use. Sprang, an interlinking technique, is attested from Viking Age England, Shetland and (probably) Norway, but there are many other, and more sophisticated, examples from different eras and regions. Using three examples of her own re-creation work, ranging from Coptic Egypt and pre-Columbian South America to Renaissance Italy, James demonstrates that exploring how the human brain works in relation to the production of sprang and the skill of makers can inform the making process, revealing short cuts, repairs, mistakes and use and wear in the original item. After giving an overview of where and when the technique was used, the author discusses the systems and length of time it takes for students to learn the technique and what this may tell us of past working methods.

The final case study brings together all that the previous chapters have explored. Chapter 11, 'From Wool to Mitten: When History Comes to Life in Your Hands', discusses a collaborative workshop by museum curator Liselotte Öhrling and practitioner Anna Josefsson, which drew on technical analysis, knowledge of past husbandry and production techniques, learning and interacting processes and sensory engagement to bring local residents closer to their surroundings and the story of their town. The project, 'From Wool to Mitten', was undertaken at Lödöse museum in Sweden. It harnessed the interest of local people in the town's medieval history, giving them a hands-on appreciation of the artefacts the museum holds through the re-creation of a medieval *nalbound* mitten excavated in Lödöse. The workshops taught people about the processes of creating the yarn and using it to make a *nalbound* mitten through experimental archaeology and a theoretical overview. The authors demonstrate that small, hands-on workshops can help galvanise enthusiasm for traditional textile crafts, keeping them alive for the next generation. They also show that by re-creating an object from the museum's collection participants felt more cemented within their community and connected to their own history.

While this book is the result of a project that has an innovative focus on the study of textiles from across the Viking North Atlantic, the editors know that this volume is only the start. It is the hope of all the contributors that their work galvanises other scholars, practitioners, museum staff and re-enactors, to name but a few, to come together and explore new or different ways in which to interpret and understand textiles, not only from the early North Atlantic but other past societies as well. By doing so, we will show how an all-encompassing study of textiles can push the boundaries of research, raising important questions and developing nuanced understandings of the social dynamics of societies and, in the process, we too can become more aware of our past, of our own worlds and of our place within them.

Note on Old Norse Characters

This book deals with places and people whose names incorporate letters that derive from Old Norse and modern Icelandic and may be unfamiliar to some readers. The list of the letters and sounds below, while not exhaustive, are those most seen within the chapters in this book: á is pronounced 'ow'; æ is said like the English 'i'; Ð/ð is a soft 'th' as in 'weather' or 'breathe' while Þ/þ, also 'th', is spoken as in 'thin' or 'thought'; é is 'ay'; ö is the same as 'u' in 'but'; Í/í is 'ee'; and ó is pronounced 'owe'.[1]

---

[1] Hayeur Smith, *The Valkyries' Loom*, p. vii; Price, *The Children of Ash and Elm*, p. xvii.

PART I

Textiles and their Interpretation

CHAPTER 1

Sheep, Wool, and Fleece Processing: Where It All Began

Carol Christiansen

Sheep have been exploited, developed, and moved across vast areas since the Bronze Age. Milk led to domestication but changes to the coat of early sheep increased the amount of wool fibre and altered the quality of fleece each animal produced.[1] Wool became a valuable economic product and breeding responded to market forces. Some breeds were raised primarily for wool, others for milk or meat, a process that continually led to changes in sheep breeds.

Product specialisation in sheep breeds was not desirable everywhere. In the far north-west fringe of Europe, characteristics found in wild sheep such as horns, a moulting fleece and hairy wool that were being eradicated elsewhere were kept. These traits were beneficial for sheep in this environment and useful to their owners. People in northern latitudes required sheep that could be relied on to produce a range of quality products and remain viable to reproduce a healthy new generation. This was particularly important for adventurers, explorers and settlers who set off from their Scandinavian homeland to establish a new life in the North Atlantic. Subsistence agropastoralism relied on versatility, not specialisation, and influenced sheep husbandry strategies and breeding.

The regular presence of caprine remains at Viking and medieval farm sites in the North Atlantic region indicates the importance of sheep and goat rearing.[2] Archaeological

ORCiD: 0000-0003-0560-4607

[1] M.L. Ryder, *Sheep and Man* (London: Duckworth, 1983), pp. 94–6.

[2] Símun V. Arge, 'Viking Faroes: settlement, paleoeconomy, and chronology', *Journal of the North Atlantic* 7 (2014), 1–17; Andrew J. Dugmore et al., 'The Norse *landnám* on the North Atlantic islands: an environmental impact assessment', *Polar Record* 41.1 (2005), 21–37 (pp. 25–32); Thomas H. McGovern, Ramona Harrison and Konrad Smiarowski, 'Sorting sheep and goats in medieval Iceland and Greenland: local subsistence, climate change or world system impacts?', in *Human Ecodynamics in the North Atlantic: A Collaborative Model*

Fig. 1.1 Shetland ewe with primitive traits: coarse wool protecting fine wool, horns, excessive pigment variation, coarse dark wool at neck and backbone. © Carol Christiansen.

investigations into farm and livestock management have regularly focused on caprines primarily as producers of milk and secondarily for meat and hides.[3] Recent attention has begun to focus on wool, not only milk and meat, as a necessary and valuable raw material for living in the northern marine environment. The majority of cloth for clothing, bedding and other textiles needed by the household, farm and community, including cloth for shipbuilding and haulage, came primarily from sheep. Wool became increasingly important by the medieval period, when it also was used to pay tithes, taxes, rents and wages.

---

of Humans and Nature through Space and Time, ed. by Ramona Harrison and Ruth Maher (Lanham, MD: Lexington Books, 2014), pp. 153–76 (pp. 159–73).

[3] Seth D. Brewington, Third Interim Report on Analysis of Archaeofauna from Undir Junkarinsfløtti, Sandoy, Faroe Islands (Brooklyn, NY: CUNY NORSEC, 2010), pp. 7–9.

The present analysis considers sheep as a living source of wool for textile making in the areas settled by Scandinavians, beginning with the Viking diaspora in the eighth century (Fig. 1.1). Knowledge gained from understanding the physical traits of northern short-tail sheep breeds, their wool and the annual cycle of husbandry governed by environmental factors can inform analysis and appreciation of ancient textiles and their production processes. This review examines the physiological responses by indigenous breeds to their northern environment and, in turn, what those responses meant for breeding new stock and producing wool. It takes the view that people in the North Atlantic past, first and foremost, created systems within farms and communities to procure the raw materials needed to make things for themselves in their otherwise unforgiving land- and seascapes. It assumes people were active agents in the reproduction or transformation of those raw materials when this was possible. The medieval Faroese farmer could obtain certain materials like wood and whale oil only by chance, when they washed up within his shoreline, and he could do nothing about their original form or condition. With sheep he (or she) had the ability to change the flock and the wool it produced through breeding choices made every year. Yet, in the North Atlantic region few significant changes appear to have been made. Even today, breeds, flocks or individuals within flocks still retain many features similar to, or not far removed from, wild sheep. This provides an opportunity to investigate fleece composition, wool structure and fibre qualities as the building blocks of textile-making in North Atlantic communities in the past.

The methodology is necessarily both 'making through thinking' and 'thinking through making'.[4] It relies on a material studies approach with a highly varied and complex material. A raw primitive fleece from a North Atlantic breed relays stories about its twelve months of life in a way that is complete, contained and holistically sensory. It has depth, density, and both dramatic and imperceptible colour differences. It smells of a body, the close scent of an animal: for example, a strong sour smell can indicate the sheep was once infested with keds (*Melophagus ovinus*, wingless flies, parasitic on sheep). Its many textures are a challenge for fingertips to discern. It is a document of annual fibre growth, weather conditions and its journeys through the landscape in the vegetation and soils it still carries. Its upper side is unrecognisable from its underside. It glistens with the animal's body oils. It will immediately warm if put in the sun. Once taken apart, it cannot be put back together again. It can provide insight and understanding of how other fleeces like it in the past grew, their wools' behaviours and qualities, the experience of deconstruction through processing and the possibilities of how hands and tools were used to make thread and cloth from it. Some of these characteristics are identifiable in recovered archaeological cloth remains.

This chapter will use modern sheep studies to examine physiological changes and responses in sheep to the environment and how this affected husbandry and the annual cycle of textile production within Norse societies. The idea that domestication necessarily became an ongoing trajectory of breeding for 'improvement' is rejected. Instead,

---

4   Tim Ingold, *Making: Anthropology, Archaeology, Art and Architecture* (London: Routledge, 2013), p. 6.

a conservative, sustained approach, putting natural forces above economic ones, was necessary for beasts to survive and reproduce. Subsistence agropastoralism in a limiting environment benefited from assurances. These could be found and maintained by respecting natural forces and breeding for robustness held in the traits of wild sheep to allow the farm's flocks the best chance of survival on limited means.

NORTHERN SHORT-TAIL BREED ORIGINS

European sheep breeds originated from wild mouflon in western Asia and travelled west and north throughout Europe in the Neolithic period.[5] Northern European breeds developed thereafter as human populations spread into regional or isolated areas. Landrace breeds in the Nordic countries and the western and northern fringes of Britain are part of the northern European short-tail type, which also includes breeds of the southern Baltic region and north-western Russia.[6] Today these breeds are considered 'primitive' or 'unimproved' types because, although domesticated, they continue to carry some characteristics also found in wild sheep.

Sheep existed already in Ireland and in Britain as far north as Shetland from the Neolithic period.[7] The fleece and wool quality of pre-Norse sheep along the North Atlantic edge is not well understood. Soay has been earmarked as a Scottish Iron Age breed (800 BCE–400 CE), and its wool colour genetics are related to Orkney and Shetland breeds,[8] suggesting that pre-Norse sheep in the Northern Isles were not completely replaced by a Norwegian breed beginning in the ninth century CE. DNA studies indicate a geographical link among sheep in southern Scandinavia, Shetland, Faroe and Iceland,[9] but there may have been other directions of travel for livestock entering into and out of Shetland before transport north. There has not yet been a systematic study on the indigenous, primitive breeds of the Scottish north and west to identify the impact of Norse settlement on pre-Norse livestock breeds for these areas.

Evidence suggests that humans and sheep were present in the Faroe Islands before the Vikings arrived in the ninth century, with a recent study suggesting human settlement with livestock three centuries earlier.[10] Historical evidence suggests settlement by

---

[5]   Miika Tapio, *Origin and Maintenance of Genetic Diversity in Northern European Sheep* (Oulu, Finland: Oulun Yliopisto, 2006), p. 22.

[6]   Ó.R. Dýrmundsson and R. Niżnikowski, 'North European short-tailed breeds of sheep: a review', *Animal* 4 (2010), 1275–82 (pp. 1276–7).

[7]   Barbara Noddle, 'Animal bones', in *Scord of Brouster: An Early Agricultural Settlement on Shetland*, ed. by Alasdair W.R. Whittle et al. (Oxford: Oxford University Committee for Archaeology, 1986), p. 132.

[8]   M.L. Ryder, R.B. Land and R. Ditchburn, 'Coat colour inheritance in Soay, Orkney and Shetland sheep', *Journal of Zoology* 173 (2009), 477–85 (pp. 478–9).

[9]   Tapio, *Origin and Maintenance*, p. 37.

[10]   Lorelei Curtain, William J. D'Andrea, Nicholas L. Balascio et al., 'Sedimentary DNA and molecular evidence for early human occupation of the Faroe Islands', *Communications Earth*

SHEEP, WOOL, AND FLEECE PROCESSING

Christian monks from Ireland or the British north, but archaeological evidence cannot confirm the point of origin for this early habitation of Faroe.

Sheep were introduced into Iceland and Greenland by the Vikings and the breed continues to flourish in Iceland today. Icelandic sheep brought to Greenland died out with abandonment in the fifteenth century, but sheep were reintroduced from Iceland in the early twentieth century.[11]

Sheep and goat remains are difficult to differentiate in archaeological contexts and reports include separate species entries and the shared subfamily designation where remains cannot be further defined. Goats were part of the domestic species initially brought from the homeland and figure in Viking sites from the early period of settlement.[12] Although goats undoubtedly were used mainly for milking and secondarily for meat and hides, modern Norwegian and Icelandic goats produce useable fibre, mainly hair but also a fine-fibred undercoat.[13] Both fibre types in these goat breeds moult, as with northern short-tail sheep breeds. Goat numbers had decreased in Iceland by the twelfth century but continued in Greenland. Textiles of heavily pigmented goat fibre have been identified in Greenland, where they were spun separately but woven with sheep's wool, including as pile threads.[14] For the sake of convenience, this analysis will focus on sheep as the primary fibre source in early North Atlantic contexts.

Today the areas of the North Atlantic, including Greenland, contain genetically related but separate, recognised breeds with some differences in fleece qualities, colouring and patterning. There is regional and farm variability developed mainly through localised flock management. In some areas there remain flocks or individuals with more pronounced primitive traits. Intra-breed differences are fewer in Iceland, where there is a national strategy to adhere to a single breed standard. The exception is the Icelandic sub-group Leader sheep, which have been bred to retain the ancient trait to lead flocks from danger and bad weather.

THE ROLE OF WOOL

Wool growth competed with milk production and lamb health across a range of grazing and fodder resources. Like foodstuffs, wool was grown, harvested, processed and formed into useable products for consumption. Farmers had to strike a balance in flock numbers

---

& *Environment* 2.253 (2021), 1–7 (p. 3). Mike J. Church et al., 'The Vikings were not the first colonizers of the Faroe Islands', *Quaternary Science Reviews* 77 (2013), 228–32 (pp. 231–2).

[11] Ryder, *Sheep and Man*, p. 549.

[12] Dugmore, 'The Norse landnám on the North Atlantic islands', pp. 27–8.

[13] Leif-Jarle Asheim and Lars Olav Eik, 'The economics of fibre and meat on Norwegian dairy goats', *Small Ruminant Research* 30 (1998), 185–90 (p. 189); S. Adalsteinsson et al., 'The Icelandic goat, a case study of a small old population', in *Proceedings of the 5th World Congress on Genetics Applied to Livestock Production*, ed. by E. Smith (1994), pp. 517–19 (p. 517).

[14] Else Østergård, *Woven into the Earth: Textiles from Norse Greenland* (Aarhus: University Press, 2004), p. 75.

between milk and lamb producers (ewes) and wool producers (ewes, wethers (castrated rams)). Milk and lambs were more valuable products from ewes, but ewes were more physiologically strained by pregnancy and lactation, producing less and poorer wool than wethers. Decisions made in the annual culling of ewes and lambs and the choice of rams ultimately could affect the amount and quality of cloth in future years.

Wool production and textile-making was embedded in everyday life, especially on farms. Women were responsible for managing and carrying out textile work in the home and girls were expected to become primary makers, overseers of production and mentors of trainees (servants, slaves, children) when setting up their own household.

Men also were skilled in aspects of textile production. Foremost they were shepherds of their own or others' flocks and participated in the wool harvest. It was vital for sea-farers, who usually journeyed without women, to be skilled in sewing to mend sails and clothing, and in spinning wool and horsehair into cords and ropes.[15] Textile-making was a necessary and constant set of tasks, with most of the population familiar with its production cycle, if not proficient in some part of it from an early age.

HUSBANDRY

The foremost concern for the farming household was to ensure the flock survived and successfully reproduced.[16] Analyses of farm sites, early laws and descriptions in the sagas indicate a wide range of strategies were used, with more diversification possible by larger farms.[17] Animals were kept near the farm but outdoors as much as possible during the winter to allow grazing on cultivated fields after harvest and therefore keeping precious fodder in reserve. Farm buildings and field walls provided protection against cold, wind and precipitation to offset cold stress, which increased the animal's need for nutrition and, as a result, had a detrimental effect on wool growth.[18]

---

[15] *The King's Mirror*, trans., intro. and notes by Laurence Marcellus Larson (New York: Twayne & American-Scandinavian Foundation, 1917), p. 84. The text is mid-thirteenth-century Norwegian, a book of advice for a future king on matters both practical and proper.

[16] Tom Amorosi, Paul C. Buckland, Kevin J. Edwards et al., 'They did not live by grass alone: the politics and palaeoecology of animal fodder in the North Atlantic region', *Environmental Archaeology* 1 (1998), 41–54 (pp. 41–2).

[17] Bernadette McCooey, 'Farming practices in pre-modern Iceland', Unpublished doctoral thesis (University of Birmingham, 2017), pp. 30–3, 37–42, 51–60, 63–6; Símun V. Arge, 'Uttangarðs: relics in the Faeroe outfield', in *'Utmark': The Outfield as Industry and Ideology in the Iron Age and the Middle Ages*, ed. by Ingunn Holm, Sonja Innselset and Ingvild Øye (Bergen: University of Bergen, [2005]), pp. 67–81 (pp. 69–70, 74–7).

[18] National Research Council, *Effect of Environment on Nutrient Requirements of Domestic Animals* (Washington, DC: National Academy Press, 1981), pp. 86, 88; M.L. Ryder and S.K. Stephenson, *Wool Growth* (London: Academic Press, 1968), pp. 65, 580. Ólafur R. Dýrmundsson, 'Shearing time of sheep with special reference to conditions in northern Europe: a review', *Icelandic Agricultural Sciences* 5 (1991), 39–46 (pp. 41–2).

Lambing took place in enclosed pens in spring and weaning occurred within six to eight weeks to enable a return to dairying. In Iceland, rams, wethers, ewe lambs and lambs were taken to hill and mountainous areas for summer grazing away from the farm to enable agriculture on the infields.[19] Milking ewes were separated to avoid suckling lambs, and in the early centuries of settlement were taken to shielings for summer grazing and dairying. Transhumance was transferred from the Norwegian homeland with emigration to Iceland, Faroe and later Greenland, although it continued the longest in Norway. Women and girls worked at dairying, but textile tools also have been identified at shieling sites.[20] In early autumn, flocks were taken back from summer pastures to fields nearer the farm. Here animals were examined for their future potential for reproduction, milking and wool. Animals were culled and slaughtered, with the remainder kept in lower pastures as winter set in.

Managing sheep flocks was usually done by shepherds, who worked with livestock owners to move animals for grazing, manage lambing and animal health, work the wool harvest and advise on culling and breeding decisions. They were a vital part of the management of large farms or where sheep were grazed by farms in common, as in Faroe. A shepherd's duty as guard was much reduced in islands, including Iceland, because of the lack of sheep predation, unlike the Scandinavian homeland, Greenland, and mainland Scotland.

SEASONAL DETERMINANTS AND ENVIRONMENTAL CONSTRAINTS

Seasonality has a strong influence over husbandry in high latitudes. Modern scientific studies of seasonal and environmental constraints on sheep provide an insight into the pressures and working methods possible to settlers in Viking areas (Fig. 1.2). Sheep in the north undergo certain dramatic physiological changes throughout the year. These changes regulate reproduction and the viability of milk, wool and lamb production. The physiological changes govern wool growth and quality, and the timing of the wool harvest. This is an area not well understood by textile historians and archaeologists, yet

---

[19] Anna Gudrún Þórhallsdóttir, Ingibjörg S. Jónsdóttir and Borgþór Magnússon, '3. Iceland', in *Sheep Grazing in the North-Atlantic Region – A Long Term Perspective on Management, Resource Economy and Ecology*, ed. by Gunnar Austrheim (Trondheim, Norway: NTNU, 2008), 22–43 (p. 26).

[20] Marit Anita Skrede, 'Shielings and landscape in western Norway: research traditions and recent trends', in Holm et al., '*Utmark*', pp. 31–41 (pp. 32–3); Tore Bjørgo, 'Iron Age house remains from mountain areas in inner Sogn, Western Norway,' in *Fra funn til samfunn: jernalderstudier tilegnet Bergljot Solberg på 70-årsdagen*, ed. by Knut Andreas Bergsvik and Asbjørn Engevik Jr. (Bergen, Norway: University of Bergen, 2005), pp. 209–28 (pp. 217–19); Ditlev L. Mahler, *Sæteren ved Argisbrekka: økonomiske forandringer på Færøerne i vikingetid og tidlig middelalder* (Tórshavn, Faroe Islands: Faroe University Press, 2007), pp. 86–7, 120–1, 208, 226–7; Paul M. Ledger, Kevin J. Edwards and J. Edward Schofield, 'Shieling activity in the Norse Eastern Settlement: palaeoenvironment of the "Mountain Farm", Vatnahverfi, Greenland', *The Holocene* 23 (2013), 810–22 (p. 820).

Fig. 1.2 A year in the life of a ewe, recorded in her fleece. © Carol Christiansen.

it has implications for understanding the type of wool and fibre excavated and the processes used to harvest and process wool. Textiles excavated at farms were likely made from wool produced on that farm or locally, yet excavated remains show that cloth qualities can have a broad range. This reflects wool variability in the indigenous breeds, as well as processing strategies to create certain end products.

Physiological reactions in livestock to the changing length of daylight and darkness (photoperiodism) govern the timing of important steps in the annual cycle of sheep rearing, including wool production. In response to decreasing daylight in autumn, hormonal changes occur, causing the onset of oestrus in ewes and an increase in sexual hormones in rams.[21] Historically, as well as today, rams were kept separate from breeding ewes and allowed access in late autumn to early winter (mid-November to January), with gestation lasting on average five months. During winter, the photoperiod slows the growth of wool in all sheep, leading to telogen, a rest phase in wool follicle growth.[22] Viking-period

---

[21] J.F. Quirke and J.P. Hanrahan, 'Differences in the breeding season of sheep', in *Endocrine Causes of Seasonal and Lactational Anestrus in Farm Animals*, ed. by F. Ellendorff and F. Elsaesser (Dordrecht, Netherlands: Martinus Nijhoff, 1985), pp. 29–43 (pp. 29–30); Lee M. Sanford et al., 'Photoperiod-induced changes in LH, FSH, prolactin and testosterone secretion in the ram', *Canadian Journal of Animal Sciences* 58 (1978), 123–8 (p. 127).

[22] G.A. Lincoln, 'Correlation with changes in horns and pelage, but not reproduction, of seasonal cycles in the secretion of prolactin in rams of wild, feral and domesticated breeds of sheep', *Journal of Reproduction and Fertility* 90 (1990), 285–98 (pp. 287–8, 291); Paul Edward Kendall,

SHEEP, WOOL, AND FLEECE PROCESSING

settlers from Norway would have been familiar with the seasonal cycle and its effect on oestrus, birth and changes to wool growth.

Keeping livestock near the farm in winter provided options for shelter against buildings and walls. Cold temperatures, wind and rain can occur on the North Atlantic islands any time of year, from any direction, and structures or walls were built in historic times to provide shelter against bad weather in the outfield.[23] Sheep are less affected by cold stress than other livestock due to their fleece, but newly shorn sheep are vulnerable. Cold stress is intensified by wind and rain, and sheep with fleeces that part along the backbone are particularly at risk when moisture soaks through to the skin.[24] The breeds of the North Atlantic tend to exhibit a mane and coarse hair behind the head and leading down the centre back. The hair is usually heavily pigmented and stands erect above the wool. The trait is more developed in rams but occurs in ewes, mainly at the back of the head. This primitive fibre growth trait will offset the central parting of fleeces and, accordingly, has been maintained in indigenous breeds in the North Atlantic.

THE WOOL

Sheep native to the North Atlantic region have fleeces with several fibre types. Such fleeces are often referred to as 'dual-' or 'double-coated' but such terms simplify their complexity. There are three types of fibre intermixed in the staple: short, fine wool; longer, coarser hair; and short, coarse kemp. Hair fibres are coarse at the distal (tip) end and fine at the proximal (skin) end (heterotype). Heterotype hair overhangs the wool and helps shed moisture, while the wool provides insulation and warmth. Kemp is short and extremely coarse, and sheds after a few months.[25] It occurs less frequently than hair and wool, and is generally found on the back thighs (britch) and belly areas but may be distributed throughout the fleece.

The heterotype formation of hair is considered a development toward fleece 'improvement' through breeding, by narrowing coarse fibres to eventually create a uniform fleece.[26] In some breeds the heterotype hair is medium fine (Shetland, Orkney, some Faroese), in others the hair is predominantly coarse (Icelandic, Norwegian Villsau). As the hair emerges from its primary follicles in late spring the fibres are coarse, and remain so during the summer when nutritional intake is at its greatest. As winter progresses, vegetation loses its nutritional benefits and wool and hair fibres begin to narrow. At the same time, hormonal changes due to photoperiodism take place and cause fibres to

---

'Prolactin and Wool Growth in the Romney Ewe', Unpublished doctoral thesis (Massey University, 1999), p. 12.

[23] McCooey, 'Farming practices', pp. 63–6; Arge, 'Uttangarðs', p. 70; Ian Laurence Tait, 'Shetland Vernacular Buildings 1600–1900', unpublished doctoral thesis (University of St Andrews, 2006), pp. 196–7.

[24] National Research Council, *Effect of Environment*, p. 86.

[25] M.L. Ryder and S.K. Stephenson, *Wool Growth* (London: Academic Press, 1968), p. 284.

[26] Ryder and Stephenson, *Wool Growth*, p. 285.

enter the telogen stage. Loss of pigment in this stage is usually more pronounced in hair fibres, contributing to their heterotype appearance. The dual effects of nutritional decline and photoperiod are more acute in pregnant ewes than rams, wethers and ewe lambs.[27] Furthermore, ewes bearing twins or triplets have shown a reduction in wool yield and fibre strength, compared to ewes carrying a single lamb.[28]

THE MOULT

The effect of living in a high latitude causes Northern short-tail type breeds to moult their wool, similar to wild sheep. This is a natural process induced by photoperiodism, which governed when wool was harvested.

The annual phases of wool growth develop from the anagen (robust growth of the fibre) stage in late spring, to a slowing and dormancy (telogen) stage in winter and finally a period of cessation of fibre growth and regression of the follicle (catagen) in early spring. During catagen, the old fibre remains in the follicle but gradually moves upward. As daylight in the north increases in length and intensity in spring, hormonal changes cause wool to enter the anagen or growth state once more. New, robust fibres, heavily pigmented in indigenous breeds, form at the base of the follicle, which lengthens. The new fibre grows upward and emerges from the follicle, while at the same time the old, thinned fibre works its way free from the skin.

The old fleece is left suspended on the animal for some weeks as the anagen phase continues to grow new wool. The old fleece is bound together by its density and suspended by a few continuously growing but extremely thin fibres. At its proximal (skin) end it is often coagulated with two secretions from the follicles, suint (thick perspiration) and grease, which bind the ends of the fibres together. As the new fleece grows rapidly and robustly, the old fleece begins to pull away from the body due to its weight, from sheep rubbing against surfaces and from lambs leaning and climbing on their mothers. This phase of the moult is sometimes called 'the rise', because the old fleece appears to rise up on the animal, signalling the period when wool removal should begin.

THE WOOL HARVEST

The process of removing wool by plucking (Old Norse, Icelandic, *rýja*; Færoese, *royta*; Shetland, *roo*) was the main method of wool harvest with sheep that naturally moult. Translations of old texts do not always make the distinction and substitute 'shear' for 'pluck', when this practice has continued into the late twentieth century. Shears are found in the archaeological record, mainly in female graves, but it is uncertain whether they were used for removing wool and they were more likely for cutting cloth.

[27]   David G. Masters, C.A. Stewart, and P.J. Connell, 'Changes in plasma amino acid patterns and wool growth during late pregnancy and early lactation in the ewe', *Crop and Pasture Science* 44 (1993), 945–57 (p. 951).

[28]   Kendall, 'Prolactin and Wool Growth', p. 15.

Knives, scissors or shears were used in areas of the fleece if the moult was not complete, but most often tools were not required. The animal was held or its legs tied and the wool was removed by pulling, in sections or by staple. The old and new fleece separated at the thinnest point of fibre growth at the proximal end. If the fleece had a good 'rise' and was whole, it could be gently coaxed away from the animal's body by inserting the hands under the old fleece to sever the remaining attached fibres. This was usually done from the lower belly toward the backbone, from where the wool was rolled back, and the animal was then turned over so the other side could be loosened and removed. The fleece was fully removed from the animal once both sides were freed at the backbone.

Moulting fleeces tended to break apart while still on the animal. This occurred more frequently when wool removal was delayed, because the new incoming fleece kept growing and the old fleece hung heavier on the animal. It is unlikely this would have happened often in the past, when wool was more valuable and crucial to the success of the farm. Fleeces were not removed in wet weather, as mould can stain and severely affect the quality of wool. Warm weather could also pose problems, since body heat and movement of the animal cotted (felted) the fine wool at the proximal end of the old fleece. Cotted fleeces had to be cut away from the animal and were difficult to process without tools such as wool combs.

In fleeces where the 'rise' had not fully taken place or the moult was not complete, the staples had to be plucked individually, coaxed apart or cut at the narrowest point of the fibres with a knife, scissors or shears. This was most common at the shoulders and the upper back legs. In some sheep the moult is gradual and the wool may come loose over a period of days or several weeks. Where sheep were kept near the farm and were tame, it was possible to remove the wool according to these natural stages to ensure it was not cast naturally and lost.

The proximal side of the old fleece, whether in large sections or by staple, often contains a layer of suint, which has the consistency and colour of beeswax. This binds together the fibre ends of the old fleece and helps to keep the wool in fleece or staple formation. Wool staples or fleece sections could be stored together or roughly sorted according to quality, based on area of the fleece, or colour. Sorting by quality was more difficult if plucked by staple, because qualitative differences were easier to determine if laid out in pelt formation or large sections.

If sheep that moult are shorn, the fleece is removed as a single pelt-shaped form, but shearing can cause harm to the wool and difficulties for further processing. The extremes in fibre diameter between the thinned old fleece and the thick, robust, incoming fleece mean that shearing can impose an additional division along the 'rise'. If shorn too close to the animal, the tip of the incoming new fleece is removed, potentially causing damage to the wool and harm to the animal during the winter. If the proximal end of the old fleece is cut off, it removes the ends of the finest fibre.

North Atlantic farmers of moulting breeds were aware of the problem with shearing and the benefit of allowing the natural cycle of the moult to take place. In December 1616, a century and a half after the Northern Isles were ceded to Scotland by the Dano-Norwegian crown, King James VI of Scotland instructed his Privy Council to end the 'rude custome ... [of] ... violently plucking the woll frome the sheepe' in Orkney and

Shetland. It was ordered that sheep must be sheared in the 'ordinaire tyme of clipping' as on the Scottish mainland or face a penalty of four shillings per sheep plucked. The islanders vehemently objected and put their case to the Privy Council of Scotland. They explained that their ancient practice was necessary because their sheep were wintered on uninhabited islands and holms without protection from the weather. By waiting for the natural moult and plucking, 'the woll ... is keeped at the full length, quhairby the awnair has the full commoditie of the woll, as is knowin by experience ...'.[29] This suggests that sheep imported from the mainland by Scottish immigrants did not moult but had to be shorn, and were shorn much earlier in the year than the natural moult took place in Shetland sheep. Imposing a different method and time scale to wool removal would have destroyed the islands' wool clip and caused livestock fatalities. Islanders argued that they would be unable to pay their taxes and might be forced to move to Norway. The Crown was made aware of the natural processes inherent in the wool harvest of Northern short-tail type breeds and the Act was withdrawn.

PROCESSING

For the same reason that a carcass was deconstructed and made into different products, fleeces were separated into their component parts and reorganised to make textiles with specific qualities: warmth, water- or wind-repellency, durability, softness, drape or strength. The wool from one's sheep had to clothe infants to adults, become outerwear for work in hills and at sea, be made into bedding, tarpaulins, sails and transport sacks. The variety of fibre types, fineness, lengths and colours in each fleece meant that different levels of hand processing were necessary or desirable before spinning took place. If fibre coarseness and length were extreme in the staple and not first separated from fine, short fibres, then spinning would be made more difficult and the usefulness of both qualities would be compromised. Thorough processing meant getting the most out of the annual clip for the purposes required.

Some processing methods are mentioned in the historical record or interpreted from archaeological finds, but the true nature is not often clear or has been misunderstood.[30] Early modern visitors to North Atlantic communities who kept diaries of their visits were men, and their interests did not always enter the sphere of detailed household processes managed by women. As more recent studies of craft practice have shown, the nuances of materials, knowledge gained through sensory responses and skills leading to certain actions are challenging to identify and record.

Processing done by the household or immediate community meant individuals worked with fleeces they were familiar with from previous years, from sheep they knew and possibly retained specifically for their wool. Wool working methods were necessarily

---

[29] *Shetland Documents 1612–1637*, ed. by John H. Ballantyne with cont. by Brian Smith (Lerwick: Shetland Times, 2016), p. 144.

[30] Marta Hoffmann, *The Warp-weighted Loom* (Oslo: Norges almenvitenskapelige forskningsråd, 1964), pp. 285, 381–2; H.P. Hansen, *Spind og Bind. Bindehosens – Bindestuens og Hosekræmmerens Saga* (Copenhagen: Ejnar Munksgaards, 1947), pp. 17–19.

Fig. 1.3 Staple separation, from l. to r.: intact Icelandic staple, separated by hand (short, fine, medium, coarse), separated by combing (comb waste, fine with some medium, medium with some fine and coarse, only coarse). © Carol Christiansen.

sequential, and once fleece deconstruction began, it could not be undone. Wool removed in sections could be graded according to staple qualities in the section, whereas wool removed by staple was more difficult to grade into lots unless this was done at the time of plucking.

Some areas of the fleece may have had a level of uniformity in the staple. This occurs mainly around the face and anus, where the fibre is usually short and fine, although it can be damaged due to its location. Most of the wool will have fibre variability in the staple, which can be pronounced. Staples must be separated to retrieve the different qualities (Fig. 1.3). The ways separation was achieved and subsequent grading of fibre types following separation are not understood from early sources and not able to be accurately determined from excavated textiles. Two methods are recorded here and their different results may inform analysis of wool processing locations in the archaeological record.

Separation by hand is possible by pulling on the coarse tip away from the proximal end. This method will ease the heterotype hair fibres away from the shorter wool fibres. Two fibre types will be created, with some gradation in the heterotype group.

Fig. 1.4 Shetland 19th-century woolcombs. Wooden handles, sheep horn bases and iron tines. Tines measure 14.5 cm long, 5 mm diameter, 5 mm spacing. Combs weigh 332 and 336 gr. Similarly made combs were used in Faroe. © Carol Christiansen.

Wool combs have been found archaeologically in Viking and medieval Norwegian contexts and are mentioned in Icelandic sagas of the thirteenth and fourteenth centuries.[31] Surviving large iron *togkambar* were used for combing only the coarse outer hair (*tog*) of the Icelandic fleece, but *þelkambar* are mentioned in records to comb the shorter and finer underwool.[32] In Faroe and Shetland, small wool combs (Fig. 1.4) with horn bases are found and were in use until the twentieth century.[33]

At the end of passing the combs through the staples several times, the hair fibres hang below. As fibres are drawn off the comb, the shorter fibres, which are generally finer, follow in a gradual sequence. The result is a long strip of wool, with coarse fibres at one end and fine fibres at the other. The drawing process is not exacting, since heterotype

---

[31] Hoffmann, *The Warp-weighted Loom*, pp. 284–5.

[32] Elsa E. Guðjónsson, 'Svolítil athugasemd ullarkambar, ekki togkambur', *Árbók Hins Íslenzka Fornleifafélags* 95 (1999), 203–6 (pp. 204–5).

[33] Hoffmann, *The Warp-weighted Loom*, p. 382; Carol A. Christiansen, 'Primitive Wool and Early Textile Production in Shetland', unpublished doctoral thesis (University of Manchester, 2003), p. 119; Hansen, *Spind og Bind*, pp. 26–7.

SHEEP, WOOL, AND FLEECE PROCESSING

fibres are drawn off as coarse fibres in the beginning of the draw and their fine ends are mixed with the fine wool fibres, which can be drawn off as a separate quality due to their shorter length. The lengths of drawn fibre are loosely wound for spinning or storage.

Using wool combs is less time consuming than separation by hand because many staples can be combed at once, but the process is less precise. Careful excavation has uncovered wool staples from medieval Shetland and Greenland.[34] They show long coarse fibres, some which appear to be heterotype. It is not clear whether there is a distinct concentration of short fine fibres at the top. In some of the excavated staples the change from coarse to fine diameters also shows a colour change to less pigmentation in the fine fibre area. These staples have not been processed with wool combs but they may be the remains of hand processing.

Concentrations of sheep ectoparasites in archaeological contexts have been interpreted as evidence of possible textile production.[35] They may mark areas where wool was processed, since the ectoparasites die within several weeks after wool is removed from the animal.[36] Their remains in specific areas suggest wool was stored for a period of months and later processed by teasing or combing. Combs completely deconstruct the staple, rather than just separate it, as hand processing does. By doing so they open the natural wool formation completely, allowing dirt, vegetation and insect remains to fall away. Teasing the wool can have a similar effect.

COLOUR

The sheep taken to the north and west Atlantic had variously pigmented fleeces: black, brown and white, or shades (e.g. fawn) or combinations (e.g. grey) of these colours. Wool colour, fleece patterning and fibre colour variation is complex in many Northern short-tail type breeds and few sheep were self-coloured (of a single, uniform fleece colour). As

---

[34] Penelope Walton Rogers, 'Textile, yarn and fibre from The Biggings', in *The Biggings, Papa Stour, Shetland: The History and Excavation of a Royal Norwegian Farm*, ed. by Barbara E. Crawford and Beverley Ballin Smith (Edinburgh: Society of Antiquaries of Scotland, 1999), pp. 194–202 (pp. 197–8); Penelope Walton Rogers, 'The raw materials of textiles from GUS, with a note on fragments of fleece and animal pelts from the same site', in *Man, Culture and Environment in Ancient Greenland*, ed. by Jette Arneborg and Hans Christian Gulløv (Copenhagen: Danish National Museum & Danish Polar Center, 1998), pp. 66–73 (pp. 68–70).

[35] Véronique Forbes, *Insect Remains of the Middle at Möðruvellir* (Quebec City: Université Laval, 2013), pp. 8, 11; P.C. Buckland and D.W. Perry, 'Ectoparasites of sheep from Stóraborg, Iceland and their interpretation', in *BugsCEP Coleopteran Ecology Package*, [ed. by] P.I. Buckland and P.C. Buckland (Boulder, CO: NOAA/NCDC Paleoclimatology Program, 2006), pp. 37–46 (pp. 38, 42–3); P.C. Buckland and D.W. Perry, 'Ectoparasites of sheep from Stóraborg, Iceland and their palaeoecological significance (Piss, parasites and people: a palaeoecological perspective)', *Hikuin* 15 (1989), 37–46.

[36] S. Crawford, P.J. James and S. Maddocks, 'Survival away from sheep and alternative methods of transmission of sheep lice (*Bovicola ovis*)', *Veterinary Parasitology* 94 (2001), 205–16 (pp. 207–11, 214–15); C.R. Toop, 'Recognition and control of lice and keds in sheep', *Journal of the Department of Agriculture, Western Australia* n.s. 4, 5 (1964), 816–24 (p. 820).

noted above, fibres can change colour during their year of growth. In coloured sheep, heterotype fibres often undergo a gradual reduction and cessation of pigment altogether during the telogen phase.[37] In addition, exposed pigmented hair forming the staple tip will often become bleached by the sun, with brown taking on a reddish or yellowish tinge. As sheep age, their fleece becomes less abundant, and in coloured sheep their wool may lose pigment or grey.

Some animals exhibit certain colour characteristics, such as black spots on a white fleece, or primitive colouring traits such as a white belly below a dark fleece ('Mouflon pattern'). The Old Norse language had an extensive vocabulary to identify sheep by their wool colours, fleece patterning and hair patterning on face, legs and tail.[38] The words mainly pertain to colour markings on the body, noting primitive traits such as white around the eyes or other facial markings in order to distinguish and discuss sheep in the flock. Subtle differences in fibre colouration are described in detailed fleece colour notation, as in the Shetlandic Norn word *sjela*, 'having wool of a dark colour (black, dark grey, bluish-grey, brown), but lighter at the points of hair, giving a lighter shade to the surface', from the Old Norse, *héla*, hoar-frost.[39]

The substantial lexicon describing fleece colouration and patterning is testimony to the variability that was allowed to continue for centuries in North Atlantic breeds, often through methods of common husbandry arrangements.

Differences in fleece and fibre colours were used to advantage in Viking and Norse fabric design. When differently pigmented hair and wool were used for warp and weft, respectively, colour patterning in cloth could be achieved. Medieval cloth remains show that dyes also were used on pigmented wools to create additional colours.[40] Most of the textiles people wore and which were used by the household were brown or grey, or a combination of differently pigmented fibres blended during processing of fleeces to prepare wool for spinning.

WOOL AMOUNTS

Fleece weight and staple length vary among the North Atlantic breeds today and the amount and length of wool sheep typically carried on their backs during the Viking migration and settlement period is unknown. Icelandic and Norwegian Villsau breeds today have heavier fleeces (1.5–2.5 kg, 3.3–5.5 lbs) with longer staples than Shetland or Orkney (1.5 kg) breeds. Faroese sheep have fleeces similar to Shetland, although in some parts of the islands there are sheep with longer-stapled fleeces similar to Icelandic. Some

---

[37] Ryder and Stephenson, *Wool Growth*, p. 288.

[38] Dánjal Jákup Mortensen, 'Seyðalitir og gásalitir í Øravík', *Fróðskaparrit* 45 (1997), 5–23 (pp. 9–21); Christiansen, 'Primitive Wool', pp. 259–64.

[39] Jakob Jakobsen, *An Etymological Dictionary of the Norn Language in Shetland* (Lerwick: Shetland Folk Society, 1985), p. 765.

[40] Penelope Walton Rogers, 'Fibres and dyes in Norse textiles', in Else Østergård, *Woven into the Earth: Textiles from Norse Greenland* (Aarhus, Oxford: Aarhus University Press, 2004), pp. 79–92 (pp. 89–91).

island communities experienced large-scale losses of native sheep in the past due to importation of diseased sheep. This was followed by further importation of neighbouring Northern short-tail type breeds in order to rebuild stocks. Today there are intra-breed variations due to breeding for specific textile products (weaving versus knitting), standards set by breed organisations or private farm initiatives to specialise in characteristics such as specific colours.

It is not known what effect, if any, the development of the lucrative *vaðmál* (woven woollen cloth) trade had on breeding for specific fleece weight and staple length in the medieval period. Five qualities of *vaðmál* were recognised in Iceland and two in Shetland,[41] but the specific nature of each in terms of fibre lengths and fleece weights would be impossible to determine. The amount of *vaðmál* leaving Iceland was more than was exported from Faroe and Shetland. *Vaðmál* shipped to Bergen from these islands in the early sixteenth century records a range of uses for the cloth, from tarpaulins and sails (Icelandic), to mittens and winter socks (Icelandic and Shetlandic), and salaries paid as cloth for clothing to male labourers, as well as caulking (Icelandic, Shetlandic and Faroese).[42] This indicates variable ranges in the quality of wools resulting from processing and workmanship, but is perhaps also a reflection of the establishment of distinct breeds in the island communities seven centuries following settlement by the Norse. Standardisation in the *vaðmál* trade in Iceland, and possibly Shetland, would indicate the need to retain certain characteristics and possibly increase fleece weights or flock numbers as the trade flourished.

CONCLUSION

In the period of the Viking emigration to the west and north, products, skills and knowledge from the homeland were carried on board. Clothing packed may have been expected to last the first years of settlement and household textiles to serve the first generation of settlers. Sheep were required for a continuation of cloth production, and to survive successfully in a new climate and landscape for meat and milk production. The producer of sheep, milk and wool also was the consumer and could influence what qualities to retain and which to eradicate. The relationship between creating the necessary raw fibre and using the cloth made from it was symbiotic and based on an exchange.

Raising sheep was ultimately governed by seasonal forces that affected the animal's ability to breed, produce milk and how and when it would produce wool. Farm and community minimised impacts on livestock through husbandry strategies, following seasonal cycles and retaining physiological characteristics inherited from much earlier, wild breeds. These traits are now of interest to livestock geneticists and environmental scientists for genetic diversity conservation and research into adaptability and the landscape impact of domesticated animals that have required only minimal interaction with farmers during centuries of settlement.

---

[41] Hoffmann, *The Warp-weighted Loom*, p. 213; Christiansen, 'Primitive Wool', p. 205.

[42] Helgi Þorláksson, *Vaðmál og Verðlag: vaðmál í utanlandsviðskiptumog búskap Íslendinga á 13. og 14. öld* (Reykjavík: Háskóli Íslands, 1991), p. 364.

CHAPTER 2

Potential Insights on Archaeological Textiles: The Nature of Preservation and the Conservator's Eye

Elizabeth E. Peacock

Cognitive and systematic examination, analysis, and documentation of textile arte-facts as part of the post-excavation investigative conservation process provide valuable insights into artefact technology, material culture, and human and material adaptation. In addition to the study of the material state and features, the conservator[1] assesses the nature and state of preservation. Through this, one gains insight into what changes have taken place to the textile, and when during the active and post-deposition lifetime of the object. There are multiple layers of evidence available, starting with diagnostic changes to the outer surfaces (e.g. loss of surface fibres), internal microstructural changes (e.g. fibre bioerosion), and chemical alterations (e.g. mineral perfusion of fibres). The state and nature of preservation of archaeological textiles testify not only to use during their active lifetime, such as wear, damage, and loss, but also to the nature of, and dynamic interaction with, their post-depositional burial environment.[2] The conser-

---

ORCiD: 0000-0002-2894-720X

[1] The term *conservator* denotes a conservation, conservation-restoration, or restoration professional.

[2] See Bill Cooke, 'Fibre damage in archaeological textiles', in *Textiles for the Archaeological Conservator*, ed. by Sonia A. O'Connor and Mary M. Brooks, *UKIC Occasional Papers* 10 (London: UKIC, 1990), pp. 5–13; Bill Cooke and Brenda Lomas, 'The evidence of wear and damage in ancient textiles', in *Textiles in Northern Archaeology*, ed. by Penelope Walton and John-Peter Wild (London: Archetype Publications, 1990), pp. 215–226; Bill Cooke, 'Creasing in ancient textiles', *Conservation News* 35 (March 1988), 27–30; Frances Pritchard, 'Missing threads from medieval textiles in north west Europe', in O'Connor and Brooks, *Textiles for the Archaeological Conservator*, pp. 15–17.

vator's expert knowledge of this complexity and interactivity of textile materials with their environment enables them to help make sense of archaeological textiles. In this respect, conservation can contribute in a substantive way to a wider cultural, archaeological, and environmental interpretation of this material.

This chapter explores the contributions that the archaeological conservator's expert knowledge and specialist conservation skills can make to the study of textile artefacts. Its scope is not restricted by time period, cultural context, burial environment, or geographical region, although many examples are drawn from the north-eastern Atlantic region. The corpus of archaeological textiles and methodological approaches for their analysis and study are briefly described. It is the conservator's naked eye and observation using equipment readily available in most archaeological conservation laboratories (e.g. microscopy, X-radiography, etc.) that is fundamental for their investigation of textile artefacts. The range of analytical equipment that augments visual observation available in today's conservation laboratory varies widely from large national museums to local and regional museums. More specialised and expensive analytical instruments to which conservation professionals in smaller institutions cannot easily obtain access are not discussed here. This chapter seeks to provide the non-conservator with insight into what an archaeological conservator's knowledge can bring to archaeological textile research, beyond standard technical analysis. Several cases demonstrate that observations made during investigative conservation of burial textiles illustrate that these materials can also be environmental markers both of the postmortem and post-depositional taphonomy[3] of the burial as well as of broader climate changes.

THE CORPUS OF ARCHAEOLOGICAL TEXTILES FOR STUDY

Finds of textiles in archaeological contexts are considered rare in comparison with finds of more durable materials such as metal and ceramics. In fact, they are found in more significant numbers than is generally assumed. The corpus of archaeological textile materials for study ranges from recently excavated materials to accessioned objects in long-established museum and archive collections. Textile materials recovered from archaeological contexts are most commonly fragmentary, and mechanically and chemically degraded at one or more levels (e.g. fibre, yarn, fabric, garment). Many of the physical and chemical properties of textiles are transformed through use and taphonomic processes in the burial environment, such that the find's resemblance to its original characteristics may be altered beyond recognition. The environmental conditions that favour their preservation are those that inhibit microbial growth, such as exceptional

---

[3] The term taphonomy was originally coined to describe the changes organisms experience after death as they leave the living world (biosphere) and enter the geological record (lithosphere). More recently it has been applied to the early changes both organisms and cultural materials undergo as they enter the archaeological record.

coldness (e.g. arctic sites), wetness[4] (e.g. deep urban environments, marine sites, bogs, burial mounds, mines), or dryness (e.g. deserts, caves, tombs, churches, secular buildings). Moreover, special circumstances can lead to the formation of mineral-preserved or carbonised pseudomorphs.[5] Textiles recovered from damp, wet, or frozen sites are commonly brown in colour, biodeteriorated to a greater or lesser extent, water saturated, and unstable unless the water is removed under controlled conditions. The potential for analysis and examination prior to controlled drying can be restricted because they are usually extremely weak. This fragility prohibits mechanical manipulation and detailed study must be delayed until the piece is freeze-dried (non-vacuum or vacuum).

Textile artefacts recovered from dry environments range from well-preserved and robust enough to handle, to friable and brittle; yet, unlike artefacts from wet environments, they are stable and often can be examined and studied extensively prior to or without conservation. Carbonised remains are extremely fragile and difficult to handle and examine, but can be stable when recovered from dry deposits.[6] Textile evidence that has been preserved as a result of interaction with mineral sources in the archaeological deposit takes a variety of forms dependent upon numerous environmental factors. In these deposits, textiles are encrusted with, infilled with, or chemically complexed with dissolved ion solutes from different sources within the surrounding environment (e.g. plaster, silicates, salts, bone) or from metal objects (iron (Fe), copper (Cu), silver (Ag)). This permineralisation or fossilisation process is most familiar in cases where the morphology of the actual textile is preserved to some extent as a positive cast. Negative casts are less commonly recorded because these are encapsulated in mineral corrosion products, and discovered only when the corrosion product is fractured.[7] Textiles recovered

---

4   A fluctuating saturated–unsaturated wet environment does not lead to favourable preservation of fibrous textile materials.

5   Mineral preservation of animal and plant tissues involves their infiltration by soluble metal salts and oxides. It takes place over a spectrum of replacement where the tissue may be barely altered, as in the flooding of pore spaces with copper ions which inhibit biological decay, through to the other extreme where metal ions perfuse the tissues fully, binding to biopolymers and filling pores – then later oxidising to an insoluble mass that preserves the morphology and dimensions of the altered (degraded) tissue. These pseudomorphs will invariably contain some traces of original organic matter.

6   For scanning electron microscope (SEM) micrograph examples of carbonised textile fibres see Antoinette Rast-Eicher, *Fibres. Microscopy of Archaeological Textiles and Furs* (Budapest: Archaeolingua Alapítvány, 2016), pp. 24–25, figs. 19–20. For carbonised textiles from wet sites see Andrea Ramírez Calderón, 'Conservation of Charred Archaeological Textiles. Consolidation Treatments and Long-term Preservation Strategies' (unpublished master's thesis, Neuchâtel: HES-SO, 2018).

7   For SEM micrograph examples of positive and negative casts of mineral-preserved textile fibres see Rast-Eicher, *Fibres*, pp. 16–17, 22, 33–35, figs. 6, 7, 14, 15, 32–35. See also, Nicole Reifarth, 'Textiles in their scientific context – interdisciplinary cooperation during the evaluation of burial textiles', in *Purpureae Vestes III. Textiles y Tintes en la Ciudad Antigua*, ed. by Carmen Alfaro Giner, Philippe Borgard, Jean-Pierre Brun and Rafaela Pierobon-Benoit (Valencia: University of Valencia, 2011), pp. 101–107.

from mines (e.g. copper, salt) can be preserved by their fibres being covered by a discontiguous dusting of mineral grains.[8] Yet another related form of preservation is textile evidence preserved as positive features in archaeological soils, which are neither particularly solid nor cohesive and disintegrate upon contact.[9] The removal of the insoluble mineral component of metal-preserved or plaster-preserved textile fibres is not possible; whereas soluble-salt-preserved fibres can be gently sprayed to remove the salts.[10]

The other main source of archaeological textiles is long-established museum and archive collections. These have a collection history in addition to their pre-deposition and excavation biography.[11] The condition of textiles in these collections can range from un-conserved, treated on site only, to conserved, and can be further influenced by post-excavation storage and display conditions; all of which will influence the extent of access to information contained within when these collections are revisited.[12] The nature of the conservation will vary as well. In older institutions, this will reflect the conservation and housing methods and approaches current during the period in which the treatment took place.[13] Consolidants have been widely used on fragile and highly deteriorated fibre

---

[8] Corentin Reynaud, Mathieu Thoury, Alexandre Dazzi, Gaël Latour, Mario Scheel, Jiayi Li, Ariane Thomas, Christophe Moulhérat, Aurore Didier, and Loïc Bertrand, 'In-place molecular preservation of cellulose in 5,000-year-old archaeological textiles', *Proceedings of the National Academy of Sciences*, 117.33 (August 2020), 19670–19676; DOI: 10.1073/pnas.2004139117, accessed 14 February 2023.

[9] These structures appear to be composed of a mix of soil components on a macroscopic scale; see Julie Unruh, 'Ancient textile evidence in soil structures at the Agora excavations in Athens, Greece', in *Ancient Textiles. Production, Craft and Society*, ed. by Carole Gillis and Marie-Louise B. Nosch (Oxford: Oxbow, 2007), pp. 167–172.

[10] The textiles recovered from the Hallstatt salt mines are an example of this type of preservation and conservation treatment. See Karina Grömer and Hans Reschreiter, 'Chapter 2: Hallstatt – 160 years of research', in *Textiles from Hallstatt: Weaving Culture in Bronze Age and Iron Age Salt Mines*, ed. by Karina Grömer, Anton Kern, Hans Reschreiter and Helga Rösel-Mautendorfer (Budapest: Archaeolingua, 2013), pp. 33–41.

[11] See, for example, Irene Skals, 'From grave to showcase: modern care for ancient textiles', in *Archaeological Conservation and its Consequences*, ed. by Ashok Roy and Perry Smith (London: IIC, 1996), pp. 162–165.

[12] See Jane Anne Malcolm-Davis, 'Shedding light with science: the potential for 21st century studies of 16th century knitting', *Journal of Dress History* 1.1 (2017), 83–91 for an example of revisiting textile collections.

[13] For studies of earlier approaches to be found in historic archaeological textile collections see Catherine Higgitt, Susanna Harris, Caroline Cartwright, and Pippa Cruickshank, 'Assessing the potential of historic archaeological collections: a pilot study of the British Museum's Swiss lake dwelling textiles', *British Museum Technical Bulletin* 5 (2011), 81–94; Kim Travis, 'A history of conservation: organic materials from the Neolithic Lake-Dwelling sites of Zurich 1850–2005', in *NESAT IX: Archäologische Textilfunde – Archaeological Textiles*, ed. by Antoinette Rast-Eicher and Renate Windle (Ennenda: Archeo Tex), pp. 17–24; Anke Grit Weidner, 'Montierung textiler Objekte unter Glas', in *Historische Textilien: Beiträge zu ihrer Erhaltung und Erforschung*, ed. by Sabine Martius and Sibylle Ruß (Nuremberg: Germanisches Nationalmuseum, 2002), pp. 129–138.

assemblies (e.g. carbonised or mineral-preserved fragments) and garments both on site and in the laboratory as well as for storage or display.[14] In numerous examples, consolidation has preserved these pieces, although there are many instances in which it has also seriously compromised later study of the material.[15]

Textile assemblies that were recovered in the field as block lifts still encased in their surrounding soil matrix (and surrounded by a plaster or other support), and which have long-since dried out, are problematic to examine and study without further treatment.[16] A notable example is the extraordinary number of textiles recovered in 1904 from the Oseberg (Norway) ship burial. These compressed, multiple layers of folded textiles encapsulated in blue clay were cut up and shovelled out in 3–4 cm thick blocks (subsequently referred to as 'cakes') and air dried shortly thereafter. When prioritised for conservation and study eight years later in 1912, these cakes were deformed, hard, cracked, and disintegrating. Anne Stine Ingstad noted in 1992 that 'Mange er så stive og utydelige at enhvert forsøk på å analysere dem er praktisk talt umulig'.[17] [Many are so rigid and indistinct that any attempt to analyse them is virtually impossible].

---

[14] A range of consolidants have been used over the years, including natural and synthetic waxes (e.g. paraffin wax, nail varnish, polyvinyl acetate, polyethylene glycol); see Rast-Eicher, *Fibres*, pp. 60–61, figs. 76–79; Travis, 'A history of conservation'; Ulrike Rothenhäusler and Betty Sacher, 'Re-conservation of the textile collection from the Swiss National Museum and Cantonal Archaeology of Zurich', in Rast-Eicher and Windle, *NESAT IX*, pp. 25–27.

[15] See Annemarie Stauffer, 'A study of the conservation problems of archaeological textiles treated with synthetic consolidants', in *Intrecci Vegetali e Fibre Tessili da Ambiente Umido: Analisi Conservazione e Restauro*, ed. by Cristina Dal Ri, Luisa Moser, and Elizabeth E. Peacock, Incontri di Restauro 4 (Trento: Provincia Autonoma, Servizio Beni Culturali, Ufficio Beni Archeologici, 2005), 174–97; Skals, 'From grave to showcase'.

[16] Imaging methods such as standard X-radiography or computerized tomography (CT), which can generate cross-sectional images, could be a first step.

[17] Anne Stine Ingstad, 'Tekstilene i Osebergskipet', in *Osebergdronningens grav. Vår arkeologisk nasjonalskatt i nytt lys*, ed. by Arne Emil Christensen, Anne Stine Ingstad and Bjørn Myre (Oslo: Schibsted, 1992), pp. 176-208 (185); English translation: http://www.forest.gen.nz/Medieval/articles/Oseberg/textiles/TEXTILE.HTM, accessed 14 February 2023. Some of the textile 'cakes' were successfully freed of their encapsulating clay coating, but the conservation was not completed for all the textile material. For a description of the textiles' post-excavation history see Margunn Veseth, 'Osebergtekstiler. Forberedende undersøkelser før et forsøk på separering av tekstilkaker' (unpublished bachelor's thesis, University of Gothenburg, 2004), pp. 17-25, 34-37, figs. 2, 4, 5, 9 and 10; Torunn Nilssen Beck, 'Tre, tekstiler og skjeletter i Osebergfunnet' (master's thesis, University of Oslo, 2014), pp. 64-70; online at https://www.duo.uio.no/bitstream/handle/10852/40846/Osebergfunnet.pdf?sequence=1, accessed 14 February 2023. The conservation dilemma of this textile material has not been resolved but is currently (2021-2025), a Research Council of Norway-funded project; https://prosjektbanken.forskningsradet.no/en/project/FORISS/316268?Kilde=FORISS& distribution=Ar&chart=bar&calcType=funding&Sprak=no&sortBy=date&sortOrder=desc&resultCount=30&offset=0&Fritekst=TexRec, accessed 14 February 2023.

There are numerous guides for field archaeologists to the handling and conservation of artefacts in the field for a range of climates, but none focuses specifically on textile materials.[18] Several publications do specifically address the on-site treatment of archaeological textiles.[19] The long-term preservation of these materials, from recovery in the field to conservation in a laboratory to housing in a research archive or museum, varies widely, dependent upon many factors (e.g. staff expertise, financing, planning, time). An on-site textile or archaeological conservator or textile specialist is not common today.[20]

TEXTILE ARTEFACT INVESTIGATION

The analysis of textile artefacts is complex. One of the main challenges is fibre degradation; fibres are frequently not fully comparable to modern or historic material. The primary method of analysis of archaeological textiles has always been – and continues to be – the same as that for historic textiles, the collection of information through visual observation and microscopy. Traditionally, this has revolved around the systematic recording of technical aspects such as identification of the raw materials, yarn properties, fabric structure and construction, thread count, borders, structural sewing, decoration, and colour description. With degraded archaeological material, this analysis is supplemented by documenting non-technical features related to a textile's state, such as creases, missing threads, and damage (e.g. wear, soiling, ingrained deposits, staining, mechanical abrasion) – visual features not captured by standard systematic technical

[18] See David Watkinson and Virginia Neal, *First Aid for Finds* (London: Rescue/UKIC Archaeology Section, 2009); Wendy Robinson, *First Aid for Underwater Finds* (London: Archetype Publications, Nautical Archaeology Society, 1998); Rosalie Scott and Tara Grant, ed., *A Conservation Manual for the Northern Archaeologist* (Yellowknife, Canada: Prince of Wales Northern Heritage Centre, 2007); https://www.pwnhc.ca/manuals-and-legislation/, accessed 14 February 2023; Katherine Singley, *The Conservation of Archaeological Artefacts from Fresh Water Environments* (South Haven, MI: Lake Michigan Maritime Museum, 1988); Catherine Sease, *A Conservation Manual for the Field Archaeologist* (Los Angeles: Cotsen Institute of Archaeology Press, 1994); https://escholarship.org/uc/item/8ft6488x, accessed 13 February 2023.

[19] See for example, Elizabeth E. Peacock, 'Fibrous materials: on site conservation', in *Archaeological Method and Theory: An Encyclopaedia*, ed. by Linda Ellis (New York: Garland Publishing, 2000), pp. 205–209; Jana Jones, Julie Unruh, Regina Knaller, Irene Skals, Lise Raeder-Knudsen, Eva Jordan-Fahrbach, and Louise Mumford, 'Guidelines for the excavation of archaeological textiles', in *First Aid for the Excavation of Archaeological Textiles*, ed. by Carole Gillis and Marie-Louise B. Nosch (Oxford: Oxbow, 2007), pp. 5–29; Jenna Tedrick Kuttruff and Mary Strickland-Olsen, 'Handling archaeological textile remains in the field and laboratory', in *Beyond Cloth and Cordage: Archaeological Textile Research in the Americas*, ed. by Penelope Ballard Drooker and Laurie D. Webster (Salt Lake City, UT: The University of Utah Press, 2000), pp. 25–50.

[20] John Peter Wild describes two cases of unsuccessful attempts of conservation in the field, John Peter Wild, 'Handling archaeological textiles. The rough guide', in Martius and Ruß, *Historische Textilien*, pp. 63–67.

analysis.[21] Also visible to the naked eye are the overall appearance and visual impression of a textile in the form of topographical features such as lustre, texture, density, thickness, transparency, and coarseness/fineness. Standard technical examination has proved consistently insufficient to describe the visual character and properties of textiles that are technically the same but which differ in appearance.[22] Hammarlund introduced the concept of applying experienced-based handicraft knowledge and skills to investigate the source of these technically complex properties and demonstrated that it is the manner of construction that influences the foundation of a fabric's appearance.[23] This interaction of handicraft factors (e.g. binding, finishing) led to a method of visual grouping of archaeological textiles.[24] Other properties embodied by the textile artefact that elude technical examination include sensory information. Reconstructions and experimental archaeology studies provide opportunities to investigate many sensory properties (e.g.

[21] See Penelope Walton and Gillian Eastwood, *A Brief Guide to the Cataloguing of Archaeological Textiles*, 3rd edn (London: Institute of Archaeology Publications, 1988), which describes fifteen aspects to be considered and recorded for each fragment; Margarita Gleba and Ulla Mannering, 'Introduction: textile preservation, analysis and technology', in *Textiles and Textile Production in Europe from Prehistory to AD 400*, ed. by Margarita Gleba and Ulla Mannering (Oxford: Oxbow, 2011), pp. 1–24, Table 0.1 at p. 4 specifies thirteen descriptive parameters that should be recorded as part of textile examination and analysis. Numerous report forms such as that of Kuttruff and Strickland-Olsen, 'Handling archaeological textile remains', pp. 43–50, have been developed to facilitate recording textile attributes. Similarly, numerous report forms have been developed for the recording of fibre attributes, such as for wool by Martha Goodway, 'Fiber identification in practice', *Journal of the American Institute for Conservation* 26 (1987), 27–44 (pp. 38–43).

[22] The objective measurement of these and similar properties historically posed difficulties for the textile industry, as well as in the evaluation of proposed conservation treatments for archaeological textiles. For example, see Elizabeth E. Peacock, 'A note on the effect of multiple freeze-thaw treatment on natural fibre fabrics', *Studies in Conservation* 44.1 (1999), 12–18.

[23] Lena Hammarlund is a trained and experienced hand spinner and weaver. See Lena Hammarlund, Heini Kirjavainen, Kathrine Vestergård Pedersen and Marianne Vedeler, 'Visual textiles: a study of appearance and visual impression in archaeological textiles', *Medieval Clothing and Textiles* 4 (2008), 69–98.

[24] Hammarlund's studies could, in fact, represent an early application of the *chaîne opératoire* model to the study of archaeological textiles. See Christophe Delage, 'Once upon a time … the (hi)story of the concept of the *chaîne opératoire* in French prehistory', *World Archaeology* 49.2 (2017), 158–73, DOI: 10.1080/00438243.2017.1300104, accessed 14 February 2023. For application of the concept of *chaîne opératoire* to archaeological textile studies, see, for example, Eva Andersson Strand, 'The textile *chaîne opératoire*: using a multidisciplinary approach to textile archaeology with a focus on the ancient Near East', *Paléorient* 38.1–2 (2012): 21–40, DOI: 10.3406/paleo.2012.5456, accessed 14 February 2023.

drape, cover factor,[25] durability) that are transformed beyond resemblance through use and taphonomic processes.[26]

Beyond the morphological, topographical, and other visible features lies a profusion of information contained within textile materials. There are many avenues of approach when investigating archaeological textiles. The identification of dyestuffs and mordants was one of the first properties of textiles to be investigated using chemical and instrumental techniques. More recently, the advancement of analytical technologies within the natural sciences has seen methods adopted/adapted not only to analyse dyes but also to extract new, previously inconceivable, types of information, including biomolecular analysis (e.g. ancient DNA, paleo-proteomics),[27] isotope tracing,[28] and radiocarbon (^{14}C) dating. Beyond the actual textile artefacts, studies of context, of associated materials such as tools and implements, together with archaeobotanical and archaeozoological remains, supported by investigations of craftmanship, and experimental archaeology all contribute to the growing field of archaeological textile research.

THE CONSERVATOR'S KNOWLEDGE

Conservators make extensive contributions to the study of archaeological textiles. Many archaeological textile finds specialists are, in fact, experienced professional archaeological conservators. They bring to their research the knowledge, experience, and the

---

[25] See Bill Cooke, Carol Christiansen, and Lena Hammarlund, 'Viking woollen square-sails and fabric cover factor', *Journal of Nautical Archaeology* 31.2 (2002), 202–210, DOI: 10.1006/ijna.2002.1039, accessed 14 February 2023.

[26] Susanna Harris, 'The sensory archaeology of textiles', in *The Routledge Handbook of Sensory Archaeology*, ed. by Robin Skeates and Jo Day (London: Routledge, 2019), pp. 210–232.

[27] See Caroline Solazzo, 'Characterizing historic textiles and clothing with proteomics', *Conservar Património* 31 (2019), 97–114. DOI: 10.14568/cp2018031, accessed 14 February 2023.

[28] Strontium isotope ratios ($^{87}Sr/^{86}Sr$) are being applied to provenance textile artefacts (e.g. Karin Margarita Frei, Ulla Mannering, Kristian Kristiansen, Morten E. Allentoft, Andrew S. Wilson, Irene Skals, Silvana Tridico, Marie Louise Nosch, Eske Willerslev, Leon Clarke, and Robert Frei, 'Tracing the dynamic life story of a Bronze Age female', *Scientific Reports* 5 (2015), pp. 1–7; DOI: 10.1038/srep10431, accessed 14 February 2023); however, more recent studies indicate that ratios for wool recovered from wet burial environments do not accurately reflect wool provenance; see Isabella C.C. von Holstein, Penelope Walton Rogers, Oliver E. Craig, Kirsty E.H. Penkman, Jason Newton and Matthew J. Collins, 'Provenancing archaeological wool textiles from medieval Northern Europe by light stable isotope analysis (δ13C, δ15N, δ2H)', *PLOS ONE*, 11.10 (2016), DOI: 10.1371/journal.pone.0162330, accessed 14 February 2023; Lihai Hu, Diego P. Fernandez, Thure R.E. Cerling and Brett J. Tipple, 'Fast exchange of strontium between hair and ambient water: implication for isotopic analysis in provenance and forensic studies', *PLOS ONE* 15.5 (2020), DOI: 10.1371/journal.pone.0233712, accessed 14 February 2023; and that modern agricultural practices can affect present-day surface waters; see Erik Thomsen and Rasmus Andreasen, 'Agricultural lime disturbs natural strontium isotope variations: implications for provenance and migration studies', *Science Advances* 5.3 (2019), DOI: 10.1126/sciadv.aav8083, accessed 14 February 2023.

practical, analytical skill set of an archaeological conservator. Quite frequently, it is the conservator who is the first responder – the first to handle, examine, and record a textile find, be it in the field or in the conservation laboratory. It may well be the only point at which the artefact is investigated in detail and microscopically. It will be the conservator who catches sight of non-technical features, especially damage and deterioration, during the investigative phase of conservation. The conservator's knowledge of the complex interactions between organic material and their surrounding post-disposition environment enables them to shed light on not only the textile remains but also the associated find context.

As pointed out earlier, the primary scientific research method of analysis in the study of textile artefacts is visual observation. Observation competency is a basic skill that the conservator learns by guided practice. It must be systematically learned, and it is a perishable skill. Conservators are trained to examine objects in detail, and conservation is a multisensory experience. Observation is most commonly associated with the sense of sight alone, but a competent conservator also uses the senses of smell, touch, taste, and hearing. An excavated textile can give off an earthy (e.g. musty, mouldy, peat-like, swampy), chemical (e.g. tar), or offensive (e.g. putrid, septic, decayed, latrine) odour. Artefacts in a museum store may have specific odours that raise alarm, for example, musty, mouldy, or indicative of actively degrading conservation materials. For most people, visual observation is deceptively simple and seemingly so trivial that it need not be learned.[29] This is a mistake. Observing is more than passively 'seeing'. 'Just looking' becomes scientific observation when questions are asked, hypotheses generated, and data interpreted on the basis of those hypotheses.[30] Visual inquiry requires a coordination of disciplinary knowledge, theory honed by experience, and the habitual practice of attention. In conservation, observation is combined with reflective thinking and the conservator's (tacit) knowledge – not unlike the craft skills of a surgeon, a weaver, or a cook.[31]

The instruments of visual observation include not only the naked eye, but also tools such as the magnifying glass, microscope, and a myriad of technologies designed to make the invisible visible. However, technology alone can never supplant the conservator whose senses, judgement and acuity are always essential to the integrity of the

---

[29] Stephen P. Thomkins and Sue Dale Tunnicliffe, 'Looking for ideas: observation, interpretation and hypothesis-making by 12-year-old pupils undertaking science investigations', *International Journal of Science Education* 23.8 (2001), 791–813, DOI: 10.1080/09500690119322, accessed 17 February 2023.

[30] Lucia Kohlhauf, Ulrike Rutke and Birgit Neuhaus, 'Influence of previous knowledge, language skills and domain-specific interest on observation competency', *Journal of Science Education and Technology* 20 (2011), 667–678, DOI: 10.1007/s10956-011-9322-3, accessed 17 February 2023; Catherine Eberbach and Kevin Crowley, 'From everyday to scientific observation: how children learn to observe the biologist's world', *Review of Educational Research* 79.1 (2009), 39–68, DOI: 10.3102/0034654308325899, accessed 17 February 2023.

[31] Salvador Muñoz-Viñas, 'Conservation science, conservation practice and the conservator's knowledge: a naïve exploration', *Journal of the Institute of Conservation* 45, no. 3 (2022), 173–189, DOI: 10.1080/19455224.2022.2112407, accessed 17 February 2023.

observation.[32] The levels of information that can be gleaned from microscopy and methods of analysis that rely on secondary visual observation (e.g. X-radiography) improve as the conservator becomes more familiar with the scope and limitations of instrumental analysis, and the best way to tease information from objects.

Conservation is a complex and evolving cultural process that Hölling characterises as 'an entanglement of theory and practice ... a complex sum of approaches and processes that refuses to fall into pre-established categories'.[33] Conservation embodies investigation, preservation (preventive and remedial) and presentation; and its boundaries extend beyond mere hands-on interventions. The field of conservation has undergone considerable changes in attitudes and practices in the opening decades of the twenty-first century, and this has had a knock-on effect for conservation education and training. The roles that conservators undertake have become increasingly diverse. There has been an undeniable shift in conservation approaches from practical to more investigative methods, and from direct intervention to more preventive conservation and collections care activities. To address these more expanded roles, conservation training attempts to fit an increasing amount of content and skills into the curriculum (e.g. disaster management, public engagement, environmental monitoring and management, project management, conservation science, and analytical methods), but delivered within the same academic time frame with scaled-back contact teaching hours. There is much handwringing and discussion in both the sector and educational establishments about these changes in the profession, especially the reduced frequency of direct intervention and, consequently, the need to develop high-level, hands-on conservation skills.[34] The conservation skills base encompasses conservation treatment skills, generic skills, and new skills. Although the demand for, and development of, interventive treatment skills is being pared down, the opposite is the case for the conservator's specialist visual observation and analytical skills, of which there is a heightened awareness and demand for both.

An important dimension of the conservator's knowledge that is not being pared down is conservation ethics. Ethics underpin the conceptual basis of the profession. Codes of ethics – accompanied by standards/guidance/rules of practice – provide guidelines and

---

[32] Lorraine Daston and Elizabeth Lunbeck, 'Introduction. Observation observed', in *Histories of Scientific Observation*, ed. by Lorraine Daston and Elizabeth Lunbeck (Chicago: University of Chicago Press, 2011), pp. 1–9.

[33] Hanna Hölling, 'The *technique* of conservation: on realms of theory and cultures of practice', *Journal of the Institute of Conservation* 40.2 (2017), 87–96 (p. 87), DOI: 10.1080/19455224.2017.1322114, accessed 17 February 2023.

[34] See Jonathan Ashley-Smith, 'Losing the edge: the risk of a decline in practical conservation skills', *Journal of the Institute of Conservation* 39.2 (2016), 119–132, DOI: 10.1080/19455224.2016.1210015, accessed 17 February 2023; Robyn Sloggett, 'Conservation skills', *Journal of the Institute of Conservation* 45.3 (2022), 157–172, DOI: 10.1080/19455224.2022.2112968, accessed 17 February 2023; Frances Halahan, 'Changes in attitudes and training in conservation', *Journal of the Institute of Conservation* 41.1 (2018), 79–84, DOI: 10.1080/19455224.2017.1417012, accessed 17 February 2023.

an ethical framework for decision making, and these evolve as the profession matures.[35] One aim is to require the conservator to consider all available options. Instilling the codes of ethics for conservation is an integral part of an emerging conservator's training, resulting in a qualified conservator addressing problems while unconsciously steered by their ingrained ethical compass.[36] Ethical considerations related to the disinterment, handling, study, and exhibition of human remains from archaeological contexts have been, and continue to be, a much-debated issue. The intimate association of textile materials with human remains recovered from archaeological contexts is not uncommon; neither has been the involvement of conservators with such finds. Previously, it was common for clothing to be removed and separated from human remains to be studied and undergo separate conservation treatment.[37] There are many case studies of the conservation of

[35] See Chris Caple, *Conservation Skills. Judgement, Method and Decision Making* (London; Routledge, 2000), pp. 59–60; European Confederation for Conservator-Restorers' Organisations (E.C.C.O.), 'E.C.C.O. Professional Guidelines (II) Code of Ethics' (2003); https://www.ecco-eu.org/wp-content/uploads/2021/03/ECCO_professional_guidelines_ II.pdf, accessed 13 February 2023; Catherine Sease, 'Codes of ethics for conservation', *International Journal of Cultural Property* 7.1 (1998), 98–115, DOI: 10.1017/S0940739198770092, accessed 17 February 2023; Salvador Muñoz Viñas, *On the Ethics of Cultural Heritage Conservation* (London: Archetype, 2020); ICOM, *ICOM Code of Ethics for Museums* (2017); https://icom.museum/wp-content/uploads/2018/07/ICOM-code-En-web.pdf, accessed 13 February 2023.

[36] Archaeological conservators are much more cautious than object conservators. They are not only aware that valuable information can be embodied in the dirt or fabric of an object but also fully comprehend the possible repercussions of their actions. Furthermore, their work is affected by the codes of archaeologists, who, additionally, may be largely unaware of the conservator's ethical restrictions; see Sease, 'Codes of ethics for conservation'. Conflicts in ethics and practice in archaeological textile conservation are widely acknowledged and debated; see Zsuzsanna Bakó, 'Consistency of ethics and practice in the conservation of archaeological textiles: the Avas Crypt finds', in *International Perspectives on Textile Conservation: Papers from the ICOM-CC Textiles Working Group Meetings, Amsterdam, 13–14 October 1994 and Budapest, 11–15 September 1995*, ed. by Ágnes Tímár-Balázsy and Dinah Eastop (London: Archetype Publications, 1998), pp. 150–154; Mary M. Brooks, 'International codes of ethics and practice and their implications for teaching and learning ethics in textile conservation education', in Tímár-Balázsy and Eastop, *International Perspectives on Textile Conservation*, pp. 74–80; Hanna Jedrzejewska, 'Problems of ethics in the conservation of textiles', in *Conservazione e Restauro dei Tessilli. Convegno Internazionale, Como, 1980. Conservation and Restoration of Textiles. International Conference, Como 1980*, ed. by Francesco Pertegato (Milan: Centro Ital. Studio Storia del Tessuto, Sezione Lombardia, 1982), pp. 99–103; Elizabeth E. Peacock, 'Study of archaeological textiles intimately associated with human remains – where is the ethical dilemma?', in Rast-Eicher and Windle, *NESAT IX*, pp. 12–16; Mary Brooks, Alison Lister, Dinah Eastop, and Tarja Bennet, 'Artifact or information? Articulating the conflicts in conserving archaeological textiles', *Studies in Conservation* 41, sup. 1 (1996), 16–21, DOI: abs/10.1179/sic.1996.41.Supplement-1.16, accessed 17 February 2023; Irene Skals, 'Exhibition of textiles from burials. An expression of ethical and political values', *Zeitschrift für Kunsttechnologie und Konservierung* 13.2 (1999), 375–378.

[37] See Elizabeth E. Peacock, 'Study of archaeological textiles'; Gunilla Lagnesjö, 'Några tankar om livet efter döden eller vem tog brallorna av Bockstensmannen eller vad handlar egentligen etikdiskussionen om eller', *SFTnytt* XXIX (1996), 7.

textiles separated from their associated remains, but few reported cases where textile and human remains have neither been separated nor subjected to remedial conservation.[38]

THE CONSERVATOR'S ANALYTICAL SKILL SET

Despite the apparently bewildering array of apparatus and methods, probably the most potent tool remains the human eye, aided by a good binocular microscope at one end and an informed brain at the other![39]

Close examination is fundamental to archaeological conservation, and excavated textile materials are no exception. It aims to identify the nature of the artefacts both as a record and for developing an informed conservation strategy. The main aim is always to collect as much information as possible non-invasively, and to minimise the number of samples to be taken for invasive destructive analysis. Critically for textile artefacts, a multi-analytical approach is vital in obtaining a clearer picture of the features and state of preservation, as no single technique may prove conclusive, although each provides information.

Non-invasive Analysis

The primary methods of investigation used by both archaeological textile researchers and conservators is macroscopic and microscopic analysis. Macroscopic examination involves observation by the naked eye, which may be augmented by a hand magnifier (10x magnification); whereas microscopic examination is carried out with a low-magnification stereomicroscope (10x to 70x magnification) or a portable digital microscope.[40] These methods are non-invasive in that no sample is removed. Low-level visual examination can be enhanced by employing a range of electromagnetic radiation wavelengths beyond the visible range (400–700 nm). Those which are most commonly used are the ultraviolet (UV: 10–400 nm), infrared (IR: 700 nm–1 mm) and X-ray (10 pm–10 nm) regions. Infrared photography and ultraviolet radiation have been common and valuable non-invasive examination tools in conservation since the early 1930s. With the advent of digital photography, ultraviolet (UV) and infrared (IR) imaging techniques are no

---

[38] See for example, Anna Javér, Dinah Eastop and Rosalind Janssen, 'A sprang cap preserved on a naturally dried Egyptian head', *Textile History* 30.2 (1999), 135–154, DOI: abs/10.1179/004049699793710598, accessed 17 February 2023; Anton Runesson, Emma Maltin, Elizabeth E. Peacock, Stina Tegnhed and Charlotta Hanner Nordstrand, 'Ett 1800-talsfynd från Åkerby. Ett nyfött barn i en svepask' [A 19th-century find from Åkerby. A newborn baby in a bentwood box], in *Årsboken Uppland 2022*, ed. by Håkan Liby (Uppsala: Upplands Fornminnesförenings Förlag, 2022), pp. 84–97.

[39] Paul Craddock and Sheridan Bowman, 'The scientific detection of fakes and forgeries', in *Fake? The Art of Deception*, ed. by Mark Jones (London: British Museum Publications, 1990), pp. 275–289 (276).

[40] Visual observation can be enhanced under raking, ultraviolet, and infrared light sources.

longer film dependent.[41] Use of IR and UV light enables the observer to see and record images in these otherwise non-visible regions.[42] For example, regions of a textile with different colourant chemistry may show selective absorption, reflectance, and fluorescence of electromagnetic radiation. IR and UV light photography were investigated to study the faded coloured patterns on some of the conserved silk fabric fragments from the aforementioned Oseberg ship grave.[43] IR imaging did not reveal complex weave structures; but UV imaging revealed coloured surface patterns that are no longer visible.

X-radiography is a rapid, non-invasive imaging technique, and X-ray systems are common in conservation laboratories that treat archaeological objects. It is a most important tool, the use of which traditionally has been closely associated with the study of metal artefacts and investigation of excavated soil blocks. Many laboratories have upgraded from analogue to digital (computed) X-radiography (CR). Conventional X-radiography records three-dimensional objects in two dimensions and this can be seen as a limitation; although experienced archaeological conservators do not find this a problem in routine investigations. In fact, the inherent versatility of digital X-radiography over traditional analogue film has reduced this.[44] With modern systems it is possible to view the X-ray image simultaneously and continuously whilst moving the object.

The application of X-ray technology to the study of ancient, historic, and museum textiles is rooted in the conservation investigation of textile artefacts in conservation laboratories with both the equipment and the archaeological conservator's knowledge of the potential of X-ray analysis. X-ray examination was carried out on textile–leather composite footwear recovered during archaeological excavations (1955 and 1960) undertaken of the eighteenth-century Russian Pomor coastal hunting station at Russekeila, Svalbard

---

[41] For an in-depth guide to digital photography in conservation see Jeffrey Warda, ed., *The AIC Guide to Digital Photography and Conservation Documentation*, 2nd edn (Washington, DC: American Institute for Conservation of Historic and Artistic Works, 2011).

[42] In addition to white LED lighting, handheld digital microscopes are available with built-in polariser and UV and IR LED lighting.

[43] Marianne Vedeler, 'New light on samite silk from Oseberg', in *NESAT XI. The North European Symposium for Archaeological Textiles XI, 10–13 May 2011*, ed. by Johanna Banck-Burgess and Carla Nübold (Rahden/Westf: Marie Leidorf, 2013), pp. 181–186 (182, fig.1).

[44] Computerised tomography (CT, micro CT, nano CT) overcomes this by recording in three dimensions; however, these systems are not commonplace in conservation laboratories. Computerised tomography is commonly employed to investigate mummies and, more recently, coffined individuals. See Sanna Lipkin, Erika Ruhl, Krista Vajanto, Annemari Tranberg and Jenni Suomela, 'Textiles: decay and preservation in seventeenth- to nineteenth-century burials in Finland', *Historical Archaeology* 55 (2021), 49–64, DOI: 10.1007/s41636-020-00270-4, accessed 17 February 2023. For investigation of blocks of soil see Ingrid Wiesner, Jörg Stelzner and Nicole Ebinger-Rist, 'Virtual analyses of Neolithic textiles', in Banck-Burgess and Nübold, *NESAT XI*, pp. 109–17. It is reported, though, that basic textile structural parameters cannot be accessed through CT scanning of a mummy bundle, M. Linda Sutherland, 'Use of computed tomography scanning in a "virtual" bioarchaeology of care analysis of a Central Coast Peruvian mummy bundle', *International Journal of Paleopathology* 25 (2019), 129–138, DOI: 10.1016/j.ijpp.2018.12.006, accessed 17 February 2023.

in the Norwegian Arctic.[45] Upon retrieval from the permafrost, the frozen artefacts were placed in paper bags and dried out naturally, retaining their distorted, as-excavated shape. The naturally coloured, well-preserved textiles and well-worn composite footwear were not examined or investigated until conserved 25 years later. X-radiographic examination of one shoe revealed stitching holes in the leather, the weave technologies of the multiple textile layers, and that the textile–leather construction was much more multilayered than the shoe itself appeared. A completely unexpected finding was the unmistakable image of the wearer's toe bones (phalanges) in correct anatomical alignment in the shoes.[46] Consequently, the conservation strategy for the shoes was preservation through appropriate housing and storage solutions.[47]

It is to be noted that in the textile history and conservation literature the issue has been raised as to whether X-rays have the capacity to change the structure of textiles by, for example, damaging any DNA that may be available for analysis.[48] Although it is correct that X-rays have the capacity to damage DNA, it is unlikely that the exposures and low doses involved in imaging textiles would constitute a significant factor in DNA degradation.[49] Any changes that do occur are at such a low level as to be undetectable in terms of alteration of their physical and chemical properties.[50]

---

[45] Elizabeth E. Peacock, 'Contribution of X-radiography to the conservation and study of textile-leather composite archaeological footwear recovered from the Norwegian Arctic', in *X-radiography of Textiles, Dress and Related Objects*, ed. by Sonia O'Connor and Mary M. Brooks (Oxford: Elsevier Science, 2007), pp. 294–301.

[46] Further investigation to localise the on-site distribution of the textile artefacts led to study of the expeditions' documentation (e.g. reports and journals) and Tromsø Museum's collection catalogue, which revealed that many of the textiles had been removed and separated from buried individuals and were now completely disassociated from the human remains; Elizabeth E. Peacock, 'Potential insights artefact studies can contribute to circumpolar research questions as illustrated by finds recovered from archaeological investigations of two Russian Pomor hunting stations on Svalbard', in *A Circumpolar Reappraisal: The Legacy of Gutorm Gjessing (1906–1979): Proceedings of an International Conference Held in Trondheim, Norway, 10–12th October 2008*, ed. by Christer Westerdahl, British Archaeological Reports (BAR) International Series 2154 (Oxford: Archaeopress, 2010), pp. 253–262 (260, fig. 5).

[47] Another example of radiographic examination of a textile artefact is Meg Chuping Wang, 'Analytical and microscopy techniques used in investigative conservation for an archaeological cap unearthed from Canterbury, England', in *Scientific Analysis of Ancient and Historic Textiles: Informing Preservation, Display and Interpretation: Postprints*, ed. by Rob Janaway and Paul Wyeth (London: Archetype Publications, 2005), pp. 250–256.

[48] Malcolm-Davis, 'Shedding light', p. 84.

[49] Sonia O'Connor and Jason Maher, 'Assessing the risks of X-radiography to textiles', in O'Connor and Brooks, *X-radiography of Textiles, Dress and Related Objects*, pp. 91–95 (92).

[50] It was concluded that excessive exposure to low-energy X-rays produced no detectable changes to the mechanical integrity of historic and modern textiles; Peter Garside and Sonia O'Connor, 'Assessing the risks of radiographing culturally significant textiles', *e-Preservation Science* 4 (2007), 1–7.

There is an ever-increasing multitude of non-invasive imaging techniques being applied to the study of artefacts, such as reflectance transformation imaging (RTI),[51] fibre optics reflectance spectroscopy (FORS), and multiband imaging techniques (MBI).[52] Although these technologies are not readily available in archaeological conservation laboratories today, the cost and availability of equipment and analyses will no doubt make these an option in future.

Invasive Analysis

Invasive analysis normally requires removal of a sample and specimen preparation. It is a vast topic, with various specific protocols developed for different analytical techniques and instrumentation. The mainstay of destructive textile analysis has been transmitted light microscopy at magnifications up to 1000x. The microscopic examination of fibre, yarn/thread, and fabric samples mounted in an appropriate mountant (temporary or permanent) is often sufficient and is minimally destructive. There are a variety of microscopy techniques, often used in combination. Methods include thin and thick longitudinal (long axis) and cross-sectional views,[53] which can be augmented by microchemical (e.g. spot) tests. Optical techniques that can aid in viewing include the use of, for example, dark-field, polarised, or UV light to enhance contrast.

Spot tests are qualitative analytical methods that are widely available and low-cost techniques. Microchemical spot testing consists of removing a microscopic sample from the textile and treating it with small amounts of chemical reagents, such as stains or solvents, with or without applied heat. These induce a visible colour change, precipitate, dissolution, or gas evolution (odour/bubbles). The resulting reaction can be done at the laboratory bench or actually under the microscope. Many tests employed for archaeological textile analysis have been adapted from those developed in the early to mid-twentieth century for the textile industry, prior to the industry's reliance on analytical techniques such as scanning electron microscopy, IR spectroscopy or X-ray fluorescence.[54] The use

---

[51]   See Emily Frank, 'Documenting archaeological textiles with reflectance transformation imaging (RTI)', *Archaeological Textiles Review* 56 (2014), 3–13; https://www.atnfriends.com/download/ATR56samlet.pdf, accessed 21 February 2023; Y. Goldman, Ravit Linn, Orit Shamir and Mina Weinstein-Evron, 'Micro-RTI as a novel technology for the investigation and documentation of archaeological textiles', *Journal of Archaeological Science: Reports* 19 (2018), 1–10, DOI: 10.1016/j.jasrep.2018.02.013, accessed 17 February 2023.

[52]   MBI encompasses both multispectral imaging (MSI) and hyperspectral imaging (HSI).

[53]   See Textile Specialty Group of the American Institute for Conservation, 'TSG Chapter V. Analysis and testing methods for textiles – Section C. Fiber identification', *Textile Conservation Wiki*; https://www.conservation-wiki.com/wiki/TSG_Chapter_V._Analysis_and_Testing_Method_for_Textiles_-_Section_C._Fiber_Identification#ref10, accessed 13 February 2023 and Cordelia Rogerson and Dinah Eastop, 'The application of cross-sections in the analysis of historic textiles', *The Conservator* 23.1 (1999), 49–56, DOI: 10.1080/01410096.1999.9995138, accessed 17 February 2023, for the application of cross-sections in the analysis of textiles.

[54]   See María Teresa Doménech-Carbó and Antonio Doménech-Carbó, 'Spot tests: past and present', *ChemTexts* 8 (2022), article 4, DOI: 10.1007/s40828-021-00152-z, accessed 17

of spot tests has diminished considerably over the years in favour of more sophisticated, and necessarily more expensive, techniques. Fibres from archaeological materials can be thick, darkly stained, and occluded with soil and other contaminants. Numerous protocols have been developed to help resolve fibre identification problems. They can be further difficult to study because of changes in their structure during use and taphonomical alteration in the burial context; the latter of which can inform on the nature and timing of degradation. Solubility and staining spot tests are especially successful for the identification of fibre classification (protein vs plant), consolidants, consolidated fibres, and mineral-preserved fibres and for highlighting fibre damage.[55]

Instrumental Analysis
Methods of analysis thus far described can be supplemented by technologically more advanced methods. There is a wide range of analytical instrumentation employed in the analysis of archaeological textiles such as Fourier-transform infrared spectroscopy (FTIR), Raman spectroscopy, X-ray diffraction (XRD), X-ray fluorescence spectroscopy (XRF), scanning electron microscopy (SEM), transmission electron microscopy (TEM), high performance liquid chromatography (HPLC), gas chromatography and mass spectrometry (GC/MS), computerised tomography (CT), and VIS/NIR hyperspectral imaging.[56] Many of these methods (e.g. FTIR, environmental SEM) accommodate micro-analysis in that the specimen is neither prepared nor destroyed in the analysis. Increasingly this instrumentation is becoming available as handheld (HH) or portable (P) analysers (e.g. Raman, XRF, and FTIR) and acquired by conservation laboratories, especially HH-XRF by archaeological laboratories. In addition to these smaller portable instruments becoming more affordable, they enable *in situ* analysis, negating the need for sampling. One needs to be circumspect, though, in choice of method(s).

February 2023; Karen Thompson, Margaret Smith and Frances Lennard, 'A literature review of analytical techniques for materials characterisation of painted textiles – Part 1: categorizing painted textiles, sampling and the use of optical tools', *Journal of the Institute of Conservation* 40, no. 1 (2017): 64–82, DOI: 10.1080/19455224.2016.1269355, accessed 21 February 2023.

[55] Felicitas Weiße and Annemarie Stauffer, 'Conservation of an early Etruscan cloak', in *ICOM-CC 12th Triennial Meeting Lyon 29 August–3 September 1999 Preprints Volume II*, ed. by Janet Bridgeland and Jessica Brown (London: James and James, 1999), pp. 667–670; Kilian Anheuser and Myrsini Roumeliotou, 'Characterisation of mineralised archaeological textile fibres through chemical staining', *The Conservator* 27.1 (2003), 23–33, DOI: 10.1080/01410096.2003.9995187, accessed 17 February 2023; Stauffer, 'A study of the conservation problems'.

[56] See Mina Magdy, 'Analytical techniques for the preservation of cultural heritage: frontiers in knowledge and application', *Critical Reviews in Analytical Chemistry* 52.6 (2022), 1171–1196, DOI: 10.1080/10408347.2020.1864717, accessed 17 February 2023, for an overview of analytical techniques applicable for the characterisation of archaeological objects; and Margaret Smith, Karen Thompson and Frances Lennard, 'A literature review of analytical techniques for materials characterisation of painted textiles – Part 2: spectroscopic and chromatographic analytical instrumentation', *Journal of the Institute of Conservation* 40.3 (2017), 252–266, DOI: 10.1080/19455224.2017.1365739, accessed 17 February 2023, for an overview of spectroscopic and chromatographic techniques applicable to the characterisation of archaeological textiles.

For example, SEM is often the go-to microscopic method for fibre analysis even though details of the medulla and lumen as well as any pigment and dye – visible using optical microscopy – are obscured.

BURIAL TEXTILES AS ENVIRONMENTAL MARKERS

In the past, humans were interred either in an earth-cut grave or within a crypt or tomb; each of which could be within or outside a place of worship. Textiles have always played a prominent role in death as clothing, bedding, or coverings/wrappings. Consequently, a not insignificant number of the corpus of archaeological textiles have been recovered from inhumation burials.

Innumerable studies of burial textile artefacts have been carried out and, traditionally, these have focused on a myriad of approaches including technology, construction, function, understanding garments, and fashion. Additionally, this material has been the subject of degradation studies of the effects that burial environments have on the nature and rate of decomposition (e.g. mineral-preservation).[57] Less attention has been directed to the bearing textile artefacts might have had on the postmortem-interval and post-depositional macro-environment or what their state of preservation can contribute to an understanding of taphonomic processes. Furthermore, just as information in textile reports might become buried in the appendices of excavation reports, so too can taphonomic evidence that is revealed during investigative or remedial conservation go overlooked in conservation reports.

The aforementioned well-preserved textile–leather composite footwear recovered in the late 1950s from a mass grave at Russekeila on Svalbard drew interest following the 2001/2 rescue excavations of another eighteenth-century Russian Pomor coastal hunting station that was located at Kapp Wijk.[58] Unlike the permafrost site conditions at Russekeila some forty-five years earlier, Kapp Wijk was being lost to the sea as a result

---

[57] For example, see Rob C. Janaway, 'The textiles', in *The Spitalfields Project. Vol. 1. The Archaeology: Across the Styx*, ed. by Jez Reeve and Max Adams, CBA Research Report 85 (York: Council for British Archaeology, 1993), pp. 93–119; Lipkin et al., 'Textiles: decay and preservation'; Karina Grömer and Martin Grassberger, 'Organic remains from archaeological contexts. Forensic taphonomy applied to prehistoric and early medieval inhumation graves', *Neues Jahrbuch für Geologie und Paläontologie* 289.2 (2018), 203–216, DOI: 10.1127/njgpa/2018/0750, accessed 17 February 2023.

[58] The west coast of West Spitsbergen is dotted with the exposed decayed wooden ruins of these hunting stations, which are surface depositions and typically were situated on a flat, raised terrace upslope from the beach and high-tide line. The Kapp Wijk site had disappeared by 2004. See Peacock, 'Potential insights'. Beyond the investigative conservation carried out by Peacock ('Potential insights') and Elizabeth E. Peacock, 'Conservation of severely deteriorated wet archaeological leather recovered from the Norwegian Arctic. Preliminary results', in *Proceedings of the 9th ICOM Group on Wet Organic Archaeological Materials Conference*, ed. by Per Hoffmann, Kristiane Strætkvern, James A. Spriggs and David Gregory (Bremerhaven: ICOM WOAM, 2005), pp. 565–578, the Kapp Wijk site and artefacts have been neither studied nor published.

of coastal erosion. The recovered Kapp Wijk artefacts, especially the work shoes, were culturally identical to those recovered at Russekeila, but unrecognisably so.[59] The textile artefacts were in a broken-down, discoloured and waterlogged state. Their condition was witness to having been in the active ground surface zone, and subjected to wave action, winter storms, and multiple freeze–thaw cycling events. The disparate states of preservation of these two textile collections, especially the work shoes, were flagged up during conservation intervention. Textile and leather, being naturally organic, are more predisposed to physico-chemical degradation than inorganic materials, and in the arctic environment of Svalbard prove a sensitive environmental marker of the rapidly changing climate of their post-depositional cultural environments.

Several medieval shrouds from burials in north-west England were conserved at the Area Museum Service Textile Conservation Laboratory in the period 1973–82.[60] The clay-embedded Quernmore (Lancaster) shroud and its log coffin – dating to the seventh–eighth century CE – had been exposed, disturbed, and damaged by a mechanical excavator while digging a drain. Finger and toe nails and locks of hair adhered to the shroud and were all that remained of the body. When received for conservation, the two dried-out pieces of the shroud had been 'washed' and disassociated from the human remains. In addition to standard technical analysis of the pieces of cloth, observations made during investigative and remedial conservation revealed the position of the body within the shroud, the wrapping technique of the shroud, and the relationship between the wrapped body and the coffin. Another two linen shrouds that formed the inner and outer wrappings of a well-preserved male corpse were discovered inside a damaged lead coffin contained within an outer wood coffin in the grounds of St Bee's Priory (Cumbria). These were also unwrapped and disassociated from the corpse prior to being received for conservation. Here too, standard technical analysis of the damp shrouds was supplemented by investigative conservation observations. Impressions and depressions on the inner shroud clearly indicated the positions of head, heels, and toes; crease marks suggested the shroud had been gathered together at the head end; and a lengthwise fold revealed the position of the body. The fabric was impregnated with a bituminous compound to which tufts of hair adhered, and fabric folds suggested the coating had been applied after the body had been bound. Similar observations were not reported for the outer shroud. Information extracted from observations of the Quernmore and St Bee's Priory shrouds provided additional insights into body decomposition, placement, and wrapping.

An informal, multidisciplinary team of specialists addressing questions related to the field of foetal loss has studied the coffins and contents of several post-medieval, secret foetal burials.[61] In 2015, during architectural restoration works on the parish church (1831)

---

[59] Peacock, 'Potential insights', p. 257, fig 3.

[60] Jeanette M. Glover, 'The conservation of medieval and later shrouds from burials in north west England', in O'Connor and Brooks *Textiles for the Archaeological Conservator*, pp. 49–58.

[61] The deliberate secret burial of a foetus, primarily in or adjacent to churches but also in other settings, was a widespread but seldom-reported tradition in Nordic Europe since the Middle Ages that continued into the twentieth century. Members of the *Nordic Research Group for*

in Gällared (Halland), Sweden a tiny, lidded wooden box (10.7 x 6.8 x 5.3 cm) was discovered in the well-aerated crawl space just beneath the floorboards.[62] Unaware of the possible significance of the box and its contents, workers on site removed its lid, revealing a dry piece of folded cloth, which was found to be wrapped around the naturally partially mummified remains of a tiny human body. The remains comprised twenty-three fragments of cartilage and skin that were adhering to the cloth.[63] The find was handed over to the county archaeologist at Kulturmiljö Halland, and the research team was later invited to study the find. Since the coffin had already been opened and the textile shroud removed, it was possible to study the contents individually – although only the textile will be discussed here. The off-white rectangular cotton textile shroud (14.7 x 8.5 cm) was intact, soft, and in good condition. Having been in a cool, dry, above-ground environment, it was not discoloured and retained much of its pre-burial characteristics. It had been carefully fashioned specifically as a shroud from a re-purposed garment or household linen. The inside was lightly stained pink in the silhouette of a tiny body along one half – probably a transfer stain resulting from contact with body fluids. The light staining indicates that the body was washed – and perhaps dried – prior to being wrapped. The burial shroud contributed significantly to the preservation of the corpse. The specific area of staining along one side points to the body being in direct, intimate contact with the shroud, and that the shroud was double folded around it. The body would have had no gut flora to accelerate putrefaction after death, nor direct contact with bacteria from soil. It became naturally partially mummified by the principal mechanism of desiccation as indicated by the presence of minute fragments of dried tissue on and the adhesion of the skeletal parts to the burial shroud. Together with the natural moisture-wicking

---

Foetal Loss in the Past are archaeologist Stina Tegnhed, Kulturmiljö Halland, Halland Museum of Cultural History; osteoarchaeologist Emma Maltin, Bohusläns Museum and Stockholm University; Professor Emerita Elizabeth E. Peacock, NTNU University Museum; historian Dr Anton Runesson, Stockholm University; and, previously, church historian Dr Charlotta Hanner Nordstrand, University of Gothenburg. The team reflects a diversity of approaches, with each member being crucial to the success of the team's work. See Runesson et al., 'Ett 1800-talsfynd från Åkerby', and Emma Maltin, Elizabeth Ellen Peacock, Stina Tegnhed and Charlotta Hanner Nordstrand, 'Dolda begravningar av foster i kyrkor under 1700- och 1800-talet: två fallstudier från Sverige' [Hidden burials of foetuses in churches during the 18th and 19th centuries: two case studies from Sweden], *META Historisk arkeologisk tidsskrift* (2021), 215–237.

[62] See Elizabeth Ellen Peacock, Stina Tegnhed, Emma Maltin and Gordon Turner-Walker, 'The Gällared Shroud and the preservation of a clandestine early 19th century foetal burial', *Archaeological Textiles Review* 62 (2020), 152–163, and Emma Maltin, Gordon Turner-Walker, Stina Tegnhed and Elizabeth E. Peacock, 'The concealed interment of a first-trimester foetus in Gällared parish church (1831), Sweden: age-estimation and reconstructed taphonomy', *International Journal of Osteoarchaeology* 32.2 (2020), 273–284, for a more detailed description of the find.

[63] Visual and microscopic analyses concluded that the foetus was miscarried in its first trimester, in week nine, making it possibly one of the youngest ever reported to be recovered from an archaeological context.

properties of the cotton fibres, the shroud was well suited to transport moisture, including body fluids, away from the body, which would have contained over 90 per cent water. It will have facilitated the drying out of the soft tissue and brought about relatively widespread desiccation of the corpse. The sign of liquid staining on the shroud confirms the dissipation of fluids leaking from the foetus. This would have been assisted by resting in the wooden coffin and being placed in a cool, dry, above-ground environment. Initially, the wrapping of the body in the shroud would have protected it from access by insects once in the coffin. With time, it restricted the scattering of the skeletal parts as the body decomposed and led to remains retaining their anatomically correct position. The formable textile wrapping protected the body, and the rigid wooden coffin – also a form of wrapping – further protected the wrapped body.

In 1992, a similar small, lidded wooden box was retrieved from a crack in an attic wall of Bringetofta (Småland, Sweden) parish church during restoration work. It was turned over to Jönköping Museum, where, when opened, it was revealed to be dry and contain small bone and cartilage fragments tightly packed in an overly large, crumpled textile. The contents underwent repeated handling whilst being investigated by a number of specialists at several institutions in the 1990s. The textile shroud (approx. 30 x 55 cm), which did not undergo remedial conservation, was identified as a long-sleeved, infant-size smock dress with an opening in the back.[64] The fabric was a worn, repaired, and torn linen. Investigative conservation of the soiled smock dress in 2020 revealed it to not have been specifically re-purposed for use as a shroud, to have crusty rust-coloured patches widely distributed in its centre, and to have adhered fragments of bone and dried-out tissue. The discoloured patches are likely dried-out foetal fluid or blood, and their distribution indicates how the smock was tightly scrunched up around the moist body. As with the Gällared shroud, the Bringetofta shroud was instrumental in the preservation of the body by natural partial mummification and reveals taphonomic changes the find underwent during the lifetime of the concealed burial. The study of the textiles intimately associated with these tiny burials testifies to the information such textile finds can contribute both to elucidating the history and evolution of the burial itself and to furthering the understanding of deliberate concealment of tiny bodies within and around churches and of infant death and grief.

CONCLUSION

The detailed examination of finds of archaeological textiles that precedes every conservation intervention, be it investigative, preventive, remedial, and/or for display, reveals not only information about their technology, construction, and use, but also valuable

---

[64] Eva Londos, 'Om askegossen från Bringetofta och döda barns begravning' [The foetus from Bringetofta and the burial of dead children], in *Från kyrkans värld: Smålåndska kulturbilder*, ed. by Klas Börjesson, *Meddelanden från Jönköpings Läns Hembygdsförbund och Stiftelsen Jönköpings Läns Museum* 65 (Jönköping: Jönköpings läns museum, 1995), pp. 49–54, figs. at 48 and 50.

evidence of interactions between the object and its immediate environment, whether that relates to specific human activities or is incidental as it adjusts to its post-depositional conditions. That which differentiates archaeological conservators from professionals in related academic fields is their strong basis in practical skills anchored in visual observation and knowledge of the complexity and interactivity of objects within a specific environment.[65] As the field of conservation continues to evolve and place more emphasis on information retrieval and investigative conservation, there is a heightened awareness of and demand for the conservator's specialist observation skills and instrumental analytical know-how. Investigation begins with the naked eye, later augmented by the use of stereo and optical microscopy, staining and solubility tests, and imaging techniques. Sophisticated and expensive analytical instruments to which many conservational professionals may not have access are not the automatic go-to methods. The ability of the conservator to extract valuable information without recourse to specialist technologies makes an invaluable contribution when they are part of a multidisciplinary team in which the exchange of knowledge and sharing of expertise in textile analysis is the cohesive force.

[65] European Network for Conservation–Restoration Education (ENCoRE), Clarification of Conservation/Restoration Education at University Level or Recognised Equivalent, ENCoRE 3rd General Assembly 19–22 June 2001, Munich, Germany; http://www.encore-edu.org/ENCoRE-documents/cp.pdf, accessed 13 February 2023.

CHAPTER 3

King Harald's Grey Cloak: *Vararfeldir* and the Trade in Shaggy Pile Weave Cloaks between Iceland and Norway in the Late Viking and Early Middle Ages[1]

Michèle Hayeur Smith

King Haraldr stayed most often in Hǫrðaland and Rogaland and so did others of the brothers. They frequently stayed in Harðangr. It happened one summer that an ocean-going ship came from Iceland, owned by Icelanders. It was loaded with sheep-skin wares, and they sailed the ship to Harðangr because they had heard that there the largest numbers of people were to be found. But when people came to do business

---

ORCiD: 0000-0003-2218-638X.

[1] I would like to thank the following institutions for contributing to the larger project (Archaeological Investigations of the Eastern North Atlantic Trade and Globalizing Economic Systems (NSF #1733914)) of which this chapter is a product: the Haffenreffer Museum of Anthropology at Brown University, Department of Earth and Environmental Planetary Sciences (DEEPS) and the Department of Geochemistry at Brown University; the National Museum of Iceland; the Greenland Museum and Archives, the Bryggen Museum, and NTNU Trondheim. The Borgund Kaupang Project (2019–2023) is supported by the Research Council of Norway (NFR 288392) and the Siftinga Sunnemøre Museum. I also thank the following individuals: Dr Robert Preucel, Kevin P. Smith, Dr Alberto Saal, Dr Soumen Mallick, Charles Steiman, Dr Gitte Hansen, Guðmundur Óláfsson, Mjöll Snæsdóttir, Dr Doug Bolender, and Guðrún Alda Gísladóttir, Howell Magnus Roberts, Dr Ramona Harrison, Dr Guðrún Sveinbjarnardóttir, Dr Gavin Lucas, Vala Garðarsdóttir, Dr Christian Koch Madsen, and Dr Jette Arneborg, Lilja Árnadóttir, Ármann Guðmundsson, Alan Coogan and Alsiosha Bielenberg. This project was made possible with the financial support of the National Science Foundation of the United States, Arctic Social Sciences, Department of Polar Programs, Archaeological Investigations of the Eastern North Atlantic Trade and Globalizing Economic Systems (Award no. 1733914).

with them, no one wanted to buy the sheepskin wares. Then the skipper goes to see King Haraldr, because he already knew him to speak to, and tells him of this problem. The king says that he will come to see them, and he does so. King Haraldr was an unpretentious person and a great one for fun. He had come there with a fully manned boat. He looked at their wares and said to the skipper: 'Will you give me a grey cloak?' 'Willingly,' says the skipper, 'or more, if you like.'

Then the king took a cloak and put it over his shoulders. Then he went down to his boat. And before they rowed away, every one of his men had bought a cloak. A few days later so many people came there, each of whom wanted to buy a cloak, that only half of those who wanted to have one got it. After this he was known as Haraldr gráfeldr (Grey-Cloak).[2]

This important event in the life of the Norwegian King Harald Greycloak (b. *c.* 935, d. *c.* 970 CE), described in Old Norse by the Icelander Snorri Sturluson in his thirteenth-century history of the Norwegian kings, *Heimskringla*, appears to lie at the root of some conclusions that have been drawn about the origins of the shaggy pile weave textiles in Norway, known as *röggvarfeldur* or *röggvarvefnaður* in Iceland.[3] *Vararfeldir* is another term used to describe woven mantles with a piled surface that had been in vogue around Northern Europe from the sixth century and survived to the late medieval period. Their true origins are to be found in Antiquity, with the earliest documented examples of this cloth type appearing in Bronze Age Sumeria, 5,000 years ago (see discussion on pp. 69–72, below).[4]

---

[2] Snorri Sturluson, *Heimskringla Volume 1. The Beginnings to Ólafr Tryggvason*, trans. by A. Finlay and A. Faulkes (London: Viking Society for Northern Research, 2016) Chapter 7 (p. 129).

[3] The authorship of Heimskringla has been questioned over the years, with a debate well presented in Diana Whaley's *Heimskringla: an Introduction* (London: Viking Society for Northern Research, University College London, 1991). While Whaley's final impression is that Snorri himself was indeed the author (despite others arguing the contrary (see Whaley, Ch. 1), she cautions: 'to call Snorri the author of Heimskringla is in my view fully justified, so long as the nature of that authorship is borne in mind. As is demonstrated elsewhere in this book, Heimskringla is both a unique work and a compilation of extracts, a masterpiece, and a stage in a process and in the same way Snorri has distinct attributes as an author but sometimes appears more as a compiler and editor'; Whaley, *Heimskringla*, p. 19. Regardless of these discussions, it is obvious that Snorri's story is not a first-hand account of what happened regarding the trade in pile-woven cloaks but offers an interesting anecdote about this garment. Of greater interest is the implied relationship between Icelanders and Norwegians, in which one has the impression that the Icelanders were unpopular, along with the wares they had for sale. With a little help from good King Harald the situation was reversed, and the Icelanders were able to sell all their textiles. This minor detail is reflective not only of the subtleties at play between these two nations but also of Snorri's agenda. The text is thought to have been intended for both Norwegian and Icelandic audiences and Snorri himself was undoubtedly well aware of the invested interest men of his standing had in visiting Norwegian courts and interacting with Norwegian royalty; Whaley, *Heimskringla*, p. 18.

[4] Else E. Guðjónsson, 'Forn röggvarvefnaður', *Árbók hins íslenzka fornleifafélags* 59 (1962), 12–71 (p. 70).

TRADE IN SHAGGY PILE WEAVE CLOAKS

Else E. Guðjónsson and Bruce Gelsinger suggested that pile weaving was quite widely practised in Iceland during the tenth and eleventh centuries and may have been a choice export item.[5] According to Guðjónsson, mantles of skin were called *skinnfeldir*, whereas the terms *vararfeldir* and *röggvarfeldir* referred to cloth woven with a piled surface.[6] Guðjónsson explains:

> The word *vararfeldur* has by some been interpreted as meaning separate sheepskins or sheepskins sewn together to the in *Grágás* specified shape [*sic*], whereas the *röggvarfledur* (mentioned in Grettis saga) was believed to have been a woven mantle with a pile surface. Also it has been maintained that there were two kinds of *vararfeldir*: those used as legal tender and those used as mantles (also just called *feldir*). The Icelandic historian, Jón Jóhannesson, examined all the relevant data, among others the price of lambskins quoted in *Grágás*, which indicated that *vararfeldir* were of a more costly material than sheepskin. Taking what seemed all possibilities into account he arrived at the conclusion that the three words, *vararfledir, feldir*, and *röggvarfeldir*, all meant woven mantles with a pile surface and that mantles of skin or fur were called *skinnfeldir* to distinguish them from the others.[7]

Vararfeldir do indeed emulate the appearance of sheepskins, but by being woven present a more resilient, waterproof, and longer-lasting equivalent. The cloth is produced as a basic woven twill or tabby, into which individual tufts of wool from the Northern short-tail sheep are interspersed at regular intervals to produce the appearance of an animal pelt. The tale of Harald Greycloak, along with other later dated sources,[8] has led to the general assumption that this type of cloth was Icelandic.[9]

Pile-woven textiles are described in detail in the medieval (twelfth- to thirteenth-century) Icelandic law code *Grágás*, reinforcing the idea that textiles were an important item of value, trade, and commerce. However, the author's own research demonstrates that, despite the later written sources briefly discussed above highlighting this type of cloth, the archaeological examples of it are extremely uncommon in the Icelandic corpus of excavated Viking Age (870–1050) and early medieval (1050–1300) textiles.

In this chapter I will present a review of the shaggy pile-woven pieces currently known from Iceland and Greenland (based on my own analysis of the material), dating from the

---

5   Guðjónsson, 'Forn röggvarvefnaður', p. 68; Bruce Gelsinger, *Icelandic Enterprise, Commerce and Economy in the Middle Ages* (Columbia, SC: University of South Carolina Press, 1st edn, 1981), p. 12.

6   Guðjónsson, 'Forn röggvarvefnaður', p. 68.

7   Guðjónsson, 'Forn röggvarvefnaður', p. 68.

8   *Laws of Early Iceland: The Codex Regius of Grágás, with Material from Other Manuscripts*, II, ed. and trans by Andrew Dennis, Peter Foot and Richard Perkins (Winnipeg: The University of Manitoba Press, 2000).

9   Frances Pritchard, 'Aspects of the wool textiles from Viking Age Dublin', in *Archaeological Textiles in Northern Europe, Report from the 4th NESAT Symposium 1–5 May 1990 Copenhagen*, ed. by Lise Bender Jørgensen and Elisabeth Munksgaard (Copenhagen: Kongelige Danske Kunstakademi, 1992), pp. 93–104 (p. 98).

Viking Age to the early modern (1600–1800) period and demonstrate that it was neither uniquely Icelandic, nor Irish, but was popular throughout Europe prior to the Viking Age. Further, examples from the late Viking and medieval site of Borgund and the town of Trondheim, both on the west coast of Norway, suggest that this cloth was widely in use in late Viking Age Scandinavia. Preliminary results from strontium isotope analysis suggest this cloth type was not imported from the North Atlantic islands but was more likely produced locally.

SHAGGY PILE WEAVING IN ICELAND

Technical Aspects

Various types of pile-woven ('pile' meaning with added tufts of wool) textiles were produced in the past, from short-napped cut pile weave, to shaggy pile weave, looped pile, and even pile made from spun yarns. The discussion here will mainly concern the shaggy pile weave, which appears more commonly in the North Atlantic corpus of archaeological textiles than other types of pile-woven cloth.

The pile itself is frequently added to a woven fabric, most often a 2 x 2 twill, though tabby weaves were also commonly used as the base weave. The pile, consisting of lightly twisted wool of the outer guard hairs (or *tog*) from a sheep were inserted into the shed between the wefts,[10] producing what is referred to as a knotless pile, or by winding the pile around the warp thread, to create a knotted pile.[11] The knotted pile method is the most common type seen in the Icelandic textile corpus, as can be observed on a large fragment of well-preserved pile-woven cloth from Heynes, Iceland, dated to the tenth century (see below p. 55, Fig. 3.1). Beyond the basic division between knotless and knotted piles, there was more than one way to knot the pile, and the frequencies of different variations appear to have varied by region.[12]

Pile-woven Textiles in Icelandic Legal Sources

Pile weaving is mentioned in the medieval Icelandic law book *Grágás*. Like *vaðmál* (a form of 2 x 2 twill), the term refers to cloth used as legal tender.[13] *Vararfeldir* could also be used as payment but was worth more than *vaðmál*, most likely due to the labour and material involved in making this type of cloth. Guðjónsson drew a distinction between

---

[10] Carolyn Priest-Dorman, 'Trade cloaks: Icelandic supplementary weft pile textiles', *Medieval Textiles* [Complex Weavers' Medieval Textile Study Group] 28 (2001), 8–14 (p. 9).

[11] Guðjónsson, 'Forn röggvarvefnaður', p. 65.

[12] Guðjónsson, 'Forn röggvarvefnaður', p. 21.

[13] *Vaðmál* is from the Norse *vað*, meaning cloth, and *mál*, made to measure; Michèle Hayeur Smith, 'Thorir's bargain: gender, *vaðmál*, and the law', *World Archaeology* 45:5 (2013), 730–746 (p. 731); Michèle Hayeur Smith, 'Vaðmál and cloth currency in Viking and medieval Iceland', in *Silver, Butter, Cloth: Monetary social Economies in the Viking Age*, ed. by Jane Kershaw, Gareth Williams, Soren Sindbaek and James Graham-Campbell (Oxford: Oxford University Press, 2018), pp. 251–277 (p. 252).

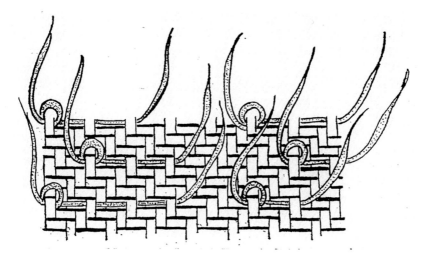

Fig. 3.1 Diagram of the method for inserting the pile, as seen on the Heynes, Iceland, fragment from the vicinity of Akranes. From Else Guðjónsson's own drawing in *Forn röggvarvefnaður*, p. 20.

vararfeldir woven as cloaks and those woven for legal tender.[14] Individual mantles mentioned in *Grágás* were called *Hafnarfeldir* and were thought to be of higher quality and produced for home consumption and export.[15] *Vararfeldir* were also described as being semi-circular in shape and were made in a variety of lengths and colours, including grey, blue, and red with border decorations.[16] Some textiles also had pile on both sides, as the author observed during the analysis of the collection from the Folkebibliotek (Public Library) site in Trondheim, Norway.

While *Grágás* (1117–1271) states that one legal ounce (1 *eyrir*) was equivalent to six ells of *vaðmál*, one 'tufted woollen cloak' (4 *þumálnir* long and 2 *álnir* wide, with thirteen strips across) was equal to 2 *aurar*. At double the value of *vaðmál*, *vararfeldir* were clearly considered a more luxurious and costlier product. But what does '4 *þumálnir* long and 2 *álnir* wide with thirteen strips across is equal to 2 *aurar*' actually mean? Thumb ell (*þumöln* singular) is a unit of measure which, according *Grágás*,[17] is likely an ell (49.2 cm/19.3 inches in modern measurements) with an additional length of a thumb added to the end of it.[18] That the ell itself underwent a number of changes over time is documented

[14] Guðjónsson, 'Forn röggvarvefnaður', pp. 67–68.
[15] Guðjónsson, 'Forn röggvarvefnaður', pp. 67–68.
[16] Guðjónsson, 'Forn röggvarvefnaður', p. 69.
[17] According to the thirteenth-century *Islendigabók*, a Norwegian settler named Úlfjótur was sent to Norway from Iceland to draft the law code (*Grágás*) based on the Norwegian legal system of the Gulathing, the legislative assembly for western Norway; Hayeur Smith, 'Vaðmál and cloth currency in Viking and medieval Iceland', p. 254.
[18] Karlsson et al., *Grágás*, p. 567.

by different definitions of the 'legal ell' in those parts of Iceland's succession of medieval and post-medieval law codes that dealt with issues of currency, changing in response to international trading standards and eventually reaching 55.6 cm (21.8 inches) for 1 ell.[19] *Búalög*, a slightly later source (thirteenth-century with even later modifications), stipulates that *vaðmál* was to be woven in panels 3.5 ells in width (roughly 1.5 metres; 59 inches).[20] The thirteen strips across refer to thirteen evenly spaced rows of locks attached through pile knots across the cloth's width, so that there would be thirteen horizontal rows when the mantle was worn[21]

Pile-woven Textiles in the Icelandic Archaeological Record
In Iceland, pile-woven textiles are surprisingly uncommon in the vast textile corpus stored at the National Museum. Research conducted by the author on North Atlantic archaeological textiles turned up twelve fragments of *vararfeldir* in a corpus of 8,000–10,000 fragments of cloth dating from the tenth and eleventh centuries into the early modern period.[22] Guðjónsson argued that the Icelandic medieval documents could be read to suggest that pile weaving disappeared in Iceland before 1200, and that when the term *feldur* (another term used to designate this type of cloth as well as fur coats) reappeared toward the end of the late medieval period (*c.* 1550) in inventories of the properties owned by Iceland's bishoprics, it related to later *vararfeldir* that were imported to Iceland.[23] While validating this assumption is impossible without re-examining each individual piece and incorporating additional isotope analysis in the study, the basic point remains that there are very few examples of *vararfeldir* from any period in the corpus of Icelandic archaeological textiles, where they represent less than two-tenths of 1 per cent (0.12–0.15 per cent) of the textiles recovered by excavations conducted across the country over the course of more than a century. This could be due to the fact that *vararfeldir* was either not produced so abundantly and more emphasis was placed on the making of *vaðmál*, which was more lucrative and a necessity; or because what was produced was traded internationally, though results from strontium isotopic studies presented below tend to suggest otherwise.

---

[19]   Hayeur Smith, 'Thorir's bargain', p. 732; *Laws of Early Iceland: Grágás: The Codex regius of grágás with material from other manuscripts*, ed. and trans by A. Dennis, P. Foote, and R. Perkins (Winnipeg: University of Manitoba Press, 1980), *Grágás I*, p. 253, *Grágás II*, pp. 155, 209, 224.

[20]   Else Østergård, *Woven into the Earth: Textiles from Norse Greenland* (Aarhus and Oxford: Aarhus University Press, 2004), p. 63.

[21]   Guðjónsson, 'Forn röggvarvefnaður', p. 69.

[22]   This work was supported by three grants from the United States National Science Foundation (Rags to Riches – An Archaeological Study of Textiles and Gender in Iceland, AD 874–1800, Award no. 1023167; Weaving Islands of Cloth – Gender, Textiles, and Trade Across the North Atlantic from the Viking Age to the Early Modern Period, Award no. 1303898; and Archaeological Investigations of the Eastern North Atlantic Trade and Globalizing Economic Systems, Award no. 1733914).

[23]   Guðjónsson, 'Forn röggvarvefnaður', p. 69.

Table 3.1, and the following discussion, provide basic information on these pieces from Iceland, along with an even smaller number of examples from the Norse Greenland colonies.[24] While a few sites remain to be studied, thirty-six or more sites were incorporated into the research project mentioned above, and the number of undiscovered fragments of *vararfeldir* can be presumed to be small. In some instances, it is impossible to be certain whether the items listed below are actually *vararfeldir*, or to be completely sure of their technical details, since wear, additional fulling, and deterioration from centuries of burial have in some cases obscured the weave or reduced the piles to short fringes or tufts.

Table 3.1   List of possible pile-woven textiles from Icelandic and Greenlandic archaeological sites.

Location	Find number	Site name	Approx. date	Base weave
Iceland	Þjms 1940	Heynes	10th–11th century	2 x 2, z/s spun, pile on one side, two pieces sewn together.
Iceland	Þjms 1940	Garðar mitten, near Heynes	10th century	2 x 2 twill with short, napped pile inserted by sewing.
Iceland	2008-32-516	Alþingisreitur	1226–1500	Short cut pile on one side; heavily felted on opposite side.
Iceland	2009-32-1235	Alþingisreitur	13th–14th century	Possibly *vararfeldir*, but entire fragment is heavily felted on both sides, making the pile difficult to discern.
Iceland	2009-99	Meiðalheimur	1300–1700	Raw wool or *vararfeldir*?
Iceland	1988-213-242	Bessastaðir	Viking Age–1900	Pile? Or clumps of raw wool? Pile is on one side, and opposite side is felted.
Iceland	1987-369	Stóraborg	1450–1600	Weave not visible, heavily felted, long pile on one side.
Iceland	Þjms 4149	Hvammur hat	16th century	Pile as on the Heynes cloth, but very matted. Similar hats have been found in Ireland.

[24]   Neither Guðjónsson nor other textile analysts has gone through, or catalogued, the substantial corpus of archaeological textiles in the National Museum of Iceland and this author wishes to make these pieces better known.

Iceland	SKH07-15797	Skálholt	Post 1600	Pile on the surface on one side and felted on the back. Weave not visible.
Iceland	ATR-32-2803	Alþinigsreitur	1500–1800?	Short cut pile on one side and felted back.
Iceland	2009-32-2807	Alþingisreitur	1500–1800?	Short cut pile, like 2803, on one side; heavily felted on opposite side.
Iceland	Þjms 14861	Þingeyrar hat	Medieval?	Coarse felt hat with pile on the outside; on permanent display.
Greenland	D5/1992.17	Ø17a Narsaq	11th century	2 x 2 twill.
Greenland	D1/1991.15	Ø149 Narsarsuaq	10th – 14th century	2 x 2 twill; evidence of reddish mauve dye.
Greenland	1950 x3095	GUS	11th century	2 x 2 twill, possibly made from goat hair. Evidence of dye with tannin.

Dates for some Icelandic examples are approximate and based on the excavators' site reports, Harris Matrices, or stratigraphic analyses of their sites rather than direct AMS dating of the textiles themselves.[25] Data and table © Michèle Hayeur Smith.

Of the pieces listed here, only four fit the description of true shaggy, pile-woven cloth with long piles: two pieces sewn together from Heynes (Fig. 3.2), located on the Akranes peninsula,[26] one specimen from Stóraborg in southern Iceland[27] and one from the bishopric of Skálholt, also in southern Iceland.[28] Based on their construction these pieces could have been made in Iceland. In contrast, all but one of the pieces from Alþingisreitur, a harbour site in the centre of Reykajvik,[29] are sufficiently different – clearly *vararfeldir* but

[25] Guðjónsson, 'Forn röggvarvefnaður', pp. 66–68; Mjöll Snæsdóttir, *Stóra-Borg: Fornleifarannsókn 1978–1990* (Reykjavik: Þjóðminjasafn Íslands, 1991); Douglas Bolender, Katherine M. Johnson, John Q. Schoenfelder and Guðný Zoëga, 'Report of the Skagafjörður Archaeological Settlement Survey 2009: Excavations at Stóra-Seyla, Area C', Unpublished excavation report (Fiske Institute, 2009); Vala Garðarsdóttir, 'Alþingisreiturinn Bindi 1 og 2', Unpublished excavation report (University of Iceland, 2010); Guðmundur Ólafsson, ed., *Bessastaðarannsókn II. Kirkjugarður og miðaldaminjar, uppgraftarsvæði 12–15 1988* (Reykjavik: Skýrslur Þjóðminjasafn Íslands, 2012), pp. 93–109; Gavin Lucas, 'Skálholt, Framvinduskýrslur/ Interim Report No. 6', Unpublished excavation report (Fornleifastofnun Íslands, 2007).

[26] National Museum of Iceland, museum number Þjms 1940; Guðjónsson, 'Forn röggvarvefnaður', pp. 14, 15, Figs. 1, 2.

[27] National Museum of Iceland, museum number 1987–369, p. 17, Fig. 3.

[28] National Museum of Iceland, museum number SKH07-15797.

[29] National Museum of Iceland, museum number 2009-32-1235.

Fig. 3.2 Two fragments sewn together from Heynes, 10th century, comprising the best-known piece of pile-woven cloth from Iceland. Photograph: Michèle Hayeur Smith, courtesy of the National Museum of Iceland.

with a short cut pile and a finish fine enough to almost resemble a coarse velvet – that it is likely that these are imports. Alþingisreitur was a harbour site and several other non-*vararfeldir* textiles from there seem to be imports, based on strontium isotope analysis.[30] Unfortunately, none of the Icelandic pile-woven specimens has yet been tested for $^{87}Sr/^{86}Sr$ isotopes (see below).

The pieces from Bessastaðir and Meðalheimur were most likely raw wool with the appearance of a shaggy pile weave, but their identification remains uncertain until further analysis. The final three Icelandic objects in the list – the mitten from Garðar and hats from Þingeyrar and Hvammur – were all discovered early in the twentieth century.[31] The hats are said to be like pile-woven hats found in sixteenth-century bog deposits at Gortmahonoge and Boolabaun, Co. Tipperary, Ireland, which are believed to be late medieval, from the fifteenth or sixteenth centuries (Fig 3.3).[32]

---

[30] Michèle Hayeur Smith, Kevin P. Smith, Alberto Saal, Charles Steinmann and Soumen Mallick, 'Bioavailable 87Sr/86Sr ratios from Icelandic wool from the Viking Age to the Early Modern period' (in prep., 2021).

[31] National Museum of Iceland, museum numbers Þjms 1940, Þjms 14861, Þjms 4149; Guðjónsson, 'Forn röggvarvefnaður', pp. 66–68.

[32] Halpin, personal communication.

Fig. 3.3   Pile-woven cloth from Stóraborg, Iceland, 1987-369, with a view of the felted underside. Photograph: Michèle Hayeur Smith, courtesy of the National Museum of Iceland.

The three Greenland examples were re-analysed by the author during the course of the projects mentioned above, with information gained supplementing Østergård's detailed descriptions of all three pieces in her thorough overview of Greenlandic textiles.[33] The piece from Narsaq[34] is very worn, to the point that the pile is barely visible on the surface. This piece was dated to the eleventh century, in keeping with Guðjónsson's statement that pile-woven cloth was most popular in the tenth and eleventh centuries based, on Icelandic finds. Iceland and Greenland were closely linked, as Icelanders settled Greenland. The fact that both display similar dates in two separate locations suggests that *vararfeldir* was popular in the North Atlantic islands during this period. Dye analysis revealed that it was originally dyed reddish-mauve with *korkje* or lichen purple.[35]

The two pieces from Narsarssuaq[36] and GUS (Gården under Sandet – The Farm beneath the Sand)[37] are similarly heavily worn: the Narsarssuaq piece was made from sheep's wool dyed reddish-mauve with *korkje*, whereas the item from GUS was thought to be made from goat hair.[38] However, the identification of goat in Greenlandic textiles has been problematic, as it is almost impossible to distinguish goat from sheep without molecular analysis. Several Greenlandic samples sent for fibre identification under the assumption that they were made from goats' hair were identified as sheep's wool through aDNA (ancient DNA) analyses.[39] The Greenlandic *vararfeldir* were knotted slightly differently from the Icelandic version and Østergård suggested that the pile knot would ultimately determine where these textiles were produced.[40]

VARARFELDIR IN NORWAY AND BIOAVAILABLE STRONTIUM RATIOS

Beyond analysing the pile knot, which is often extremely difficult to see, another avenue for determining the possible provenance of textiles is the use of $^{87}Sr/^{86}Sr$ isotope analysis. However, this technique is informative about the provenance of the wool, not where the textiles were made.

As sheep graze, they absorb isotopic signatures from elements in the soil into their wool. In part, this signature arises from elements and isotopes found in the vegetation they graze upon and the water they drink, but more comes from soil ingested directly

---

[33] Østergård, *Woven into the Earth*, pp. 73–74.

[34] Greenland Museum and Archives, museum number, D5/1992.17.

[35] Østergård, *Woven into the Earth*, p. 73.

[36] Østergård, *Woven into the Earth*, pp. 233–52.

[37] Greenland Museum and Archives, museum number, 1950 x 3095.

[38] Østergård, *Woven into the Earth*, p. 73.

[39] Mikkel-Holger Sinding, Filipe Garrett Vieira and Michèle Hayeur Smith, 'Unmatched DNA preservation prove arctic hare and sheep wool in Norse Greenlandic textile from "The Farm Beneath the Sand"', *Journal of Archaeological Science: Reports* 14 (2017), 603–608.

[40] Østergård, *Woven into the Earth*, p. 74.

while feeding. Consequently, the elemental and isotopic signatures of sheep's wool, and other animals' hair, vary from place to place around the world, and from region to region within larger, geologically complex zones. But whereas skeletal elements and teeth provide isotopic signatures of the places an individual human or animal lived when that tooth or bone completed its growth, wool and hair are produced continuously through the animal's lifetime, and in agricultural settings wool is shorn annually and then regrows, providing a record of grazing locations on an annual basis. Assuming that wool was woven soon after being shorn, since leaving wool stored for months or years could lead to moth and other insect infestations, strontium isotopes in wool most likely represent a single year's grazing signature.

As a test of the idea that *vararfeldir* were imported to Norway from the North Atlantic, $^{87}Sr/^{86}Sr$ isotopic analyses were performed on a small suite of *vararfeldir* samples excavated from the coastal Norwegian site of Borgund in the vicinity of present-day Ålesund,[41] along with samples of modern sheep's wool and archaeological textiles from Iceland. Borgund was an early urban site and marketplace that was founded late in the Viking Age and continued into the late medieval period. The site was excavated over several decades during the mid-twentieth century, and the analysis of this substantial legacy collection forms the core of a large collaborative project, the *Borgund Kaupang Project*, run from the University of Bergen under the direction of Dr Gitte Hansen.[42]

Historical sources suggest that cloth was a central item in commerce from the North Atlantic islands to the European continent, and especially Norway, from the end of the Viking Age until the eighteenth century. Gelsinger argued that cloth was exported from Iceland primarily between 930 and 1264 CE, the end of the Icelandic Commonwealth period.[43] While this might be true for trade between Trondheim and the North Atlantic, Knut Helle has stressed that North Atlantic trade flourished in the thirteenth century, particularly with Bergen as its focal port.[44]

The type of cloth most commonly exported from Iceland, the Faroe Islands, Shetland, and Orkney was a coarse, woollen 2 x 2 twill known as *vaðmál*, that served as currency within Iceland and was subject to stringent rules regulating its length, width, and thread count. This cloth, later known as *wadmal*, *wadmol*, or *wedmol* in harbour records and archival sources across Europe, was in high demand in Norway and England, and made its way to Germany, France, Poland, Austria, the Baltic countries, and elsewhere in

---

[41] Asbjørn E. Herteig, *Kaupangen på Borgund* (Ålesund: Borgundkaupangens Venner, 1973); Asbjørn E. Herteig, *Borgund Kaupangen på Sunnmøre* (Ålesund: Borgundkaupangens Venner, 1974).

[42] The site of the project is called Borgund whereas the project has been named Borgund Kaupang. Michèle Hayeur Smith, *The Textiles from Borgund Norway* (forthcoming).

[43] Gelsinger, *Icelandic Enterprise*, pp. 149–180.

[44] Knut Helle, 'Bergen's role in the medieval North Atlantic trade', *AmS-Skritfer* 27 (2019), 43–51 (pp. 43–44).

Europe.[45] However, Gelsinger and others have suggested that pile-woven cloaks were also important in this trade:

> The most important exports were the sheep products of undyed tweed-like *vaðmál*, and cloaks called *röggvarfeldir* or *vararfeldir* made by braiding shaggy tufts of wool to imitate as much as possible the pelts of squirrels and of other wild animals. The fact that *vaðmál* was used as a standard of payment in Iceland testifies not only to its importance there but also its acceptance abroad in exchange for other goods.[46]

Borgun's corpus of approximately 306 fragments of cloth includes thirty-seven fragments of *vararfeldir*. This is not only a larger sample of shaggy pile weave than is known from all excavated Icelandic and Greenlandic sites combined, but also represents a much larger percentage of the site's textile assemblage (12.1 per cent) than in the Icelandic corpus, where it accounts for just 0.12–0.15 per cent of excavated textiles. The thirty-seven fragments from Borgund included 2 x 2 twills, 2 x 1 twills and tabbies used as base weaves, and one of these items was piled on both sides (Table 3.2).

Table 3.2 Weave types used for producing pile-woven fabrics at Borgund Kaupang, Norway.

Weave type	Number of pile-woven cloth fragments
2 x 2 twill	26
2 x 1	2
Tabby weave	4
Unidentified	5
Total	37

Data and table © Michèle Hayeur Smith.

Not all *vararfeldir* from Borgund is of the shaggy pile type: one exception is a unique piece made from spun yarns fastened into a knotted pile.[47] This piece of cloth was reproduced and technically analysed by weavers from the Østeroy Museum and from Shetland (Fig. 3.4). Woven as a 2 x 2 twill with z/s spun yarns and a thread count of 8/7, the pile consisted of single z spun yarns. Other researchers and weavers who are members of the Borgund Kaupang Project[48] speculated that this unique pile-woven textile

---

[45] Charles Steinman and Michèle Hayeur Smith, 'The North Atlantic wool trade, c. 1000–1400: historical sources and a strontium isotope approach', forthcoming.

[46] Gelsinger, *Icelandic Enterprise*, p. 12; other evidence from Helgi Þórláksson, *Vaðmál og verðlag: vaðmál í utanlandsviðskiptum og búskap Íslendinga á 13. og 14. öld* (Reykjavik: Fjölföldun Sigurjóns, 1991); Marta Hoffman, *The Warp Weighted Loom: Studies in the History and Technology of an Ancient Implement* (Oslo: Universitetsforlaget, 1964), and the author's research.

[47] University of Bergen, 0001/61/002055/001

[48] Hayeur Smith, *The Textiles from Borgund Norway* (forthcoming).

Fig. 3.4 Pile-woven cloth from Borgund Kaupang, Norway, woven as a 2 x 2 with yarns that are spun rather than the customary shaggy pile. Photograph: Michèle Hayeur Smith, courtesy of the Bryggen Museum, Bergen.

may have originated elsewhere, with Ireland or Scotland's Western Isles as possibilities, on the grounds that this type of cloth is not present in the North Atlantic corpus.

Of these thirty-seven fragments, seven were analysed for $^{87}Sr/^{86}Sr$ isotope ratios, following methods pioneered by Karin Frei[49] and successfully reproduced at Brown University and a commercial laboratory, Isobar Laboratories, located in Miami, Florida. These textile samples were collected from deposits ranging in age from tenth to twelfth century as part of the Archaeological Investigations of the Eastern North Atlantic Trade and Globalizing Economic Systems project. The age of the deposits that produced these textiles, therefore, overlapped the periods during which trade in North Atlantic, especially Icelandic, textiles is thought to have begun and the period during which historic

[49] Karin Margarita Frei, Ulla Mannering, Margarita Gleba, M.-L. Nosch and H. Lyngstrøm, 'Provenance of ancient textiles – a pilot study evaluating the strontium isotope system in wool', *Archaeometry* 51.2 (2009), 252–276 (pp. 254–255); Karin Margarita Frei, Ina Vanden Berghe, Robert Frei, Ulla Mannering and Henriette Lyngstrøm, 'Removal of natural organic dyes from wool – implications for ancient textile provenance studies', *Journal of Archaeological Science* 37 (2010), 2136–2145 (pp. 2139–2140); Karin Margarita Frei, 'Provenance of archaeological wool textiles: new case studies', *Open Journal of Archaeometry* 2:5239 (2014), 1–5 (p. 2).

sources suggest it was most active and also during which imports of North Atlantic *vararfeldir* would be expected.

However, most of these textiles returned results consistent with local Norwegian baselines of >0.7095–0.7107 and none matched baselines for bioavailable strontium in wool from Iceland, which exhibit a range of 0.7042–0.7086 (Table 3.3, Fig. 3.5). Therefore, there is no indication that these textiles from Borgund are Icelandic. It seems likely that if these were not produced from sheep that grazed near the town itself, they are from somewhere in Norway.

Table 3.3 ^{87}Sr/^{86}Sr strontium ratios from Borgund Kaupang's pile-woven textiles that were analysed in the course of the project.

Bryggen Museum number	^{87}Sr/^{86}Sr ratio
0001/56/000287/002	0.7102196
0001/56/000283/002	0.709644
0001/57/000558/001	0.7101726
0001/57/000570/002	0.7099086
0001/57/000563/001	0.71078791
0001/61/002055/001	0.7106593
0001/56/000287/002	0.709456

Data and table © Michèle Hayeur Smith.

Although it seems clear that none of the Borgund *vararfeldir* were produced from Icelandic wool, the interpretation that they were locally produced requires more analysis. More samples have been collected from the region around Borgund and Ålesund and while considerable regional variation was noted among the strontium isotope ratios in the entire region, the textiles still fall between the Borgund plant data (0.7112) and coastal rain water (0.7092).[50] Borgund's ratios are surprisingly consistent, with ^{87}Sr/^{86}Sr ratios between 0.7090–0.7107 (see Table 3.3, Fig. 3.5), and are far more homogeneous than slightly later textile assemblages from medieval Bergen, which show considerably more diversity in ^{87}Sr/^{86}Sr ratios, undoubtedly due to the influx of trade goods in that larger, and later, harbour city.[51]

---

[50] Research in collaboration with Kristoffer Dahl is ongoing, and more baselines from the surrounding areas have been collected. Samples of plants and modern wool taken from areas around Ålesund are showing more regional variation than expected. We attribute this variation to proximity to the coast and quaternary geology. Despite this regional variation, textiles show no evidence of North Atlantic imports in the corpus. Michèle Hayeur Smith and Kristoffer Dahl, 'Baa, baa black sheep, have you any wool? Late Viking and early medieval wool trade networks evaluated through strontium isotope analyses at Borgund Kaupang, Norway' (paper given at the European Archaeological Association, September, 2021).

[51] Michèle Hayeur Smith and Gitte Hansen, *The Borgund Textiles* (University of Bergen forthcoming, 2023).

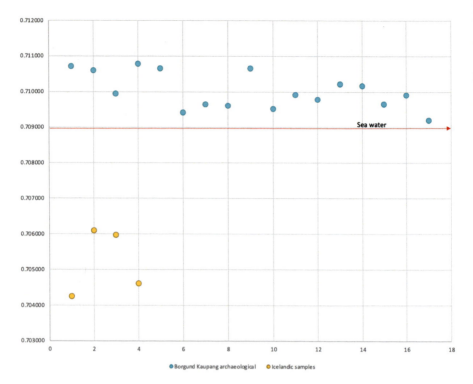

Fig. 3.5 $^{87}Sr/^{86}Sr$ ratios for analysed textiles from the site of Borgund Kaupang (blue), plotted in comparison with four Icelandic baseline samples (yellow). ©Michèle Hayeur Smith.

The homogeneity in strontium isotope values for the samples from Borgund was surprising, given the scholarly assumption that Iceland was selling *vararfeldir* to Norway at this time, based on the story of King Harald's cloak, and due to the diversity of base weaves and knotting approaches present at the site. However, the strontium isotope data suggest that the production of *vararfeldir* was alive and well in Norway and that local wool from Borgund and its vicinity, or wool from elsewhere within Norway, was being used to produce a relatively diverse range of pile-woven fabrics; the diversity encountered in the pile weaves could also be reflective of the movement of makers across regions.

However, overlaps do exist between Borgund's strontium values and those from Ireland. These may be attributable to similarities in geological formations in these two areas but do add more complexity to the overall picture. Doug Price et al. reported strontium isotope values from Irish basalts (which are always lower than bioavailable ratios) between 0.704–0.706 (bedrock ratios).[52] Hair, such as wool, tends to absorb elements

---

[52] Doug Price, Karin Margarita Frei and Elise Naumann, 'Isotopic baselines in the North Atlantic region', *Journal of the North Atlantic, Viking Settlers of the North Atlantic: An Isotopic Approach Special Volume* 7 (2015), 103–136.

rapidly and discard them more quickly, and values tend to be higher. Bone or tooth enamel absorbs elements such as strontium and other contaminants, such as lead, more slowly and, it would seem, more permanently.[53] Due to a lack of wool ratios for Ireland, we have to use Price et al.'s basalt rock ratios, which are comparable to our results from Borgund. Analysis of eleven pig bones from Dublin produced ratios around 0.7094, and on human tooth enamel, 0.7010, while Price et al. obtained ratios of 0.709 at Waterford, Republic of Ireland, 0.709 at Tintern Abbey, Wales, and at Armagh, Northern Ireland.[54]

Vararfeldir in other Norwegian sites
Folkebibliotek, one of the main archaeological sites excavated within Trondheim, exposed the area of this important medieval town that was involved in trade between Norway and other parts of the Northern Atlantic, and provided the closest parallel textile assemblages for comparisons with those from Borgund and Bryggen (Bergen's medieval harbour), thus helping us understand the role of *vararfeldir* within the North Atlantic textile trade. Trondheim, or Nidaros as it was known during the later Viking and early medieval periods, was the seat of the bishop of Nidaros, and after Iceland's initial period as a free state (the Commonwealth Period) ended, the island fell under the control of the bishop of Nidaros and the king of Norway in 1264. Taxes were paid regularly to the bishop of Nidaros in fish, wool, falcons, and other commodities that came from Iceland, and in walrus ivory and furs from Greenland. It is thought that most of the Faroese textiles ended up there as well. As a hub of North Atlantic trade, it provides an interesting place to track the trade in cloth.

Twenty-four pieces of pile-woven or potentially pile-woven textiles were identified among a sample of 886 fragments analysed from an assemblage of approximately 3,000 textile fragments recovered during excavations at Folkebibliotek. Most of these textiles were not analysed as thoroughly as the rest of the collection because they were oversized and because of insufficient time. Weave assessment is therefore approximate.

The Folkebibliotek site is said to span several hundred years, from approximately the eleventh to the seventeenth centuries.[55] A review of the pile-woven textiles' locations and stratifications on site suggests that they all derive from earlier phases of the town. All pieces identified in the sample appear to belong in the eleventh- and twelfth-century layers, much in keeping with the date of *vararfeldir* from Borgund and with

---

[53] Garvin Williams, Lincoln Hall and Jonas Addae, 'Increase in hair lead, but not blood lead content of occupationally-exposed workers', *Environmental Geochemistry and Health* 20 (1998), 239–243 (p. 242).

[54] Price et al., 'Isotopic baselines', p. 121.

[55] See Excavation Reports: A. Christophersen, E. Jondell, O. Marstein, S.W. Nordeide and I.W. Reed, *Utgravning, Kronologi og Bebyggelsesutvikling, Meddeleser no. 13 fra prosjektet Forntiden i Trondheim Bygrunn: Folkebibliotekstomten* (Trondheim: Riksantikvaren, Utgravningskontoret for Trondheim, 1988), p. 42; A. Christophersen, E. Jondell, O. Marstein, S.W. Nordeide and I.W. Reed, *Excavation, Chronology and Settlement Development, Meddelelser nr. 17, fra prosjektet Forntiden i Trondheim Bygrunn: Folkebibliotekstomten* (Trondheim: Riksantikvaren, Utgravningskontoret for Trondheim, 1989).

Guðjónsson's conclusion that this type of cloth disappeared in Iceland by the twelfth century. *Vararfeldir* account for just 2.7 per cent of the analysed assemblage from the eleventh- to twelfth-century deposits at Folkebibliotek and are far less common there than at tenth- to twelfth-century Borgund; yet pile-woven cloth is nearly twenty times more frequent at Folkebibliotek than in the Icelandic corpus, even when accounting for differences in the size of those excavated assemblages (Table 3.4). Unfortunately, the COVID-19 pandemic of 2020–21 made it impossible to return and collect samples from Folkebibliotek, to run either AMS dates or $^{87}Sr/^{86}Sr$ isotope analyses, or to re-examine individual pieces; therefore, a determination of where the *vararfeldir* were produced remains problematic.

Table 3.4   Selection of possible pile-woven textiles from Folkebibliotek, Trondheim, Norway.

Specimen number	No. of fragments	Weave	Approx. date based on the phasing at Folkebibliotek
N94110 (FU 485 B)	1	Felted	1025–75
N94110 (FU 485 C)	1	2 x 2	1025–75
N33775 (FH 547)	1	Not analysed	1075–1175
N41042 (FA 772)	1	Not analysed	1025
N56322 (FP 217 B)	3	2 x 2	1075–1175
N58017 (FP 349)	1	Not analysed	1025
N34801 (FH 532)	4	Twill	1075–1175
N59009 (FP 398)	2	Not analysed	1025
N40595 (FA 728 B)	1	Felted	1025
N94082 (FW 700)	1	Twill, not analysed	1125–1225
N94106 (FU 469)	1	Twill, not analysed	1025–75
N94108 (FN 1000)	6	2 x 2	1075–1175
N59708 (FS 324 A)	1	2 x 1	1025

Data and table ©Michèle Hayeur Smith.

The scarcity of *vararfeldir* in Icelandic site assemblages, coupled with these preliminary results from strontium isotope analyses, raises questions about the role of *vararfeldir* in trade between the North Atlantic and Norway's emerging towns. Gelsinger argued that the textile trade was most important during the tenth to thirteenth centuries, yet Helle felt that trade with the North Atlantic really began to develop in the twelfth century and was more firmly established by the thirteenth.[56] During the period 1180–90, trade conducted from Norwegian towns such as Bergen is thought to have been largely focused on cod, which is supported by Icelandic archaeological evidence for the intensified

---

[56]   Helle, 'Bergen's role', p. 47.

production of stockfish (dried fish) for export markets.[57] Helle states that in 1180 Bergen was described as 'packed with dried cod' and merchants from all over Europe came to purchase fish in exchange for their own goods.[58] He adds that as Bergen developed into an important node in trade across Northern Europe and as a gateway for Icelanders or others who wanted to exchange their goods, Icelanders and Faroese were also there seeking commodities scarce in the North Atlantic.[59] However, in the 1260s, according to Helle, Iceland and the North Atlantic islands fell under Norwegian control, with Bergen as the political and administrative centre from which they were administered.[60] A source from the fourteenth century provides a glimpse of North Atlantic trade with Bergen and mentions textiles, especially *vaðmál*, along with other goods circulating in the town.[61]

While it is unclear how much cloth was imported prior to the fourteenth century, Helle's observations suggest that it is possible that the textile assemblages from both Borgund and Folkebibliotek are a bit early for documenting the main influx of North Atlantic textile trade goods to Norway. Our own research into medieval sources mentioning '*vaðmál*' as a term, along with its variant forms, suggests that the thirteenth century seems to be the starting point of this textile trade.[62]

However, the archaeological data from Borgund and Folkebibliotek suggest that *vararfeldir* were present at both of these harbour towns prior to the main period of imports from the North Atlantic, that it was present there at much higher frequencies than in Iceland, and that none of the samples analysed presented isotopic evidence linking them to Iceland. All of these observations suggest that *vararfeldir* present at both of these Norwegian sites appear to be the result of local production. Future research will help add to this growing dataset and confirm or lead to revisions to these conclusions.

PILE WEAVING ELSEWHERE IN EUROPE

The Mediterranean Region

A review of the history of pile weaving suggests it was not specific to one location but was, rather, woven widely across Europe and Scandinavia prior to the Viking Age.

As outlined earlier (see p. 52), Guðjónsson argued that pile weaving dated back to the Sumerian cultures of Mesopotamia approximately 5,000 years ago, with other examples known from early dynastic Egypt, approximately 4,000 years ago, as well as ancient

---

[57] Sophia Perdikaris and Thomas McGovern, 'Codfish and kings, seals and subsistence: Norse marine resource use in the North Atlantic', in *Seeking a Richer Harvest: The Archaeology of Subsistence Intensification, Innovation and Change*, ed. by T.L. Thurston and C.T. Fischer (New York: Springer Science and Business Media, 2007), pp. 193–216; Gunnar Karlsson, *Iceland's 1100 Years History of a Marginal Society* (London: Hurst, 2017).

[58] Helle, 'Bergen's role', p. 47.

[59] Gelsinger, *Icelandic Enterprise*, p. 111.

[60] Helle, 'Bergen's role', p. 47.

[61] Helle, 'Bergen's role', p. 44.

[62] Steinman and Hayeur Smith, 'The North Atlantic wool trade'.

Persia, Asia Minor, and Greece.[63] The Sumerian examples were referred to as *kaunakès*, and discussions about this type of cloth have led to a debate over whether it was a woven textile with added pile, or whether it referred to sheepskins.[64]

Emile Cherblanc, curator of the Musée d'Art Industriel of Lyon, published a volume in 1937 dedicated to this type of cloth, sparking disagreement on the nature of these textiles and contradicting earlier interpretations by Léon Heuzey, conservator at the Musée du Louvre. (Heuzey's ideas were more in line with Guðjónsson's interpretation.) Some of these earlier theories saw connections with looped textiles recovered from Egyptian Coptic tombs, and suggested that the Greek *flokati* is a possible surviving type of *kaunakès*.[65] Cherblanc felt that the garments depicted on Sumerian statues were not woven textiles at all, but were actual skins of sheep or goats, but he felt that the term *kaunakès* should also apply to these materials, creating further confusion.[66] Leon Legrain pointed out that in this region, wool was reserved for clothing, while skins were intended for rug trimmings.[67]

A more recent review of the question by Catherine Breniquet reopened the debate and rejected Cherblanc's argument that the *kaunakès* was simply a sheepskin. One problem regarding the debate over the cloth and garment described as *kaunakès* pertains to the researchers' reliance on iconography rather than actual textiles, since organics preserve poorly in that part of the world. Breniquet even went so far as to suggest that the *kaunakès* may have been a figurative iconographic element with no bearing on reality.[68] But the potentially early examples, such as a Coptic linen pile-woven textile dated to the fourth or fifth century CE, a fifth-century statue of St John the Baptist from Ravenna wearing a pile-woven shawl, and 'Vandals', on an ivory diptych now housed in the Bargello Museum, Florence, wearing shaggy pile-woven robes from *c*. AD 450 all point towards the Mediterranean as a place of origin for this type of cloth.[69] How it reached Northern Europe is less clear.

Ireland

Frances Pritchard described the presence of heavyweight tabby textiles, z/s spun with traces of pile preserved from Viking Age Dublin. She confirmed that the pile hung face down and was inserted into the weave, not unlike similar Viking Age finds from the Isles

---

[63] Guðjónsson, 'Forn röggvarvefnaður', pp. 32, 33.

[64] See L. Legrain, Review: '*Le Kaunakès* (Histoire Génerale du Tissu. Document II: Tissus Anciens, Première Partie) by Emile Cherblanc', *American Journal of Archaeology* 44.1 (1940), 150–152.

[65] Legrain, Review: '*Le Kaunakès*', p. 151.

[66] Catherine Breniquet, 'Que savons-nous exactement du kaunakès mésopotamien?', *Revue d'Assyriologie et d'Archéologie Oriental* 110 (2016) 1–22 (p. 5).

[67] Legrain, Review: '*Le Kaunakès*', p. 151.

[68] Breniquet, 'Que savons-nous', p. 13.

[69] Guðjónsson, 'Forn röggvarvefnaður', p. 38.

of Eigg and the Isle of Man,[70] tenth- and eleventh-century York[71] and Viking Age Birka in Sweden, where at least three pile-woven textiles were found in burials.[72] They are also known from Lund, Sweden,[73] and Wolin, Poland.[74] However, Pritchard also confirmed the presence in Viking Age Dublin of shaggy pile weaves similar in appearance to the Icelandic ones, woven as 2 x 1 or 2 x 2 twills incorporating the characteristic long, shaggy piles. Even so, she concluded that the textiles from Dublin were of Irish origin, based on a long-lived reputation for their manufacture during the medieval and early modern periods, and because such cloth is often referred to in Old Irish literature.[75]

According to Pritchard, this type of cloth was quite widespread across Europe but displayed a variety of weaves – 2 x 2 twill (including broken lozenge twills) and 2 x 1 twills – not unlike the situation described in the assemblage of textiles from Borgund. Further, she argued that the differences in twist or pile and the methods by which they were inserted suggest that no standardisation existed in the making of this type of cloth.[76] Finally, she saw similarities between the Irish Viking Age pile-woven textiles and that from Heynes, Iceland, and concluded that such a strong connection existed between these two Viking Age colonies that the technique may have come to Iceland via Ireland, concluding that: 'Both Iceland and Ireland were renowned for shaggy cloaks – the use of an uncommercial red dye rather than madder points to a rural production centre.'[77] But where this rural production centre, or centres, might have been remains unclear.

In the same volume, Elizabeth Wincott Heckett provided a good overview of Irish pile-woven textiles and their unique characteristics but also acknowledged their prior widespread production throughout Europe and could not pinpoint where they were first

---

[70] G.M. Crowfoot, 'Textiles from a Viking grave at Kildonan on the Isle of Eigg', *Proceedings of the Society of Antiquaries of Scotland* 83 (1949), 24–28 (p. 25).

[71] J. Hedges, 'Textiles', in *Anglo-Scandinavian Finds from Lloyds Bank, Pavement and other Sites*, ed. by A. MacGregor, *The Archaeology of York* 17.3, (1982), 102–127 (pp. 113–114); Pritchard, 'Aspects of the wool textiles', p. 98; Frances Pritchard, 'Textiles from Dublin', in *Kvinner i Vikingtid*, ed. by Nancy Coleman and Nanna Løkka (Oslo: Scandinavian Academic Press, 2014), pp. 225–242 (p. 203).

[72] Pritchard, 'Aspects of the wool textiles', p. 98.

[73] Märta Lindström, *Medeltida textilfynd från Lund* (Lund: Kulturen, 1970).

[74] Jerzy Maik, 'Frühmittelalterlichen Textilwaren Wolin', in *Archaeological Textiles: Report from the 2nd NESAT Symposium, 1.-4.V.1984*, ed. by Lise Bender Jørgensen, Bente Magnus and Elisabeth Munksgaard, Arkaeologiske Skrifter 2 (Copenhagen: Arkaeologisk Institut, 1988), pp. 162–186.

[75] Pritchard, 'Textiles from Dublin', p. 231.

[76] Pritchard, 'Aspects of the wool textiles', p. 98.

[77] Pritchard, 'Aspects of the wool textiles', p. 98.

produced in Ireland.[78] She confirmed that pile weaving was known in both Greece and Rome and referred to as *villosa* by Pliny the Younger.[79]

In Ireland, it seems that shaggy pile weaves were produced in abundance, with accounts of their export to France in the fourteenth century, and with a possible Irish example appearing in Belgium (on the mantle of St Brigid).[80] Of interest is the curly nature of the pile on some of the cloaks discussed, which Wincott Heckett traces as an Irish characteristic. She presents evidence by A. Lucas,[81] who described techniques using teasels to brush up the nap, with the intention of creating a 'curled pile', where either a fleece or spun yarns look curly.[82] How the curly-looking fibres were actually created is unclear. Was the pile woven into the cloth and then curled, or added after weaving? Were the curled piles of spun yarns, or locks of wool? One might think that the pile-woven textiles from Borgund with spun curly piles (Bryggen Museum number 0001/61/002055/001), described above, could be such an example of this type. However, the overlap between strontium ratios from Norway and Ireland makes it currently unclear.

The Irish shaggy pile-woven cloak appears to have become a part of Irish traditional dress from the early Middle Ages to the late seventeenth century, when it was eventually abandoned.[83] This period of use coincides with the ages of later Icelandic pile-woven textiles, which date roughly to the early modern period. These Icelandic textiles are also distinct in their construction and do not resemble the earlier tenth-century examples, suggesting, in accordance with Guðjónsson, that they may actually have been imported, possibly from Ireland. The records of the property owned by both of the Icelandic episcopal sees, Skálholt and Hólar, during the sixteenth and seventeenth centuries include descriptions of shaggy pile-woven textiles used both as bedding and as cloaks.[84]

CONCLUSION AND THOUGHTS ON
THE ORIGINS OF *VARARFELDIR*

The origins of shaggy pile-woven textiles and cloaks seem clearly to be found in Antiquity and in the Mediterranean region. The technique probably made its way across the Europen continent and became popular during the Iron Age in Northern Europe and persisted in Ireland through the Middle Ages, though we have no evidence as to how it travelled.

---

[78] Elizabeth Wincott Heckett, '"Shaggy pile" fabric of the 16th century – an Insular survival?', in Jørgensen and Munksgaard, *Archaeological Textiles in Northern Europe*, pp. 58–168 (p. 160).

[79] Wincott Heckett, '"Shaggy pile" fabric', p. 160.

[80] Wincott Heckett, '"Shaggy pile" fabric', p. 162.

[81] A. Lucas, 'Cloth finishing in Ireland', *Folklife Journal* 6 (1968), 19–67.

[82] Wincott Heckett, '"Shaggy pile" fabric', p. 162.

[83] Wincott Heckett, '"Shaggy pile" fabric', p. 166.

[84] Guðjónsson, 'Forn röggvarvefnaður', p. 28.

Clearly, in the Icelandic context, pile-woven textiles were locally produced during the Viking and Medieval periods, but whether they were exported, as possibly inferred from the short description of King Harald's acquisition of them in *Heimskringla* and in records of their value in medieval Icelandic law codes, remains unclear. Further it is still unclear if the technique came to Iceland via Ireland or from Norway with Iceland's early settlers. It now well established by Helgason et al. that mtDNA of Icelanders as well as other groups of North Atlantic islanders reflects origins and lineages not only from Scandinavia but also from Britain and Ireland.[85] The preliminary strontium isotope data from Borgund suggests that Norway had its own tradition of pile weaving during the late Viking Age, if not before, and that *vararfeldir* do not seem to have been a significant component of the textile trade between Iceland and Norway when it intensified after the thirteenth century.[86]

Possibly the most important aspect of the shaggy pile weave is its persistence and lengthy survival as item of material culture in Scandinavia and Northern Europe, largely because it was so well suited to the climatic conditions of the North Atlantic. Apparently, such cloaks were relatively impermeable, since the pile would keep out rain during the inclement weather that characterises the North Atlantic's land- and seascapes.[87] While Wincott Heckett called it the 'raincoat' of the Irish, I would suggest it was the 'Viking raincoat' and that the visual cliché of hairy Vikings crossing the North Atlantic on their ships really reflects them wrapped in their pile-woven cloaks!

[85] Agnar Helgason, Eileen Hickey, Sara Goodacre, Vidar Bosnes, Kári Stefánsson, Ryk Ward and Bryan Sykes, 'mtDNA and the islands of the North Atlantic: estimating the proportions of Norse and Gaelic ancestry', *American Journal of Human Genetics* 68 (2001), 723–737 (p. 724).

[86] Steinnam and Hayeur Smith, 'The North Atlantic wool trade'.

[87] Wincott Heckett, '"Shaggy pile" fabric', p. 164; also see Kearney, Chapter 7 this volume.

CHAPTER 4

Re-clothing the Inhabitants of Tenth-century Dublin based on Archaeological Evidence[1]

Frances Pritchard

The style of dress worn by Viking settlers in the North Atlantic and Irish Sea zone has received considerable attention from scholars. The evidence for this has been based mainly on pagan burials around the coast of Scotland and in England from Cumbria southwards to Wales.[2] The clothing has often been likened to the attire of Scandinavians, especially in western Norway, a region from which some of the early marauders actually came. However, there is a need for more nuanced regional and chronological differences to be established,[3] as the Viking world was not a unified empire and people of diverse ethnicity lived in many places, not least in Dublin.[4] By the tenth century the influence of native Irish dress is also likely to have been assimilated to some degree.[5]

---

[1]   I am very grateful to Dr Patrick F. Wallace, former Director of the National Museum of Ireland, for enabling me to research the excavated textiles from Dublin. The dye analyses mentioned in the text were undertaken by Penelope Walton Rogers.

[2]   David Griffiths, *Vikings of the Irish Sea: Conflict and Assimilation AD 790–1050* (Stroud: The History Press, 2010), pp. 72–99.

[3]   Inga Hägg, 'Einige Beobactungen über die Birkatracht', in *Archäologische Textilfunde, Textilsymposium Neumünster*, ed. by Lise Bender Jørgensen and Klaus Tidow (Neumünster: Textilmuseum Neumünster, 1982), pp. 249–265 (249); James Graham-Campbell and Colleen E. Batey, *Vikings in Scotland. An Archaeological Survey* (Edinburgh: Edinburgh University Press, 1998), pp. 151–154.

[4]   Christina Lee addressed aspects of this subject in 'Costumes and contact: evidence for Scandinavian women in the Irish Sea Region', in *The Vikings in Ireland and Beyond: Before and After the Battle of Clontarf*, ed. by Howard B. Clarke and Ruth Johnson (Dublin: Four Courts Press, 2015), pp. 284–296, but she took little account of the excavated textiles from Dublin.

[5]   There have been a number of studies of indigenous early medieval Irish dress based chiefly on figurative art, ancient Irish laws and literary sources. Among the most recent are Maria A.

Interpreting textiles recovered from the Wood Quay/Fishamble Street series of excavations in Dublin directed by Patrick F. Wallace from 1974 to 1981 for the National Museum of Ireland forms the core of this chapter. However, as the textiles derive from rubbish deposits within the town, close to the banks of the river Liffey, they provide a less coherent indication of the garments worn by the inhabitants than if they had come from furnished graves, where it is often possible to reconstruct much of the burial clothing, although even this can give a false impression of dress worn in everyday life as opposed to death, where ritualistic elements need to be taken into account.[6] Matters of status and occupation are also easier to deduce from grave-goods. Nevertheless, the difficulty of interpreting burial clothing has recently been highlighted by the project 'Fashioning the Viking Age', a collaboration between the National Museum of Denmark, the Centre for Textile Research at the Saxo Institute, University of Copenhagen, and the Land of Legends Centre for Historical-Archaeological Research and Communication in Lejre.[7] This has involved a re-examination and re-interpretation of the textile fragments recovered from two burials in Jutland dating to the second half of the tenth century that were excavated in 1868–69 and 1880, with the garments worn for burial by the chieftain at Bjerringhøj, Mammen now taking on a very different appearance from those suggested by an interdisciplinary study undertaken only twenty-five years previously.[8] Unsurprisingly, therefore, an element of conjecture exists in this present discussion.

Furnished burials from Dublin and its environs have been researched in detail but, as they date to an earlier period than that being considered here, they will not be used to indicate mid- to late tenth-century styles of dress.[9] However, they do demonstrate the transfer of dress as a means of identity from one far distant region to another, as it had nothing in common with indigenous Irish clothing. This is, for example, apparent in the clothing of a woman of high status buried at Finglas in the hinterland north of Dublin, who wore a pair of ostentatious, silver inlaid, oval brooches decorated with bear heads that are paralleled by examples from graves in Birka, Hedeby and Fristad, Rogaland, and which it has been suggested link her to a possible bear cult.[10] Scientific techniques

---

FitzGerald, 'Insular dress in early Medieval Ireland', *Bulletin of the John Rylands Library* 79.3 (1997), 251–261; and Niamh Whitfield, 'Aristocratic display in early medieval Ireland in fiction and fact: the dazzling white tunic and purple cloak', *Peritia* 27 (2016), 159–188.

[6] Neil Price, *The Children of Ash and Elm: A History of the Vikings* (New York: Basic Books, 2020), p. 248.

[7] Ulla Mannering, 'Fashioning the Viking Age', *Archaeological Textiles Review* 60 (2018), 114–117 (p. 115); Ulla Mannering, 'Fashioning the Viking Age: status after the first three years', *Archaeological Textiles Review* 63 (2021), 139–144 (pp. 141–143).

[8] Elisabeth Munksgaard, 'Kopien af dragten fra Mammengravern', in *Mammen. Grav, kunst og samfund i vikingetid*, ed. by Mette Iversen, Jysk Arkæologisk Selskabs Skrifter 28 (Aarhus: Aarhus University, 1991), pp. 151–153.

[9] Stephen H. Harrison and Raghnall Ó Floinn, *Viking Graves and Grave Goods in Ireland*, Medieval Dublin Excavations 1962–81, Series B, vol. 11 (Dublin: National Museum of Ireland, 2014).

[10] Maeve Sikora, 'The Finglas burial: archaeology and ethnicity in Viking-Age Dublin', in *The Viking Age: Ireland and the West. Papers from the Proceedings of the Fifteenth Viking Congress, Cork, 18–27 August 2005*, ed. by John Sheehan and Donnchadh Ó Corráin (Dublin: Four Courts Press, 2010), pp. 402–417 (407–414).

including oxygen and strontium isotope analyses of tooth enamel further confirm documentary sources that some of the inhabitants of Dublin grew up elsewhere, including the Scottish islands as well as Scandinavia.[11] Thus, like the woman buried at Finglas, they may have possessed a different taste in dress, although by the second half of the tenth century interaction and intermarriage at various levels of society between the Scandinavian settlers and native Irish led to hybridisation and to some extent a distinctive Hiberno-Norse culture had evolved, which has been noted as well from certain inland settlement sites such as Ballinderry crannóg, Co. Westmeath.[12] Other factors such as the increasing conversion to Christianity by the Viking immigrants in the tenth century probably also affected clothing and associated dress accessories, such as a change from wearing a pendant in the shape of Thor's hammer to a cross, ornaments that in Dublin were often made locally from imported amber.[13]

THE TEXTILE EVIDENCE

The textiles recovered from four rubbish deposits (open areas) from plots 2 and 3 at Fishamble Street, with the earliest dating to c. 930 to 950, two dating to c. 960 to 980 and the fourth c. 980 to 1000, provide the nucleus of the evidence in this discussion, in addition to the textiles retrieved from inside a sequence of buildings, many of which were probably houses. The actual place of origin of the textiles cannot easily be determined. A survey of woven textiles from sites throughout north-west Europe published by Lise Bender Jørgensen in 1992 provided a broad indication of initial production centres for particular types of cloth up to AD 1000.[14] However, it is doubtful if any but the most specialised products were confined to a few workshops, especially as the use of slave labour meant that craft skills, such as wool processing, spinning and weaving, were transmitted across the seas from one place to another. This is reflected in the experience of the fictional Irish poet, Moriuth, who traced his enslaved wife to a spinning workshop in Vaudreuil, near Rouen in northern France, in the early eleventh century.[15]

---

[11] Linzi Simpson, 'Viking warrior burials: is this the longphort?' in *Medieval Dublin VI. Proceedings of the Friends of Medieval Dublin Symposium 2004*, ed. Seán Duffy (Dublin: Four Courts Press, 2005), pp. 11–62 (pp. 50–53).

[12] Ruth Johnson, 'Ballinderry crannóg No. 1: a reinterpretation', *Proceedings of the Royal Irish Academy* 99c.2 (1999), 23–71 (pp. 65–67).

[13] Patrick F. Wallace, *Viking Dublin. The Wood Quay Excavations* (Sallins, Co. Kildare: Irish Academic Press, 2016), pp. 289–296.

[14] Lise Bender Jørgensen, *North European Textiles until AD 1000* (Aarhus: Aarhus University Press, 1992).

[15] Elisabeth M.C. van Houts, 'Scandinavian influence in the Norman literature of the eleventh century', *Anglo-Norman Studies* 6 (1983), 107–121 (pp. 107–108).

Analysis of wool fibres by various methods, including measuring the diameter of fibres, helps identify the fleece type, a system developed by Michael Ryder in the 1960s;[16] more recently stable-isotope analysis is providing an indication of the terrain where the sheep grazed.[17] In 2013 a project was undertaken to assess the source of two different types of wool fabrics represented among the textiles from Dublin and whether any chronological differences could be ascertained based on ten textiles of each weave type, making forty samples in total. They were fine, open-textured tabby-woven fabrics of the type used for headwear and good quality, three-shed diamond twills woven throughout from combed z-spun wool, with one exception that had z-spun wool in one system and s-spun wool in the other. Currently, the results remain inconclusive in respect of the geographical place of origin, but analysis of the fleece types indicated that the wool selected for the tabby-woven bonnets and scarves was consistently a semi-fine fleece type, which was only very rarely identified among the other textiles in Dublin at this period.[18] A wad of raw fleece of similar type was also recovered from a late tenth-century deposit,[19] thus indicating that this special type of cloth could have been locally produced.

With respect to the actual clothing, no attempt is made here to debate the terminology of garments worn in Dublin. Outer garments worn by men and women are considered first, followed by inner garments, headwear and legwear. Accessories including belts, jewellery and shoes are mentioned only briefly as they have been studied in depth by other specialists.[20]

OUTER GARMENTS

The easiest garment to characterise in terms of its cloth is the cloak woven in chunky wool yarn, usually z-spun in the warp and s-spun in the weft and bound in tabby weave, 2 x 2 twill or 2 x 1 twill, although occasionally they are either z-spun or s-spun throughout. Many were probably used for cloaks, which then doubled as bedding, a practice that continued for centuries. A few of these textiles from Dublin preserve edges bound

---

[16] Michael L. Ryder, 'Changes in the fleece of sheep following domestication (with a note on the coat of cattle)', in *The Domestication and Exploitation of Plants and Animals*, ed. by Peter J. Ucko and G.W. Dimbleby (London: Duckworth, 1969), pp. 495–521.

[17] Karin Margarita Frei, 'Provenance studies of ancient textiles: a new method based on the strontium isotope system', in *The North European Symposium for Archaeological Textiles XI (NESAT XI)*, ed. by Johanna Banck-Burgess and Carla Nübold (Rahden, Westphalia: Marie Leidorf GmbH, 2013), pp. 145–149; Isabella C.C. von Holstein, 'An introduction to carbon, nitrogen and hydrogen stable isotope provenancing for archaeological wool', in Banck-Burgess and Nübold, *NESAT XI*, pp. 150–154.

[18] Penelope Walton Rogers, 'Fleece types in further textiles from Viking Age Dublin', *Anglo-Saxon Laboratory Report*, 3 October 2013, unpublished.

[19] Penelope Walton Rogers, 'A fragment of unprocessed fleece from Viking Age Dublin, E190:7428', *Anglo-Saxon Laboratory Report*, 11 January 2013, unpublished.

[20] The specialists include Paula Harvey (amber) and the late Dáire O'Rourke (footwear).

Fig. 4.1   Tabby-woven wool cloth with pile on the reverse (all yarn s-spun yarn, 3–4/4 threads per cm) bound with a tabby-woven band, width 30 mm (z/s-spun yarn, 24/11–12 threads per cm), from Fishamble Street, Dublin. National Museum of Ireland, E172:3374. (Photo: Michael Pollard).

with sewn-on tablet-woven bands, which provided a firm finish,[21] or, alternatively, fine, worsted, tabby or twill-woven bands (Fig. 4.1). Occasionally traces of pile are preserved in some of these heavyweight cloths. The pile is always inserted so that it hangs on only one face of the cloth, in imitation of a sheep's fleece. Very similar pile-woven cloths that were worn as cloaks have been recorded from the graves of Viking warrior-farmers on the Isle of Eigg and Isle of Man,[22] and a piled fabric bound with a tabby-woven band was also recovered from Coppergate, York.[23] Weave structures in 2 x 1 and 2 x 2 twill that incorporate long, shaggy wool pile from Dublin have a slightly higher number of warp threads (ranging from 5 to 10 per cm) compared to the examples in tabby weave that mainly have three or four warp threads per cm. One example in 2 x 2 twill recovered from a late tenth-century rubbish deposit has a warp dyed with an unidentified plant dyestuff producing a red hue and a weft and pile yarn of naturally pigmented wool, indicating that colour effects were characteristic of some of them.[24] It is likely that most of the shaggy cloaks were Irish in origin, as the country gained a long-lived reputation for their manufacture throughout the medieval and early modern periods and they are frequently referred to in Old Irish literature. For example, in the epic tale *The Destruction*

[21]   Frances Pritchard, 'Evidence of tablet weaving from Viking-Age Dublin', in *Crafting Textiles. Tablet Weaving, Sprang, Lace and Other Techniques from the Bronze Age to the Early 17th Century*, ed. by Frances Pritchard (Oxford and Philadelphia: Oxbow Books, 2021), pp. 37–52 (p. 42, fig. 3.5).

[22]   Grace M. Crowfoot, 'Textiles from a Viking grave at Kildonan on the Isle of Eigg', *Proceedings of the Society of Antiquaries of Scotland* 83 (1949), 24–28 (p. 25).

[23]   Penelope Walton, *Textiles, Cordage and Raw Fibre from 16–22 Coppergate*, The Archaeology of York The Small Finds 17/5 (London: The Council for British Archaeology, 1989), pp. 319–321, fig. 128 and pl. XVIII.

[24]   Frances Pritchard, 'Aspects of the wool textiles from Viking Age Dublin', in *Archaeological Textiles in Northern Europe, NESAT IV, Tidens Tand 5*, ed. by Lise Bender Jørgensen and Elisabeth Munksgaard (Copenhagen: Det Kongelige Danske Kunstakademi, 1992), pp. 93–103 (pp. 95–98, fig. 3).

of Da Derga's Hostel, a woman, who was as tall and her shins as black as a weaver's beam, is described as wearing a 'very fleecy striped mantle'.[25]

No traces of fur remained on any of the cloak-weight textiles; therefore no fur linings can be postulated from the surviving archaeological evidence, although this does not mean that fur linings, edgings or separate capes should be dismissed from consideration. Indeed fragments of a fur outer garment trimmed with a gold and silver tablet-woven band, which has been interpreted as a cape, were recovered from the burial of a high-status woman at Hvilehøj, Jutland that is coin-dated to some time after 962.[26] Furs would have been traded to Dublin from the Baltic region and further north. In addition, among the species of native wild animals identified from the bones at the Wood Quay complex are fox, otter, hare and stoat, the skins of all of which could have been used in clothing. However, the cut marks and bone selection are mostly suggestive of meat eating rather than skinning for fur pelts.[27] Badgers are an exception, also cats, which had light cut marks on their skulls above the nose, indicative of skinning. Later in the medieval period there was a flourishing trade in animal pelts from Ireland to England, where they were imported into Chester and Bristol,[28] when beautifully marked dark grey or black cat (*genette*) skins were among the most sought after; so the trend for this type of fur may have originated in earlier centuries.

The length of the cloaks worn by the inhabitants of Dublin also cannot be determined from the archaeological record. Men's cloaks fastened on the shoulder, usually with ringed pins made from copper alloy, most of which were probably made locally.[29] One ring-headed pin has a length of silk cord still wound round its head.[30] A small pennanular brooch also has silk thread wound round its hoop,[31] indicating that sufficient surplus supplies of imported silk thread were available in Dublin to use in this manner.

There is no evidence that the front-opening jackets, coats or kaftans that have been identified from ninth- and tenth-century burials in Birka[32] were worn by either men or women in Dublin. If these items were made from fur, as recently deduced for the

[25] J. Gantz, *Early Irish Myths and Sagas* (Harmondsworth: Penguin Classics, 1981), p. 76. See also Chapter 7 in this volume.

[26] Anne Hedeager Krag, 'Denmark – Europe: dress and fashion in Denmark's Viking Age', in *Northern Archaeological Textiles NESAT VII*, ed. by Frances Pritchard and John Peter Wild (Oxford: Oxbow, 2005), pp. 29–35 (p. 29); Mannering, 'Fashioning the Viking Age', p. 116, fig 2; Mannering, 'Fashioning the Viking Age: status after the first three years', pp. 142–143, fig. 5.

[27] Wallace, *Viking Dublin*, pp. 218–219.

[28] Elspeth M. Veale, *The English Fur Trade in the Later Middle Ages* (London: Oxford University Press, 1966), pp. 60–61.

[29] Tom Fanning, *Viking Age Ringed Pins from Dublin*, Medieval Dublin Excavations 1962–81, Series B, vol. 4 (Dublin: Royal Irish Academy, 1994), p. 117.

[30] Fanning, *Viking Age Ringed Pins*, pp. 41 and 125.

[31] Wallace, *Viking Dublin*, p. 280, fig. 8.9.

[32] Hägg, 'Birkatracht', p. 249.

chieftain at Bjerringhøj,[33] none is preserved. Fragments of jackets from Hedeby were made from twill fabrics with a fur-like roughened nap,[34] but twills of this type are absent from the Dublin assemblage.

INNER GARMENTS

Tunics

More than one tunic may have been worn at any one time depending on the climate and season of the year. The weight of the cloth and type of fabric selected may also have varied. The wool cloth chosen for male and female tunics in the tenth century was probably most often a twill-woven fabric. In Dublin, 2 x 2 twill and 2 x 1 twills are represented, with self-patterned diamond weaves in both structures being commonplace. Fabrics woven in four-shed diamond twill, usually with displacement in the warp and weft, occur throughout tenth-century deposits in Dublin. Pattern repeats are often not consistent in a single cloth, although the displacement in the weft frequently occurs after nine picks (Fig. 4.2). Most are woven with a z-spun warp and s-spun weft, although a few woven throughout from z-spun yarn are generally slightly finer.[35] The finest example of a 2 x 2 broken diamond twill recorded from the site, with 29 x 16 threads per cm, has mixed spinning. This is very similar to the quality of a diamond twill dress fabric in a woman's grave at Cnip (Kneep) on the Isle of Lewis.[36] The woman, who was in her late thirties, appears to have died in the tenth century. She was a Viking colonist of high status, and wore a leather girdle fastened round her waist with a distinctive Insular buckle and strap-end that is paralleled by metalwork at Fishamble Street,[37] and a Hiberno-Norse ringed pin of the type most common in Dublin.[38] Therefore, the burial clothing of this woman appears to provide some indication of the style of dress of some of the better-off inhabitants

---

[33] Mannering, 'Fashioning the Viking Age: status after the first three years', p. 142.

[34] Inga Hägg, *Die Textilfunde aus dem Hafen von Haithabu*. Berichte über die Ausgrabungen in Haithabu 20 (Neumünster: Karl Wachholtz, 1984), pp. 73, 81–83; Ulla Mannering, *Iconic Costumes: Scandinavian Late Iron Age Costume Iconography* (Oxford and Philadelphia: Oxbow, 2017), p. 158.

[35] Frances Pritchard, 'Twill weaves from Viking Age Dublin', in *Archaeological Textiles – Links between Past and Present, NESAT XIII*, ed. by Milena Bravermanová, Helena Březinová and Jane Malcolm-Davies (Liberec and Prague: Technical University of Liberec, Faculty of Engineering and Institute of Archaeology of the CAS Prague, 2017), pp. 115–123 (pp. 117–118).

[36] Lise Bender Jørgensen, 'The textile remains', in 'A Viking burial from Kneep, Uig, Isle of Lewis', by R.D.E. Welander, Colleen E. Batey and Trevor G. Cowie, *Proceedings of the Society for the Antiquaries of Scotland* 117 (1987), 165–168 (pp. 167–168).

[37] Caroline Paterson, 'Insular belt-fittings from the pagan Norse graves of Scotland: a reappraisal in the light of scientific and stylistic analysis', in *Pattern and Purpose in Insular Art. Proceedings of the Fourth International Conference on Insular Art held at the National Museum & Gallery, Cardiff 3–6 September 1998*, ed. by Mark Redknap, Nancy Edwards, Susan Youngs, Alan Lane and Jeremy Knight (Oxford: Oxbow, 2001), pp. 125–132 (pp. 129–131).

[38] Fanning, *Viking Age Ringed Pins*, p. 25.

Fig. 4.2 Seamed fragments of a wool 2 x 2 broken diamond twill (z/s-spun yarn, 14/7 threads per cm) bound with a band woven in 2 x 2 warp chevron twill (z/s-spun yarn, 15/11 threads per cm), maximum height of textile 90mm, from a deposit dating to 960-980 at Fishamble Street, Dublin. National Museum of Ireland, E172:10579. (Photo: Michael Pollard).

in Dublin at the same period.[39] However, details of the actual cut and construction of such a dress remain elusive.

An example from Dublin of a garment-weight 2 x 2 broken diamond twill (E190:7444) with 21 x 12 threads per cm retains four panels of the cloth of varying widths carefully seamed together so that the pattern is aligned. It is hemmed in herringbone stitch sewn in two-ply red thread. This, and many other textiles with seams, suggests that a considerable amount of shaping went into the garments, although some of the stitching may represent repairs or recycling of fabrics. Traces of seams and hems show that the stitching was often carried out in thread of a contrasting colour, which would have provided a decorative effect. In addition, sometimes a narrow worsted band was added to a seam, probably as a form of reinforcement.[40] Fabrics were not necessarily monotone: alternately spun yarns were occasionally used in the weft, which may have been dyed different colours; and stripes sometimes remain visible to the eye, such as a 2 x 1 diamond twill with stripes formed from dark brown pigmented wool next to red that was dyed with lichen purple.[41]

[39] Somewhat surprisingly, the woman was also buried wearing two oval brooches; Richard Welander, 'The contents of the grave', in 'A Viking burial from Kneep', pp. 153–165 (pp. 154–156 and 160–161) and a more recent reappraisal of the grave-goods has suggested an earlier date for the burial; Graham-Campbell and Batey, *Vikings in Scotland*, p. 74.

[40] Pritchard, 'Aspects of the wool textiles', p. 100, fig. 7.

[41] Pritchard, 'Aspects of the wool textiles', pp. 96 and 98, fig. 4.

Fig. 4.3 Fine quality wool 2 x 1 diamond twill (all yarn z-spun, 50/22 thread per cm), maximum height 68 mm, from a deposit dating to 960-980 at Fishamble Street, Dublin. National Museum of Ireland, E172: 10576. (Photo: Jon Bailey).

Written sources also imply that woven cloth seized as loot at this period was notable for its colour as well as for its variety.[42]

Finer wool fabrics tend to be woven in 2 x 1 diamond twill using combed wool that has been expertly z-spun (Fig. 4.3),[43] and they match the quality of those recovered from Birka, where they were apparently restricted to female burials.[44] The fragments preserved are usually smaller in size than the slightly chunkier 2 x 2 broken diamond twills and they

[42] Lee, 'Costumes and contact', p. 295 quoting the Munster tract, *Cogadh Gáedhel re Gallaibh*.
[43] Pritchard, 'Twill weaves', p. 119.
[44] Agnes Geijer, *Birka III. Die Textilfunde aus den Gräbern* (Uppsala: Almqvist and Wiksells, 1938), pp. 26–29, but this generalisation is based on only eight examples.

are more numerous, indicating that cloth of this type was readily available in Dublin, where more of it has been recorded than anywhere else.

The extent to which any of the wool tunics were decorated is difficult to determine. Most of the stitching of the hems and seams appears to have been carried out in two-ply sewing thread of a contrasting colour. Apart from narrow bands in tabby weave or 2 x 2 chevron twill used to trim edges, no applied decoration in the form of embroidery or strips of silk (as interpreted as a feature of the woman's tunic from Hvilehøj)[45] was identified, although many plain woven ribbons as well as strips of samite (weft-faced compound twill) were available in Dublin for such a purpose if so desired.

Trousers

In her discussion of Scandinavian late Iron Age costume Ulla Mannering states that trousers constituted an integral part of Scandinavian male costume at this period (covering an era that extends to 1050).[46] However, at present it is difficult to argue persuasively whether there are any fragments of trousers among the many textiles from Dublin. It therefore remains speculative based on evidence from visual sources and excavated material from sites such as Hedeby and, more recently, Bjerringhøj, where re-examination of the textiles and bones from the burial indicates that the high-status man was attired in long-legged trousers made from a cellulose plant fibre such as linen or hemp around which he wore padded silken ankle cuffs.[47] It is, indeed, possible that trousers were a practical garment that the Vikings partly adopted from the native Irish, who had a tradition of wearing trews (*truibhas*) stretching back to their Celtic origins, as later depicted for example in the Book of Kells (*Codex Cenannensis*, Dublin Trinity College Library, A.I. [58]), which dates to the late eighth or early ninth century.[48]

Shirts/Chemises

Due to the unfavourable, anoxic (without oxygen) soil conditions, only tiny amounts of linen, or textiles woven from other types of plant fibres, are preserved from Dublin. A few carbonised fragments are all tabby woven from z-spun yarn and of a medium quality, with the finest having 22/19 threads per cm. There is no pleated linen, which, it has been asserted, was a common feature of women's clothing and often worn in combination with a wool dress secured with shoulder straps (and oval brooches) in many parts of the Viking world and enduring into the tenth century in Birka, Sweden.[49] In discussing the pleated linen from Birka, Inga Hägg traced its origin to southern Slavic territories.

Often associated with linen are slickstones made from balls of glass that could have been used to impart sheen to the surface of linen, as well as for pressing pleats and

---

45 Mannering, 'Fashioning the Viking Age: status after the first three years', pp. 142–143, fig. 5.

46 Mannering, *Iconic Costumes*, p. 170.

47 Charlotte Rimstad, Ulla Mannering, Marie Louise S. Jørkov and Marie Kanstrup, 'Lost and found: Viking Age human bones and textiles from Bjerringhøj, Denmark', *Antiquity* 95 (2021), 735–752.

48 FitzGerald, 'Insular dress', pp. 252–255 and 260–261.

49 Hägg, 'Birkatracht', p. 249.

seams.[50] Two fragments of these glass balls were recovered from late tenth- and early eleventh-century deposits inside buildings on Plot 9 at Fishamble Street,[51] one of which was a well-constructed house, with a wooden front door, that also contained other textile tools including part of a wooden weaving sword and fragments of a bone weaving tablet as well as remnants of silk trimmings (a ribbon and strip of samite) and pieces of a fine wool scarf.[52] Round balls of glass designed to produce a shiny finish on cloth had a long tradition of use in north-west Europe and can be traced back at least to the Roman world.[53] Consequently, the tool cannot be claimed to indicate Viking influence, although its use was held in sufficient esteem in the Viking world to be a considered a status symbol in female burials, where it was sometimes placed alongside exquisite whalebone smoothing boards, which were often decorated with pairs of confronted animal heads, as on an example from the cemetery at Kilmainham, Dublin.[54]

The only evidence preserved for linen garments among the urban rubbish material derives from the strips of silk samite, as it appears that most were stitched to linen fabrics. This is because occasional traces of brittle, degraded cloth and sewing thread are visible in the folded edges. Consequently, it is possible to suggest that various linen garments, especially men's shirts and perhaps trousers, were sometimes trimmed with exotically patterned silk fabrics. Regarded as a sign of status, these silks would have been conspicuously positioned round the neck opening or at the wrists or, if trousers, at the ankles. It was evidently the silk itself, rather than the design, that was considered important, as sometimes the strips were stitched inside out and two different scraps were even placed side by side to make a wider trimming.[55] In view of the number of trimmings of patterned silk recovered from rubbish deposits in Dublin, it may be suggested that they were worn more widely by the inhabitants than perhaps in other towns, which may partly explain why the town was described by the Danish historian, Saxo Grammaticus, as being in the tenth century 'filled with the wealth of barbarians'.[56]

---

[50] Penelope Walton Rogers, *Textile Production at 16-22 Coppergate*, The Archaeology of York The Small Finds 17/11 (York: The Council for British Archaeology, 1997), p. 1775.

[51] Accession numbers E190:7259 and E190:7129.

[52] House FS 88. For a description of this building see Patrick F. Wallace, *The Viking Age Buildings of Dublin*, Medieval Dublin Excavations 1962–81, Ser. A, vol. 1, (Dublin: Royal Irish Academy, 1992), pp. 178–181. For the scarf see Elizabeth Wincott Heckett, *Viking Age Headcoverings from Dublin*, Medieval Dublin Excavations 1962–81, Ser. B, vol. 6 (Dublin: Royal Irish Academy, 2003), DHC22, p. 34, fig. 32.

[53] John Peter Wild, *Textile Manufacture in the Northern Roman Provinces* (Cambridge: University Press, 1970), p. 85.

[54] Harrison and Ó Floinn, *Viking Graves*, pp. 169–170, 396–397, ill. 234, and 402–403, ill. 297.

[55] Frances Pritchard, 'Silk braids and textiles of the Viking Age from Dublin', in *Archaeological Textiles. Report from the 2nd NESAT symposium 1984*, ed. by Lise Bender Jørgensen, Bente Magnus and Elisabeth Munksgaard, Arkæologiske Skrifter fra Historisk Museum, Universitet i Bergen 4 (Copenhagen: Arkæologisk Institut, Københavns universitet, 1988), pp. 149–161 (p. 159).

[56] Alfred P. Smyth, *Scandinavian York and Dublin. The History and Archaeology of Two Related Viking Kingdoms*, vol. 2 (Dublin: Templekieran Press, 1979), p. 210.

HEADWEAR

A considerable number of items of headdress were recovered from the Fishamble Street excavations.[57] The most common item was a cap or bonnet-like head covering made from tabby-woven silk or wool and shaped with a dart at the centre back. Examples in silk were recovered from levels two and four at Fishamble Street, thus dating no later than the mid-tenth century.[58] It appears that the style was then copied locally in finely spun wool. This sequence of events peculiar to Dublin may perhaps explain why similar head coverings from York and Lincoln in eastern England have only been found made from silk and not wool.[59] Hairnets of knotted silk mesh were also worn[60] and a hairnet discarded in the early eleventh century is an unshaped length made in an openwork sprang technique from silk thread that was dyed with lichen purple, a dyestuff widely favoured in Dublin at the time.[61]

There are also fragments of scarves with tasseled ends and possible headbands. Whether they formed part of male or female dress is not easy to determine. There are no traces of stitch holes along any edges of the narrow, gold-brocaded tablet-woven bands (Fig. 4.4); consequently it is very likely that they were worn as headbands, as indicated by tenth-century burials in Norway and Sweden.[62]

Attention to hair and hair styling was evidently an important consideration, since numerous composite combs, many of which were made in workshops nearby, were recovered from the excavations.[63] Women do not appear to have worn their hair in the glamorous pony-tail style depicted in earlier, mainly Scandinavian sources, associated with pagan iconography. However, a bone plaque shows a bearded man with his hair tied in a bun at the back of his head.[64]

LEGWEAR

One type of textile that changed little with the vagaries of fashion was a wool band that was used as both a leg wrapping and garter. Similar bands were produced over a long period and appear to have been worn throughout northern Europe from at least the

---

[57] Wincott Heckett, *Viking Age Headcoverings*.

[58] Wincott Heckett, *Viking Age Headcoverings*, pp. 67–70. Accession numbers E172:13590 and E172:14370.

[59] Walton, *Textiles, Cordage and Raw Fibre*, pp. 360–367.

[60] Pritchard 'Silk braids and textiles of the Viking Age', p. 156.

[61] Frances Pritchard, 'Textiles from Dublin', in *Kvinner i vikingtid*, ed. by Nancy L. Coleman and Nanna Løkka, pp. 224–240 (pp. 235–236, fig. 11); Penelope Walton, 'Dyes of the Viking Age: a summary of recent work', *Dyes in History and Archaeology* 7 (1989), 14–20 (p. 18).

[62] Marianne Vedeler, *Silk for the Vikings* (Oxford and Philadelphia: Oxbow, 2014), pp. 42–43; Geijer, *Birka III*, p. 143, figs. 39–41.

[63] Wallace, *Viking Dublin*, p. 301.

[64] Wallace, *Viking Dublin*, p. 297, fig. 8.32.

Fig. 4.4 Gold-brocaded silk tablet-woven band, width 9 mm, from Fishamble Street, Dublin. National Museum of Ireland, E190:1194. (Photo: Valerie Dowling).

eighth to the eleventh centuries.[65] Ranging in width from approximately 70 to 100 mm, the bands were often woven in 2 x 2 broken chevron twill (Fig. 4.5). Evidence from the man's burial at Bjerringhøj suggests that more elaborately patterned garters were tablet woven,[66] but, although the equipment and skill existed in Dublin for making them in this technique,[67] none has been positively identified from the town.

Foot wrappings, like leg wrappings, probably made any form of sock unnecessary. However, a fragment of needle coiling (or *nalebinding*) made from two-ply (zz/S) wool yarn dyed with lichen purple[68] may have formed part of a sock or shoe lining similar to that excavated from a tenth-century backyard deposit at Coppergate, York,[69] or it may be a remnant of a mitten, another item that lent itself to this particular technique. Thus various options with respect to footwear, as with other items of dress, were probably available to a proportion of the inhabitants.

DRESS ACCESSORIES

No ensemble was complete without accessories, which conveyed as much about cultural identity as actual clothing. The accessories were practical as well as distinctive,

[65] Walton, *Textiles, Cordage and Raw Fibre*, p. 340.
[66] Lise Ræder Knudsen, 'Det uldne brikvævede bånd fra Mammengraven', in Iversen, *Mammen*, pp.149–150.
[67] Pritchard, 'Evidence of tablet weaving', p. 38.
[68] Pritchard, 'Aspects of the wool textiles', p. 102, fig. 11.
[69] Walton, *Textiles, Cordage and Raw Fibre*, pp. 341–342.

Fig. 4.5 Detail of a wool 2 x 2 warp chevron twill band (z/s spun yarn, 15/11 threads per cm), width 72mm, from a deposit dating to 980–1000 at Fishamble Street, Dublin. National Museum of Ireland, E172:12064. (Photo: Jon Bailey).

indicating status, gender and aspects of ethnicity. Silver was the preferred precious metal, as reflected in many hoards of the time. However, two gold finger rings were recovered from the excavations at Fishamble Street and a pair of twisted wire gold armlets were found during the excavations at High Street.[70] Other jewellery included brooches, cloak fasteners mostly in the form of ring-headed pins, and amber beads and pendants, which were mainly crafted locally from imported raw material. Needle cases made from bird bones or copper alloy were fitted with a ring to enable them to hang from a necklace. Other implements were attached to belts or placed in leather pouches. Belts were mainly leather, but wool tablet-woven bands were also very strong and could be made in suitable widths. Strap-ends and buckles with elongated, waisted buckle-plates were another Dublin speciality.[71] This is not an exhaustive list; it merely hints at some of the range of items that were worn at the time in Dublin.

CONCLUSION

Based on the finds from the excavations in Dublin an attempt has been made to reconstruct the clothing of a man and woman in the tenth century (Figs 4.6 and 4.7). That aspects of clothing and appearance were considered important signifiers at the time is conveyed even at a very basic level by the nicknames given to various rulers who had

[70] Wallace, *Viking Dublin*, pp. 281 and 296, figs. 8.26, 8.27 and 8.28.
[71] Paterson, 'Insular belt-fittings', pp. 129–131; Wallace, *Viking Dublin*, p. 344, figs. 9.52 and 9.53.

Fig. 4.6 Reconstruction of a woman's clothing in 10th-century Dublin. (© Christina Unwin).

Fig. 4.7 Reconstruction of a man's clothing in 10th-century Dublin. (© Christina Unwin).

links with Ireland such as Sigtryggr Silkbeard (d. 1042) and Magnus Barelegs (d. 1103). Much remains conjectural, but they take into account the different types of textiles and accessories recorded from the Wood Quay complex. Men's garment fabrics included a range of twills for tunics, shirts edged in silk, and heavier cloths, often with pile on the inside, for cloaks that fastened on the shoulder with a ringed pin. Women's clothing is less easy to determine. The shaping of tunics appears to have changed: no longer were they worn as pinafores with oval brooches at the shoulders and greater emphasis was placed on wearing girdles round the waist.

The clothing worn in daily life would not have matched the quality of textiles associated with the elite, and much of what has been recovered was patched and repaired. Attempting to perceive cultural identity and gender differences from old, discarded rags is a considerable challenge. That contrasts in dress existed within the Viking diaspora is evident by comparing late tenth-century textiles and clothing in the eastern and western peripheries of the Viking world. The burial garments of a woman of high rank on the bank of the river Dnieper near Gnëzdovo included a silk gown of oriental style,[72] whereas in Dublin there is nothing similar and wool was the dominant fibre. Yet, exceptionally, both places yielded examples rare in the northern world at this period of probable headwear made in sprang, in Dublin using silk thread and in Gnëzdovo linen thread, proving that easy assumptions about exotic fabrics and dress can be misleading.

---

[72] Olga Orfinskaya and Tatyana Pushkina, '10th century AD textiles from female burial Ц-301 at Gnëzdovo, Russia', *Archaeological Textiles Newsletter* 53 (2011), pp. 35–51 (pp. 37–43).

CHAPTER 5

The Sensory Archaeology of Early Medieval Fabrics from the North Atlantic[1]

Alexandra Lester-Makin

Textiles are by their very nature tactile sensory objects. They encompass the whole human sensorium: the five senses according to Aristotle – sight, sound, taste, smell and touch – but also other sensorial perceptions such as movement and emotion. Textiles create relationships between themselves and people, between individuals and between groups of people. While they interact with us as we wear or handle them, textiles also interact with their makers through their creation, from the processing of raw materials into fibres, to the handing over of the finished product to its owner. Archaeological textiles interact with professionals from excavation or discovery, through analysis and conservation to storage or display, while examples that are exhibited engage, from a distance, those who interact with the displays.

Within the discipline of archaeological textiles sensory theory is a recent phenomenon, with most developments being made by those specialising in the pre-historic and classical periods.[2] While it can be suggested that sensorial methodologies are particularly

---

ORCiD: 0000-0002-6871-5745.

[1]   I would like to thank Susanna Harris and Gale Owen-Crocker for reading earlier versions of this chapter.

[2]   See, for example, Lise Bender Jørgensen, 'Towards textile textures', in *Considering Creativity: Creativity, Knowledge and Practice in Bronze Age Europe*, ed. by Joanna Sofaer (Oxford: Archaeopress, 2018), pp. 133–141; Ida Demant, 'From stone to textile: constructing the costume of the Dama de Baza', *Archaeological Textiles Newsletter* 52 (2011), 37–40; Ida Demant, 'Making a reconstruction of the Egtved clothing', *Archaeological Textiles Review* 59 (2017), 33–43; Karina Grömer and Helga Rösel-Mautendorfer, 'Catalogue of the Hallstatt textiles', in *Textiles from Hallstatt; Weaving Cultures in Bronze Age and Iron Age Salt Mines. Textilien aus Hallstatt;*

useful for studying societies that left little or no written record, they also have the potential to help researchers unlock and define the 'mindset' of societies which left incomplete records, to 'read' and understand that which was not documented but was intrinsically understood by people at the time. As Susanna Harris has stated:

> a sensory archaeology of textiles is both an analysis of the multiple sensations of ancient textiles (the artefact of study) and an interpretative framework that seeks to understand people's perceptions of such textiles in their sensory environment (the contextual interpretation). It has relevance to how textiles are contextualised in the past and how they are analysed and presented in the present.[3]

Using sensory archaeology to study early medieval textiles from across the North Atlantic therefore has the ability to unlock a deeper understanding of innate early medieval societies' relationships with textiles: to answer the bigger questions about the development and structure of societies, their interactions with others and their journeys across this geographical area. As a result, it also has the potential to help develop interdisciplinary research questions that incorporate knowledge from makers, analysts and researchers, creating unique and potentially vibrant international working communities.

The rest of this chapter is divided into three parts. The first section outlines what sensory archaeology and sensory textile archaeology are. The second explores the early medieval sensorium with particular focus on textiles from Viking communities of the North Atlantic and the Sámi, nomadic peoples that lived, and still live, in Scandinavia and with whom the Vikings shared encounters which impacted on their understanding of textiles. This survey then forms the basis of a discussion about the bigger relationships early medieval societies had with textiles, and how sensory textile archaeology can help researchers answer these questions and consider these themes in more nuanced ways.

Gewebt Kultur aus den Bronze-und Eisenzietlichen Salzbergwerk, ed. by Karina Grömer, Anton Kern, Hans Reschreiter and Helga Rösel-Mautendorfer (Budapest: Archaeolingua, 2013), pp. 243–574; Susanna Harris, 'Smooth and cool, or warm and soft: investigating the properties of cloth in prehistory', in *North European Symposium for Archaeological Textiles X*, ed. by Eva B. Andersson Strand, Margarita Gleba, Ulla Mannering, Cherine Munkholt and Maj Ringgaard (Oxford: Oxbow, 2010), pp. 104–112; Susanna Harris, 'Sensible dress: the sight, sound, smell and touch of Late Ertebølle Mesolithic cloth types', *Cambridge Archaeological Journal* 24.1 (2014), 37–56, DOI: 10.1017/S0959774314000031, accessed 16 February 2023; Susanna Harris, 'From value to desirability: the allure of worldly things', *World Archaeology* 49.5 (2017), 681–699, DOI: 10.1080/00438243.2017.1413416, accessed 16 February 2023; Sylvia Mitschke, 'Textile Qualitäten im römische Heer de Rheinprovinzen', in *Die Macht der Toga: in DressCode Römischen Weltreich*, ed. by Michael Tellenbach, Regine Schulz and Alfried Wieczorek (Regensberg: Schnell and Steiner GmbH, 2013), pp. 229–237.

3 Susanna Harris, 'The sensory archaeology of textiles', in *The Routledge Handbook of Sensory Archaeology*, ed. by Robin Skeates and Jo Day (Abingdon: Routledge, 2020), pp. 210–232 (211).

SENSORY ARCHAEOLOGY

Archaeological theorists have been exploring the potential of sensorially studying past societies since the 1990s.[4] At its basic level, sensory archaeology is about incorporating and exploring how humans interact with their material and cultural surroundings through the senses. It is part of a move away from simply applying technical details such as measurements and constituent material parts to, for example, objects, an issue which Harris has stated is particularly true of textile archaeology.[5] This theoretical approach has the ability to unlock more nuanced understandings of cultures, particularly those that may not have followed the Aristotelian doctrine of the five senses, which now dominates Western society. Yannis Hamilakis has pointed out that different cultures recognise differing numbers of senses and, therefore, a wider number of ways in which they sensorially experience the world around them.[6] Of interest here is the wide range of experiences that different cultures, both modern and those in the past, think or thought of as sensory. They may include, for example, movement itself or the act of eating, not just the taste, textures and smells that eating produces. One of the things Hamilakis is trying to do is open our minds to the possibility that previous cultures may have thought of senses and perceived and interacted with and within their worlds very differently from how we do today.

Research within this field has been diverse, including the study of buildings and spaces, naturescapes, sound, food and its consumption, ritual and objects.[7] By developing and using sensorial methodologies, archaeologists studying different aspects of past societies are able mentally to immerse themselves within these different sensoria, helping to develop their understanding of how cultures conceptualised the world they lived in. However, we must be mindful that no matter how sensorially immersive the research, scholars will never truly have the same experiences as the original populace. Individual sensory concepts and understandings are developed from childhood, by the cultures and environments in which that person lives, but as Delong, Wu and Park discovered, they can change over time, if social perceptions or new knowledge cause them to do so.[8]

---

[4] For discussions on the development of sensory studies, particularly within archaeology, see Jo Day, 'Introduction: making senses of the past', in *Making Senses of the Past: Toward a Sensory Archaeology*, ed. by Jo Day (Carbondale, IL: Southern Illinois University, 2013), pp. 1–31; Yannis Hamilakis, *Archaeology and the Senses: Human Experience, Memory, and Affect* (Cambridge: Cambridge University Press, 2014); Robin Skeates, *An Archaeology of the Senses: Prehistoric Malta* (Oxford: Oxford University Press, 2010); Robin Skeates and Jo Day, 'Sensory archaeology: key concepts and debates', in Skeates and Day, *The Routledge Handbook of Sensory Archaeology*, pp. 1–17.

[5] Harris, 'The sensory archaeology of textiles', pp. 211–213.

[6] Hamilakis, *Archaeology and the Senses*, pp. 73–110.

[7] See, for example, chapters in Day, *Making Senses of the Past*; Skeates and Day, *The Routledge Handbook of Sensory Archaeology*.

[8] Sonja Andrew, 'Textile semantics: considering a communication-based reading of textiles', *Textile* 6.1 (2008), 32–65 (p. 39), DOI: 10.2752/175183508X288680, accessed 16 February

There have also been debates around the issue of isolating individual senses. Theorists have argued that when we sensorially experience the world we do so on a multi-sensory and innate level. Thus, separating each sense and focusing research on the senses as individual entities, effectively isolating them, imposes false parameters and removes us from the all-encompassing actuality of sensory encounters.[9] Despite these difficulties, the idea of a sensory archaeology has gained momentum since the late 1990s, with a number of journal articles, monographs, edited volumes and conference sessions being devoted to the subject.[10]

TEXTILE ARCHAEOLOGY AND THE SENSES

Within textile archaeology there has been, according to Susanna Harris, a 'dulling of the senses'. She has argued that the study of archaeological textiles has developed into an exercise of data gathering. While she agrees that this is important, she suggests that it is limiting, isolating researchers' experiences of the textiles they study. She believes that people associate certain complex and often subtle ideas with textiles based on their material properties and interactions with them, creating relationships with them. In turn, the way people interact with a textile is impacted by the way in which its properties perform,[11] thus having the potential to alter the relationship over time as the properties of the textile change. Therefore, using sensorial methodologies to study textiles, our own

---

2023; Marilyn Delong, Juanjuan Wu and Juyeon Park, 'Tactile response and shifting touch preference', *Textile* 10.1 (2012), 44–59 (pp. 55–57), DOI: 10.2752/175183512X13267336595278, accessed 16 February 2023; Skeates, *An Archaeology of the Senses*, p. 3.

[9] Day, 'Introduction', pp. 7–9; Hamilakis, *Archaeology and the Senses*, pp. 73–101, 113–114;

[10] See for example, Chris Gosden, 'Making sense: archaeology and aesthetics', *World Archaeology*, 33.2 (2001), 163–67, DOI: 10.1080/00438240120079226, accessed 16 February 2023; Catherine Frieman and Mark Gillings, 'Seeing is perceiving?', *World Archaeology* 39.1 (2007), 4–16; Linda Hurcombe, 'A sense of materials and sensory perception in concepts of materiality', *World Archaeology* 39.4 (2007), 532–45, DOI: 10.1080/00438240701679346, accessed 16 February 2023; Lena Hammerlund, Heini Kirjavainen, Katherine Vestergård Pedersen and Marianne Vedeler, 'Visual textiles: a study of appearance and visual impression in archaeological textiles', *Medieval Clothing and Textiles* 4 (2008), 69–98; Hamilakis, *Archaeology and the Senses*; Skeates, *An Archaeology of the Senses*; Skeates and Day, *The Routledge Handbook of Sensory Archaeology*. Conference sessions and seminars include 'Integrating Theory and Science in Archaeology' at Archaeology Theoretical Group (TAG) conference, Chester University, 2018; 'From Fibre to Decorated Textiles' at IONA Islands of the North Atlantic conference, Simon Fraser University, Vancouver, Canada, 2019; 'Exploring the Senses Day Seminar', First Millennia Studies Group, University of Edinburgh, 2019. Day, *Making Senses of the Past*; *Sense and Feeling in Daily Living in the Early Medieval English World*, ed. by Maren Clegg Hyer and Gale R. Owen-Crocker (Liverpool: Liverpool University Press, 2020); Alexandra Lester-Makin, 'Embroidery and its early medieval audience: a case study of sensory engagement', *World Archaeology* 52.2 (2021), 298–312.

[11] Harris, 'Smooth and cool, or warm and soft', p. 104.

understanding of the people who made the textiles, the societies in which they were produced, used and had meaning can be greatly enhanced.[12]

To put this into perspective, when studying early medieval embroidery the traditional scientific approach does not allow one to answer questions about how an embroidery felt to the touch or when worn; how it moved if worn or was hung on a wall; or the visual engagement and interpretation brought about by the early medieval mind, something so different from our own. On a practical level, did embroidery smell because of the materials used in its creation and the chemical interaction between it, the creator and then the user or wearer? What noises could be heard when it was made, then used? Did the worker's fingers, wrists, back and/or neck hurt after spending hours sat over the embroidery? On a metaphorical plane, did the embroideries imbue other meanings such as the imagined power held by the motifs embroidered on them? Or did people believe the embroidery gave power to the user or wearer? Could the embroiderer impregnate charms, curses or messages into the work? To answer such questions a deeper sensory engagement is needed with the embroideries, while multidisciplinary approaches to working are required. These questions oblige us not to suspend our modern belief systems or understanding of the world but to be open to engaging with different types of reality and sensory perceptions.

However, Harris acknowledges the difficulties of this. Archaeological textiles are often preserved as small, fragile fragments that do not retain their original properties, due to decay,[13] thus forming a barrier to sensory engagements. Harris convincingly explores the possibilities of using macroscopic and microscopic images, scientific analysis and reconstruction and experimental archaeology for overcoming these barriers.[14] She suggests that researchers can also overcome these problems by analysing the original textiles and comparing the results with modern equivalents, but she warns of the difficulties in understanding which aspects of fibre and textile properties were actually valued.[15] Lise Bender Jørgensen has tried to do just this by analysing and then examining authentically made reproductions of a number of Bronze and Iron Age textiles from Hallstatt, Austria, and Scandinavia. She discovered that during the period of so-called Hallstatt culture (1200–800 BCE) people making textiles were innovating with techniques and materials, and she believes the makers were not only interested in the practical function of the textiles but also their aesthetics, their attractiveness.[16] Bronze Age makers were, therefore, also interested in the sensory qualities of the textiles they were producing.

Corresponding to the rise in the sensory analysis of *actual* textiles has been a gradually increasing interest in exploring wider aspects of textiles and the senses within past societies. Magdalena Öhrman examined the sensory experiences of textile production

---

[12] Harris, 'The sensory archaeology of textiles'.

[13] Harris, 'Smooth and cool, or warm and soft', p. 104.

[14] Harris, 'The sensory archaeology of textiles', pp. 213–223.

[15] Harris, 'Smooth and cool, or warm and soft', pp. 104, 109–110.

[16] Bender Jørgensen, 'Towards textile textures', pp. 139–140.

expressed by male writers in the Roman world. She concluded that while literary sources portray textile activities and training as an all-female activity, evidence shows that these processes often took place within the *atrium*, where women and children gathered together. Women would produce textiles while looking after younger children and training older girls. Öhrman goes on to state that in higher-ranking households gender definitions between boys and girls were not prominent when they were young and so both boys and girls would have played together within the female domestic space. As such, the sounds, smells and sights of weaving and working with textiles would have been part of a young boy's daily experience. Öhrman points out that a male toddler would have been able to explore weaving tools and associated materials as he played. Thus, when Roman adult males wrote about weaving as a sensory experience, they were actually accessing memories of their own childhood, however unconscious of that they may have been.[17] Öhrman's work demonstrates that a multidisciplinary approach to studying the available evidence can enlighten our understanding of wider sensory perceptions regarding textiles within past societies. Gale R. Owen-Crocker has also demonstrated this in her chapter, 'Smelly sheep, shimmering silk: the sensual and emotional experience of textiles'. Here she uses evidence from archaeological and textual sources to draw a picture of both negative sensory experiences endured by textile makers and the sensory pleasures textiles gave people within early medieval England.[18]

There has also been an expansion in studying humans' innate knowing of making, wearing and using textiles. Naomi Braithwaite has worked with modern shoe designers, trying to discover how they learn and/or know. The designers stated that they simply 'knew' how to react to each manipulation of the leather, unconsciously perceiving what the fingers felt, the smell of the materials and the noises made by materials and equipment. Yet, the designers could not explain *how* they knew.[19] Hilary Davidson has also discussed this in relation to her historical dress research and re-creations. She argues that, 'making literally changes the way the body works and the mind thinks as creative action becomes embodied in the maker'.[20] Lise Bender Jørgensen has suggested something similar: 'tacit knowledge, [the] possible links between technological practice and beliefs and superstitions, and the interplay between the body (mind and muscles) and practice', and 'movements, especially when in sequence, assist memory. They also hold memory.'[21] Elyse

[17] Magdalena Öhrman, 'Textile work in shared domestic spaces in the Roman house: the evidence from Latin poetry', *Fasciculi Archaeologicae Historicae* 31 (2018), 93–101.

[18] Gale R. Owen-Crocker, 'Smelly sheep, shimmering silk: the sensual and emotional experience of textiles', in Hyer and Owen-Crocker, *Sense and Feeling*, pp. 197–218.

[19] Naomi Braithwaite, 'Sensing creativity: the role of materials in shoe design', *The Senses and Society* 12.1 (2017), 90–94, DOI: 10.1080/17458927.2016.1223786, accessed 16 February 2023.

[20] Hilary Davidson, 'The embodied turn: making and remaking dress as an academic practice', *Fashion Theory* 23.3 (2019), 329–362 (pp. 331, 347), DOI: 10.1080/1362704X.2019.1603859, accessed 16 February 2023.

[21] Lise Bender Jørgensen, 'Introduction to Part II: technology as practice', in *Embodied Knowledge: Historical Perspectives on Belief and Technology*, ed. by Marie Louise Stig Sørensen and Katharina Rebay-Salisbury (Oxford: Oxbow, 2013), pp. 91–94 (p. 91).

Stanes explored innate knowledge of clothing with a group of individuals for her work on contemporary fashion consumption. She discovered that participants often unconsciously understood whether a fabric or piece of clothing was 'good' not only through simply touching it but also through familiar and/or social conditioning, personal ideals, a personal knowledge of making and its particular stage of wear. Stanes found that the sensory properties of the clothes and the participants' sensory engagement with them were fluid, as they evolved from new to old. While participants were able to express the broad concepts of their sensory engagements, some were innate, working on a subconscious holistic sensory comprehension of the textiles they were interacting with.[22]

THE EARLY MEDIEVAL SENSORIUM

Early medieval society in the British Isles understood its material culture through multilayered sensory and perspectival lenses.[23] Within Christianised Anglo-Saxon society the Aristotelian doctrine of the five senses was followed. Sight was given the most importance, as shown on the ninth-century Fuller Brooch.[24] The brooch's design depicts Sight as the largest, central figure. The other four senses are depicted equally sized, surrounding Sight. However, early medieval prose, poetry and riddles tell us that in reality the other four senses were ranked – hearing, taste, smell and touch, each with

---

[22] Elyse Stanes, 'Clothes-in-process: touch, texture, time', *Textile* 17.3 (2019), 224–245, DOI: 10.1080/14759756.2018.1548553, accessed 16 February 2023.

[23] See chapters in Hyer and Owen-Crocker, *Sense and Feeling*; also Meg Boulton, '"The end of the world as we know it": viewing eschatology and symbolic space/s in Late Antique and Insular art', in *Making Histories: Proceedings of the Sixth International Conference on Insular Art*, ed. by Jane Hawkes (Donington: Shaun Tyas, 2013), pp. 279–290; Dieter Bitterli, 'Strange perceptions: sensory experience in the Old English "Marvels of the East"', in *The Five Senses in Medieval and Early Modern England*, ed. by Annette Kern-Stähler, Beatrix Busse and Wietse de Boer (Leiden: Brill, 2016), pp. 137–162; Javier E. Díaz-Vera, 'Coming to past senses: vision, touch and their metaphors in Anglo-Saxon language and culture', in Kern-Stähler et al., *The Five Senses in Medieval and Early Modern England*, pp. 36–66; Katherine Hindley, 'Sight and understanding: visual imagery as metaphor in the Old English *Boethius* and *Soliloquies*', in Kern-Stähler et al., *The Five Senses in Medieval and Early Modern England*, pp. 21–35; Katherine O'Brien O'Keeffe, 'Hands and eyes, sight and touch: appraising the senses in Anglo-Saxon England', *Anglo-Saxon England* 45 (2016), 105–140; Meg Boulton, 'Art History in the Dark Ages: (re)considering space, stasis, and modern viewing practices in relation to Anglo-Saxon imagery', in *Stasis in the Medieval West? Questioning Change and Continuity*, ed. by Michael D.J. Bintley, Martin Locker, Victoria Symons and Mary Wellesley (New York: Palgrave Macmillan, 2017), pp. 69–86; Meg Boulton, 'Looking down from the Rothbury Cross: (re) viewing the place of Anglo-Saxon art', in *Insular Iconographies: Essays in Honour of Jane Hawkes*, ed. by Meg Boulton and Michael D.J. Bintley (Woodbridge: Boydell, 2019), pp. 217–134; Catherine E. Karkov, *The Art of Anglo-Saxon England* (Woodbridge: Boydell, 2011), pp. 135–178.

[24] Images of the Fuller Brooch can be accessed at https://www.britishmuseum.org/collection/object/H_1952-0404-1, accessed 30 January 2023.

its own positive and negative values, while law codes give us the monetary values for material damage or loss of the human appendage associated with each sense.[25]

Early medieval theologians believed that the senses, especially sight, could be used to gain spiritual enlightenment, but they also warned that their misuse could lead to corruption.[26] Objects discovered in the archaeological record prove that, despite these theological misgivings, early medieval society in England enjoyed a sensorial, stimulating world.[27]

There has been little research investigating Scandinavian sensory perceptions. Kata Sepp has stated that sensory perceptions in the Norse world were 'quite personal',[28] while Sandra Straubhaar has established that the colour spectrum and its resulting meanings in Old Norse do not match those in modern English.[29] Insights into Viking Age understandings of the senses, particularly in relation to textiles, have to be gleaned by exploring notions of dress and textiles in the Norse and Icelandic sagas, archaeological evidence and the results of experimental archaeological projects and dress re-creations. A survey of this evidence has been drawn together below.

Several articles have explored the use of clothing in sagas in relation to the wearer's role. While there is a need to be aware of clothing descriptions as a literary convention, it is possible to draw some conclusions about the sensory perceptions of clothing in real life. Icelandic and Norse saga writers use the term 'scarlet cloth' (*skarlati*) not to describe a colour but a type of precious material.[30] It is consistently used to demonstrate wealth, status and bonds of allegiance and friendship within Icelandic elites. While the fabric was considered precious and worthy enough to be given by kings, it could be further

---

[25] Elizabeth Coatsworth and Michael Pinder, 'Sight, insight and hand: some reflections on the design and manufacture of the Fuller Brooch', in *The Material Culture of Daily Living in the Anglo-Saxon World*, ed. by Maren Clegg Hyer and Gale R. Owen-Crocker (Exeter: University Press, 2011), pp. 258–274; O'Keeffe, 'Hands and eyes, sight and touch', pp. 106, 111–117.

[26] See Bitterli, 'Strange perceptions', pp. 137–146; Hindley, 'Sight and understanding'; Richard G. Newhauser, 'Foreword: the senses in Medieval and Renaissance intellectual history', *The Senses and Society* 5.1 (2010), 5–9 (pp. 6–7), DOI: 10.2752/174589310X12549020528013, accessed 16 February 2023; O'Keeffe, 'Hands and eyes'; Eric Palazzo, 'Art, liturgy, and the five senses in the early Middles Ages', *Viator* 41.1 (2010), 25–56 (pp. 29–30), DOI: 10.1484/J. VIATOR.1.100566, accessed 16 February 2023; Herbert L. Kessler, *Seeing Medieval Art* (Toronto: Toronto University Press, 2011), p. 172.

[27] Lester-Makin, 'Embroidery and its early medieval audience'.

[28] Kate Sepp, personal communication.

[29] Sandra Ballif Straubhaar, 'Wrapped in a blue mantle: fashions for Icelandic slayers?', *Medieval Clothing and Textiles* 1 (2005), 53–65 (p. 54).

[30] Throughout the Middle Ages the term 'scarlet cloth' was used to identify a certain type of broadcloth and, at a later stage, a vivid red colour. See John H. Munro, 'The medieval scarlet and the economics of sartorial splendour', in *Cloth and Clothing in Medieval Europe: Essays in Memory of Professor E.M. Carus-Wilson*, ed. by Negley B. Harte and Kennth G. Ponting (London: Heinemann, 1983), pp. 13–70; John Munro, 'Scarlet', in *Encyclopedia of Medieval Dress and Textiles of the British Isles c. 450–1450*, ed. by Gale Owen-Crocker, Elizabeth Coatsworth and Maria Hayward (Leiden: Brill, 2012), pp. 477–481.

enhanced with lavish embellishments and/or embroidery and fur. Heroes and heroines portrayed as wearing scarlet clothing are often described as elegant, outshining others and, in one instance, flamboyant enough to be called a peacock.[31] While we have no details describing the texture, sound, drape or movement of scarlet cloth, it is possible to imagine the wearer dazzling onlookers, especially as the social connotations of the fabric seem to have been well known. Indeed, one hero, Bolli of *Laxdæla Saga*, dazzled onlookers when he and his men arrived home from Byzantium, and it is probable that he was wearing the exotic fashions and materials of that far-flung empire, which may have included silk.[32] If so, we can imagine the visual impact these clothes would have had from surviving examples, combined with the noise of rustling fabrics, the clinking of metal decorations and clanking of weaponry as the wearer moved. Sepp has also stated that the sagas imply sensory differences between expensive and cheaper clothing and textiles; for example, in *Eyrbyggja Saga* onlookers have a sense of wonder at Þórgunna's finely made English sheets, silken quilt, bed curtains and full canopy that she brings with her to Iceland from the Hebrides.[33]

Kate D'Ettore has explored the connections between clothing and violence within the sagas. She argues, for instance, that descriptions and references to the clothing of men assembled ready for violence are used to heighten tension and contribute to the overall sensory mood of what is to come. For women, especially those on the threshold of marriage, similar descriptions are used to give a sense of unease and misgiving.[34] In these instances the clothing speaks to the readers, drawing them into the sensory orbit of the saga characters, helping them feel as the characters do. While the clothes may be described in elaborate sensory terms, it is not only their physical properties that are sensorially engaging with characters or readers, but also the meanings behind them. Thus, a garment that should have been comfortable may have physically felt uncomfortable due to the connotations of the situation it is alluding to; for example, in chapter 33 of *Laxdæla saga*, Guðrun Ósvifrsdóttir dreams of her marriages, stating of one, 'I had a crooked coif on my head, and I thought it misfitted me, and I wished to alter the coif, and many people told me I should not do so, but I did not listen to them, and I tore the hood from my head, and cast it into the brook …'. She was told that her dream indicated that she would not love her future husband.[35] Clothing was also associated with shape-shifting.

---

[31]   Olaf the Peacock appears in several Icelandic sagas, especially the mid- to late thirteenth-century *Laxdæla saga*; Anna Zanchi, '"Melius abundare quam deficere": scarlet clothing in *Laxdæla Saga* and *Njáls Saga*', *Medieval Clothing and Textiles* 4 (2008), 21–37 (pp. 23–24, 26, 27, 28, 31, 34–36).

[32]   Zanchi, '"Melius abundare quam deficere"', p. 32.

[33]   Kata Sepp, personal communication. Also see, Anonymous, *Story of the Ere-Dwellers* (*Eyrbyggja Saga*), trans. by William Morris and Eirikr Magnusson (London: Bernard Quaritch, 1892), chapter 50; https://sagadb.org/eyrbyggja_saga.en, accessed 28 January 2023.

[34]   Kate D'Ettore, 'Clothing and conflict in the Icelandic family sagas: literary convention and the discourse of power', *Medieval Clothing and Textiles* 5 (2009), 1–14 (pp. 3, 4).

[35]   Anonymous, *Laxdæla Saga, Translated from the Icelandic*, trans. by Muriel A.C. Press (London: Dent, 1964), p. 99.

In *Nibelungenlied* and *Volsunga Saga* certain clothes alter the wearer's body shape once they are worn. For the purposes of the narrative the wearers are often 'turned' into the animals the clothes represent or were made from, taking on the traits of the animal and/ or being seen as that animal by anyone they encounter and thus hiding the true identity of the clothed individual.[36] While these descriptions are not explicitly sensory, they infer the change a body undergoes when it is covered in clothing and how people perceive others depending on what they wear.

Archaeological evidence has been used to shed some light on how Migration Period (AD 400–550) and Viking Age (AD 800–1050) women sensorially engaged with the world around them. Dress evidence from a burial at Sande farm in Norway suggests the interred was a woman, although no skeleton survives. The clothes are consistent with high status, while evidence of a fur-lined cloak indicates the woman was identified as an adult by her community. The clothes are tight fitting, suggesting restricted movement, but silver rings and beads located near the great brooch that held the cloak in place and metal items attached to the girdle would have made noises as the wearer moved and went about her daily business. The brooch itself would have reflected light, while the two colours, blue and red, incorporated into her clothes would have given the wearer a visual presence within her community.[37]

A woman interred in a Scandinavian-style burial at Ketilsstaðir in north-eastern Iceland was clothed in textiles that were older than she was but which had been made into clothes at approximately the time of her death, in the later tenth century. The zs spinning technique, used to make the yarns woven into the straps of her overdress, is known to have been used in urban areas within the British Isles and some Viking-Age Scandinavian sites during the ninth to tenth centuries, while zz-spun threads dominate Icelandic assemblages of the same period.[38] It has been suggested that the yarn used to weave the straps of the overdress indicate the deceased was either from or had links to Britain, and this has been related to the fact that mitochondrial DNA studies of modern Icelanders show a considerable number of native British among female Icelandic settlers. However, the tablet-woven starting border of the woman's garment is made from Icelandic wool worked in a Norwegian form and the style of her clothes is Scandinavian. In death the woman visually told onlookers of her interconnectedness with the wider

---

[36] M.A. Nordtorp-Madson, 'Dress, disguise, and shape-shifting in *Nibelungenlied* and *Volsunga Saga*', in *Refashioning Medieval and Early Modern Dress: A Tribute to Robin Netherton*, ed. by Gale R. Owen-Crocker and Maren Clegg Hyer (Woodbridge: Boydell, 2019), pp. 45–57 (pp. 52–53, 57).

[37] Marianne Vedeler, Elna Siv Kristoffersen and Ingunn Marit Røstad, 'Dressed for ritual, dressed for life. A Migration-Period grave from Sande in Norway', *Medieval Archaeology* 62.1 (2018), 1–27.

[38] Lise Bender Jørgensen, *North European Textiles until AD 1000* (Aarhus: University Press, 1992), pp. 39, 40, 41; Penelope Walton, *Textiles, Cordage and Raw Fibre from 16–22 Coppergate*, The Archaeology of York: The Small Finds, 17/5 (London: Council for British Archaeology for the York Archaeological Trust, 1989), p. 334.

Viking world, while displaying her status and affiliation with the elite of Norse Iceland.[39] Thus, this burial demonstrates that Viking visual perceptions of status were linked to the quality and style of the clothes they wore, just as the saga narratives involving scarlet clothes intimate.

Those engaged in re-creating textiles and clothes as a form of experimental archaeology primarily focus on the technical details of material properties and construction but there are hints of the sensory engagement, which give us a window into the sensorial worlds of the original clothes and wearers. Through a process of making, Katherine Vestergaard Pederson ascertained that the medieval textiles used to create garments would have felt like modern upholstery fabrics.[40] Marianne Guckelsberger learnt that while her re-creation of a fur-lined *surcot* was aesthetically 'beautiful', it weighed almost 2.8 kg but did not hinder her arm movements and was practical, being warm. When she re-created an overdress based on the Herjólfsnes dress from Greenland, she found that the four-metre-plus circumference of the hem and the turn shoes she wore with the dress influenced her posture and gait.[41]

Eva Andersson Strand recorded spinners with Motion Capture, a computer programme that records and analyses movement through markers that are placed at strategic points on the person or object being observed.[42] She and her team explored the minute actions undertaken by two spinners to understand how they affected the resulting thread, and the physical and sensory engagement between spinner, tool, fibre and even place. The results of the initial tests showed that a wobbling spindle resulted in irregular work from the spinner and an unevenly spun yarn. The results of the second test, which compared working methods and resulting yarns of the two spinners, demonstrated that while each spinner used a slightly different spinning technique, the resulting yarns were actually similar enough that they could be used to weave the same textile.[43]

---

[39] Michèle Hayeur Smith, Kevin P. Smith and Karin M. Frei, '"Tangled up in blue": the death, dress and identity of an early Viking-Age female settler from Ketilsstaðir, Iceland', *Medieval Archaeology* 63.1 (2019), 95–127.

[40] Kathrine Vestergaard Pedersen, 'Spotlight on medieval Scandinavian dress: sources and interpretations', in *Dressing the Past*, ed. by Margarita Gleba, Cherine Munkholt and Marie-Louise Nosch (Oxford: Oxbow, 2008), pp. 86–97 (p. 95).

[41] Marianne Guckelsberger, 'A Norse Greenlandic woman 1000–1500: how I recreated my costume' (unpublished report); https://www.academia.edu/35051133/A_Norse_Greenlandic_Woman_1000_1500_How_I_recreated_my_costume_docx, accessed 30 January 2023.

[42] Eva Andersson Strand, Stefan Lindgren and Carolina Larsson, 'Motion capture and textile experimental archaeology, a possible combination', *Origini* 40 (2017), 129–140 (p. 131).

[43] Eva Andersson Strand, Stefan Lindgren and Carolina Larsson, 'Capturing our cultural intangible textile heritage, MoCap and craft technology', in *Digital Heritage: Progress in Cultural Heritage: Documentation, Preservation, and Protection*, 6th International Conference, EuroMed 2016, Nicosia, Cyprus, 31 October–5 November 2016, Proceedings, Part II, ed. by Marinos Ioannides, Eleanor Fink, Antonia Moropoulou, Monika Hagedor-Saupe, Antonella Fresa, Gunnar Liestøl, Vlatka Rajcic and Pierre Grussenmeyer (New York: Springer, 2016),

The handweaver Anna Nørgaard has discovered that while fibres may look 'right' they do not always have the correct properties, for example, creating finished garments that are too stiff. When working on a re-creation of the Huldremose Skirt for the National Museum of Denmark, Anna *felt* at one with the people who had woven the original cloth, being able to imagine how the weavers had sat at the loom and gossiped. When she moved on to weaving the accompanying scarf, Anna innately understood that it had not been woven with the same expertise as the skirt. She also learned that her working practices were similar to the weavers of the scarf, creating a skewed effect in the weave, but because no two people work in exactly the same way, Anna's piece was not skewed as much as the original.[44]

Re-creations and experimental archaeology have the potential to help us understand not only technical processes and the material properties of fibres and finished textiles but also the sensory experiences, both conscious and innate, of makers. They may also create bridges, helping us to enter the mindset and creative worlds of the makers, exploring their physical and mental highs and lows.

The Sámi nation of northern Scandinavia and the Kola Peninsula of Russia have their own textile traditions. Archaeologists now agree that while the populations that would eventually identify themselves as Sámi have been present in these regions since the Stone Age, Sámi ethnicity seems to have developed gradually, and partly as a result of contact with different societies to the south. While Sámi social identity appears to have evolved during the early part of the first millennium CE, it was probably consolidated as a result of relationships with Viking societies and the resulting social and economic stress for resources, including an intensified fur trade.[45] Although archaeology has been able to shine a light on many aspects of Sámi culture, textiles have received less attention and Sámi sensorial engagement with textiles has received none. During the research process for this chapter, researchers, Sámi artists and Sámi museums were contacted on a number of occasions. Unfortunately, there was either no reply or, after introductory e-mails, contact ceased. As a result, it has been possible to draw together only a scant amount of information regarding Sámi textiles and their sensorial and cultural meanings.

In 1992 Tom Svensson wrote that Sámi clothing is one of the nation's most prominent non-verbal messages about identity, and Sámi people have used it in their fight for their nation's rights over many years. He went on to state that the development of clothing was influenced by not only the climatic conditions in which the Sámi live, but the need for free movement when working. Even so, Svensson found that clothing was often

---

pp. 10–15, DOI: 10.1007/978-3-319-48974-2_2, accessed 16 February 2023; Andersson Strand et al., 'Motion capture and textile experimental archaeology', pp. 133–134.

[44] Anna Nørgaard, 'A weaver's voice: making reconstructions of Danish Iron Age textiles', in Gleba et al., *Dressing the Past*, pp. 43–58 (pp. 48, 49, 52, 53).

[45] For a detailed discussion on these points see Bjørnar Olsen, 'Belligerent chieftains and oppressed hunters? Changing conception of interethnic relationships in northern Norway during the Iron Age and early Medieval period', in *Contact, Continuity, and Collapse: The Norse Colonization of the North Atlantic*, ed. by James H. Barrett (Turnhout: Brepols, 2003), pp. 9–31.

embellished with silver decorations that denoted wealth and status, and embroidery that also acted as a reinforcement at points of weakness.[46]

When Emilie Demant Hatt spent time with two Sámi families between 1907 and 1908, she noted that clothing was often embellished with silver, brass and glass decorations that sparkled in the light. At the time of Demant Hatt's writing, silver decorations were believed to have protective qualities. Children's cradles were made from hollowed-out spruce wood that was covered in tanned reindeer hide. Trinkets and bells made of silver were often placed inside the cradle's lining, where they were meant to keep the child from being kidnapped by 'Uldas' (underground people), but Demant Hatt also noted that as the child was rocked, the cradle would jingle.[47] Metals including pewter may have played a similar role during the Viking period. In her work on textile finds from Birka, Agnes Geijer argued that the trading town's inhabitants had learnt how to make pulled metal threads from the Sámi, who created this type of thread out of pewter. The Sámi used it to embroider decorations in 'couched work' onto their dress.[48] It is possible that this type of embroidery was used as a form of protection, possibly to keep evil spirits at bay and/ or protecting areas prone to weakness. I have argued elsewhere that looped stitch, which was used throughout the early medieval period, had amuletic properties.[49] There is an extant example of looped stitch worked in pulled silver metal thread that dates to *c.* AD 878–900. This piece was excavated from the cremation burial of a probable warrior associated with the Viking Great Army. While the burial is located at Ingleby, Derbyshire, in the United Kingdom, it is not unlikely that this warrior originally came from or travelled through Birka or a similar trading town, and acquired the pulled metal with its symbolic power at the same time.[50]

Most Sámi clothing appears to have been made from fur, reindeer and seal skins. For example, in the Icelandic *Bárðar Saga*, which was written down in the fourteenth century, the origin story of a Sámi boy nicknamed Þorkell Skinnvefja (Skin-swathed) states that the child was wrapped in seal-skins to keep warm.[51] However, archaeological

---

[46] Tom G. Svensson, 'Clothing in the Arctic: a means of protection, a statement of identity', *Arctic* 45.1 (1992), 62–73 (pp. 63, 64, 65, 68, 70–72).

[47] Emilie Demant Hatt, *With the Lapps in the High Mountains: A Woman among the Sami, 1907–1908*, ed. and trans. by Barbara Sjoholm (Madison, WI: University of Wisconsin Press, 2013), pp. 39–40, 120.

[48] Agnes Geijer, 'The textile finds from Birka: Birka III, die Textilfunde aus den Gräbern', *Acta Archaeologica* 50 (1979), 209–222 (p. 216).

[49] See Alexandra Lester-Makin, 'Looped stitch: the travels and development of an embroidery stitch', in *The Daily Lives of the Anglo-Saxons*, ed. by Carole Patricia Biggam, Carole Hough and Daria Izdebska (Tempe, AZ: Arizona Center for Medieval and Renaissance Studies, 2017), pp. 119–136.

[50] Lester-Makin, 'Looped stitch', p. 132; Alexandra Lester-Makin, *The Lost Art of the Anglo-Saxon World: The Sacred and Secular Power of Embroidery* (Oxford: Oxbow, 2019), pp. 51, 126–127.

[51] Kata Sepp, personal communication. Also see *Bárðarsaga Snæfellsáss, Viglundarsaga, Þórðarsaga, Draumavitranir, Völsaþáttr*, ed. by Guðbrandur Vigfússon, Nordiske Oldskrifter 27, det Nordiske Literatur-Samfund (Copenhagen: Berlingske, 1860), chapter 3.

excavations at the eleventh- to twelfth-century Sámi burial sites of Vivallen and Långön Island in Ångermanland, northern Sweden, give us an intriguing insight into expressions of high-status Sámi clothing. At both these Viking Age sites, male graves contained textiles made from linen and wool, which had to be imported from Norse communities. As a result, it appears that wool and linen textiles became representative of status within Sámi communities.[52]

One grave at Vivallen stood out from the rest. This biologically male burial incorporated objects that would be classified as typical of both 'male' and 'female' dress. The 'male' artefacts included a sword, and a belt that mimicked examples of warrior belts from the Steppes but which have also been found in both Norse and Sámi contexts. The 'female' artefacts included a necklace made from glass and rock-crystal beads, a silver brooch and finger ring and a needle-case. However, the most intriguing object was the 'female' linen dress that the deceased was buried in. This type of garment has also been found in rich female burials at Birka.[53] The transgender nature of this burial, a Sámi man dressed as a Norse female with conventional male Sámi accessories, points to the deceased being a shaman.[54] Neil Price has argued that the female dress and jewellery were probably made within the Viking world for Nordic women but at some point they moved into the Sámi community, where they acquired a completely different cultural meaning.[55] This person would have looked strikingly different from those around him, just as the previously mentioned probable woman from Sande in Norway would have done with her distinctive dress (see p. 100, above). As such, this linen dress would have taken on different sensorial meanings for those seeing it, hearing the sound of the fabric and possibly touching it, as compared to the linen and wool garments worn by the community's elite.

The *Historia Norwegiae* (History of Norway) includes a reference to a shaman using a cloth to cover himself while he prepared for a ritual.[56] Clive Tolley has analysed this particular incident, concluding that the cloth may have represented the heavens that were going to be crossed during the ceremony.[57] But it also did another fundamental

---

[52] Inger Zachrisson, 'The Sámi and their interaction with Nordic peoples', in *The Viking World*, ed. by Stefan Brink in collaboration with Neil Price (London: Routledge, 2012), pp. 32–39 (p. 36).

[53] Inger Zachrisson, *Möten i gränsland: samer och germaner i Mellanskandinavien* (Stockholm: Statens Historiska Museum, 1997), pp. 61–71.

[54] For a discussion about the traditions of cross-dressing and sexual ambiguity within circumpolar region shamanism see Neil Price, *The Viking Way: Magic and Mind in Late Iron Age Scandinavia*, 2nd and fully revised edn (Oxford: Oxbow, 2019), pp. 123, 175, 177, 222–224, 249–251.

[55] Price, *The Viking Way*, p. 228.

[56] Carl Luke Phelpstead, *A History of Norway and the Passion and Miracles of the Blessed Óláf*, trans. Devra Kunin (Exeter: Short Run Press, 2001), p. 54, lines 27–29. For a discussion about the dating of the text, which scholars think could date from as early as the mid-twelfth century to no later than 1266, see pp. ix–xvii.

[57] Clive Tolley, 'The shamanic séance in the Historia Norvegiae', *Shaman* 2 (1994), 114–136 (p. 121).

thing; it hid the shaman from view as he changed both his clothing and his mental state. This would have been an important sensory dis-engagement from the everyday world and the people watching him, while he physically and sensorially prepared himself for the spiritual space that he was about to enter.

It appears that everyday clothing could also be imbued with magical powers. Else Mundal notes the use of magical clothing to defeat enemies in both the Sámi and Old Norse cultures.[58] However, it appears that it was the Sámi who had the power to turn ordinary clothes into magical ones. One example of such magic can be found in the Icelandic *Heimskringla saga*, which is thought to have been written *c.* 1230. In this example one Þórir Hundr obtained, from Sámi he had been trading with, magical reindeer-skin coats that could not be pierced or cut by weapons. The saga goes on to tell us that he was wearing one of these coats during the battle of Stiklestad, a historical battle that took place during the eleventh century. When King (Saint) Olaf Haraldsson struck Þórir across the shoulders, the sword did not penetrate the coat, with only dust-like particles rising from the garment in response. During the ensuing fight, the king's sword was unable to pierce the reindeer coat but it did cut Þórir's hand, which was not protected.[59] In this instance it can be argued that the everyday fabric of reindeer skin had taken on magical properties associated not only with shamans but with their exotic textiles as well.

This extremely brief outline of Sámi textile culture is in no way complete, but it does give us an intriguing glimpse into how the Sámi engaged with textiles and the multi-sensory impact they had within Sámi communities and those they encountered from other societies. Everyday clothing and utility objects were made from skins and fur but they could be imbued with protective qualities through decorative motifs of embroidery and silver or through magic. Textiles made from linen and wool had to be imported. The evidence from surviving examples indicates that the difficulty in obtaining these textiles resulted in their association with elite status, while their rarity and 'otherness' associated them with shamans. This is not hard to understand. The difference in textures, visual properties, drape and movement, the noise they would have made, and possibly even their colour, would have been completely alien to the sensory engagements Sámi had with their native everyday fabrics and fibres. Thus, for the Sámi, textiles could be a part of this world while also being a part of their spiritual cosmology.

CONCLUSIONS AND DEVELOPMENT

The survey of Viking Age societies' sensory perceptions of textiles and clothes highlights the diverse nature of different cultures' understanding of the actuality of sensing and interpreting sensations. It is therefore important that people who engage in sensory

---

[58]   Else Mundal, 'The perception of the Saamis and their religion in Old Norse sources', in *Shamanism and Northern Ecology*, ed. by Juha Pentikäinen (Berlin: M. de Gruyter, 1996), pp. 97–116 (p. 112).

[59]   Snorri Sturluson, *Heimskringla volume II, Óláf Haraldsson (The Saint)*, trans. by Alison Finlay and Anthony Faulkes (Exeter: Short Run Press, 2004), ch. 193, 228.

textile archaeology understand these differences and engage with them when exploring past societies' sensory interactions with textiles. By doing so, those involved in the exploration and dissemination of these ideas can give a tangible link, a greater sense of connection, to our ancestors.

It is apparent from the Norse and Icelandic sagas that clothing and textiles imbued many metaphorical ideas and social connotations. There are the obvious cultural aspects such as luxurious textiles demonstrating one's status within society, and there are the gendered, for instance the beauty of women as represented by their elaborate and brightly coloured clothing. Textiles and clothing also told viewers where an individual was from and which group they were a member of, in a complex world of inter-territorial group ties and geographical associations. However, there is also a sense of otherness and magic. Clothing made of skin could force or enable the wearer to take on and hide behind animalistic traits, or clothing could be imbued with protective qualities: ideas that could, crucially, travel between and be understood by disparate cultures.

Archaeological evidence provides material insights not only for the more usual ideas of social status, community allegiance and interconnectivity but also for how onlookers would have sensorially engaged with the wearer. The use of native and exotic clothing worn in slightly different, often physically restrictive ways from the rest of the community, and the incorporation of accessories which would have made a noise when the wearer moved, all combined to give that individual an aura of otherness, of magic. The same can be seen in the identity of Sámi shamans as non-gendered or third gendered, expressed not only through cross-dressing but also by wearing exotic materials and styles of clothing.

Experimental archaeology and re-enactors who make and wear accurate replicas of clothing can add to our understanding of the written and archaeological sources: the bodily movements when spinning thread or weaving; the aching, pains and possibly even the resulting change in body shape that these time-consuming, repetitive motions induce. A good example of such bodily changes is seen in the skeleton of an elderly lady buried in a late ninth- to tenth-century ship burial at Scar on the island of Sanday, Orkney. This woman was buried with spindle whorls, a weaving beater, needles and needle case and a plaque for smoothing linen, presenting her as a textile worker, an image confirmed by her skeleton. She had routinely sat cross legged, and the ligaments of her right hand had been affected by the motion repetitive spinning created.[60] The noise of creation, particularly weaving, envelops anyone in the vicinity of the work. Once made, the weight of wearing the garments alters the wearer's posture and gait, visually and physically engaging with the senses of not only the wearer but those who witness them.

This brief outline demonstrates the collaborative nature of exploring Viking Age textiles through the senses. Literary historians, historians, archaeologists, anthropologists, re-enactors and craftspeople with intimate knowledge of their specialism can draw out different nuances and understandings of the textiles and their sensory impact.

---

[60] Olwyn Owen and Magnar Dalland, ed., *Scar: A Viking Boat Burial on Sanday, Orkney* (East Linton: Tuckwell Press, 1991); D.H. Lorimer, 'The bodies: the female skeleton', in Owen and Dalland, *Scar*, pp. 56–58.

A good example of an exploration of sensory engagement between textiles and people can be seen through the migration-period costume of the deceased female buried at Sande farm in Norway. This woman was interred in clothing that denoted high status, yet it was closely fitted, suggesting restricted movement that may have been part of everyday life or of the burial rite. Textile archaeologists have analysed the fibres and construct of the textiles. Their results tell us that the garments were made of wool and an unidentified fur. The wool was variously undyed or dyed blue from woad, and red, probably from madder. The red threads were woven with some of the blue threads, forming one textile. The weaves were 2 x 2 twills woven from zz-spun yarn and had varying counts of 10/12, 12/12 and 14/14 threads per cm.[61] This scientific data gives insights into how the woman would have been perceived metaphorically. In the later sagas blue was associated with nature, metallic objects and the place of the dead. Its association with shades of black probably also describes the range of tones created when dyeing textiles. As a dye for textiles, it was deemed special because it involved an expensive process.[62] In Old Norse sources, red appears to have been associated with luminosity and lustre;[63] so this woman, clothed in blue and red, probably incorporated ideas of death, expense, speciality and luminosity. She was special, literally glowing as she went about her daily life, the drape and folds of her expensively dyed clothes 'shimmering' and creating new patterns as they moved.

The production and fit of the clothes can be explored through experimental archaeology and by re-enactors. By making and wearing replica garments, the time and effort, both physically and sensorially, involved in collecting the fibres, spinning them into yarn, dyeing the yarn and weaving the fabric can be ascertained. Questions such as what smells and sounds resulted from these activities and how they may have been interpreted by those close enough to hear and understand them can also be investigated. Indeed, the sagas suggest that these processes were understood to be magical in themselves.

The reality of wearing such possibly restrictive clothing can be explored as both a physical and sensory engagement, helping to answer the question of whether the costume was worn in this way during life as well as death. Information gathered from the sagas suggests that if this woman did wear her clothing differently from the norm, she could have held a religious or magical role within her community. This position would have been sensorially established and cemented by her clothes, and accessories that reflected light and tinkled as she moved. The accessories and jewellery denoted the deceased's membership as part of the local community elite, but by incorporating objects that came from different geographical territories within the Viking world she was also 'telling' onlookers of her connections and access to exotic resources through wide-ranging networks of trade and/or exchange and, possibly, that she herself had travelled.

---

[61] Vedeler, Kristoffersen and Røstad, 'Dressed for ritual, dressed for life', pp. 14, 17.

[62] Straubhaar, 'Wrapped in a blue mantle', pp. 55, 63, 64; Kirsten Wolf, 'The color blue in Old Norse-Icelandic Literature', *Scripta Islandica* 57 (2006), 55–78.

[63] Jackson Crawford, '*Bleikr, Gulr*, and the categorization of color in Old Norse', *The Journal of English and Germanic Philology* 115.2 (2016), 239–252 (p. 245); Kirsten Wolf, 'Some comments on Old Norse-Icelandic color terms', *Arkiv för nordisk filologi* 121 (2006), 173–192 (p. 177).

Thus, through a sensory engagement with textiles this woman secured and kept her place in society in both life and death; and through collaborative sensory research, we can unravel her story and that of textiles in Viking Age societies across the North Atlantic. As Sharon M. Fortney states, 'objects can tell us many things about the people who make and use them; we only have to listen [sensorially engage]'.[64]

---

[64] Sharon M. Fortney, 'Identifying Sto:lo Basketry: exploring different ways of knowing material culture', unpublished Master of Arts thesis (University of British Columbia, 2001), p. 48. Phrase in square brackets author's insertion.

CHAPTER 6

The Function of Written Textiles in the *Íslendingasögur*

Rachel Balchin

The *Íslendingasögur* (the *Sagas of Icelanders*) is a generic term which encompasses approximately forty early medieval narratives. Like much of the literature from this period, the *Íslendingasögur* are thought to have their origins in oral tradition. They were first written down in the vernacular during the thirteenth and fourteenth centuries, but recount stories of people and events from the Viking Age some three hundred years before.[1] They centre on the day-to-day existence of the earlier settlers of Iceland, focusing on legal disputes, social structures and familial relations (the reason they are also referred to as the 'Family Sagas').[2] Within these accounts are an abundance of allusions to textiles, but these references are often overlooked or misread. Until recently, it was an accepted belief that descriptions of textiles in the sagas were authenticating details at best, or unnecessary and irrelevant at worst.[3] This chapter will show how and why this is not the case, agreeing with Anita Sauckel's suggestion that textiles in the *Íslendingasögur* have an important literary function.[4] In order to do this I will first explore the importance of textile terminology in the *Íslendingasögur* and outline some of the methodological challenges of investigating written textiles. 'Written textiles' are defined here as written

[1] The accepted date range is *c.* 870–1030 CE. See Heather O'Donoghue, *Old Norse Icelandic Literature: A Short Introduction*, Blackwell Introductions to Literature (Oxford: Blackwell, 2004), p. 23; cf. Robert Kellog, 'Introduction', in *The Complete Sagas of Icelanders Including 49 Tales*, 5 vols., Viking Age Classics Series ed. by Viðar Hreinsson, Terry Gunnell, Keneva Kunz and Bernard Scudder (Reykjavik: Bókaútgáfan Leifur Eiríksson, 1997), I, pp. xxix–lv (p. xxx).

[2] O'Donoghue, *Old Norse Icelandic Literature*, pp. 23–24.

[3] Anita Sauckel, *Die Literarische Funktion von Kleidung in den* Íslendingasögur *und* Íslendingaþættir, Ergänzungsbände zum Reallexikon der Germanishen Altertumskunde 83 (Berlin: de Gruyter, 2014), pp. 1–2, citing Hans Kuhn, *Das alte Island* (Dusseldorf: Diederichs, 1971).

[4] Sauckel, *Die Literarische Funktion von Kleidung*, p. 5.

representations of textile-making processes, such as spinning, weaving and embroidery, and the material results of those processes, such as clothing. I will suggest a potential resolution to the challenge posed by the written – as opposed to the physical or material – nature of textiles, in the form of the Old Norse vestimentary code.[5]

Written textiles have not received as much attention in scholarship as some of their material counterparts, such as the textile fragments from the Oseberg Ship Burial, or even the later Bayeux Tapestry.[6] I argue that Old Norse textile terminology is imbued with a wealth of culturally contingent meanings that, when used in saga narrative, act as signifiers for a broad range of significations. However, examining textile terminology in isolation does not reveal the function of written textiles, but merely illustrates the relationship between written object and an abstract social or cultural phenomenon. In order to ascertain what purpose textiles serve, and understand why they are important devices within literature as a whole, it is necessary to examine the textile terminologies within their Old Norse narrative and cultural contexts. In addition to investigating the machinery of how written textiles generate meaning, I will also explore the potential for written textiles to function as 'material memory' and sites of emotional expression, qualities that Peter Stallybrass has incorporated in the term 'worn worlds'.[7] Furthermore, amidst a growing understanding of the modes of emotional expression in the *Íslendingasögur* (a genre which is typically understood to be emotionally constrained), I will show that textiles play an important role in transmitting emotion within the framework of what Sif Rikhardsdottir has called 'emotive scripts' and 'horizons of feeling'.[8]

Before exploring the emotive potential of written textiles, however, it is first necessary to outline some of the unique challenges that are posed by the texts. There is not adequate space here to discuss fully the complexities of the transmission, circulation, reception and translation of the *Íslendingasögur*, all of which influence the function of written textiles. Although Barthes' methodology can be helpfully adapted in order to examine written textiles in the sagas, one of the main limitations of the Old Norse vestimentary code is that it simply does not work universally. For this reason, the textual examples I discuss are intended to be illustrative – what can potentially be gained from

---

[5] This framework is an adaptation of work done by Roland Barthes in his analysis of the semiology of written fashion in mid-twentieth-century fashion magazines. Roland Barthes, *The Fashion System*, trans. by Matthew Ward and Richard Howard (New York, NY: Penguin Random House, 2010).

[6] Marianne Vedeler, 'The textile interior in the Oseberg burial chamber', in *A Stitch in Time: Essays in Honour of Lise Bender Jørgensen*, ed. by Sophie Bergerbrant and Sølvi Helene Fossøy (Gothenberg: University Press, 2014), pp. 281–300; Marianne Vedeler, *The Oseberg Tapestries* (Oslo: Scandinavian Academic Press, 2019); Gale R. Owen-Crocker, *The Bayeux Tapestry: Collected Papers* (Farnham: Ashgate Variorum, 2012); Shirley Ann Brown, *The Bayeux Tapestry: A Sourcebook* (Turnhout: Brepols, 2014).

[7] Peter Stallybrass, 'Worn worlds: clothes, mourning and the life of things', in *The Textile Reader*, ed. by Jessica Hemmings (New York: Berg, 2012), pp. 68–77.

[8] Sif Rikhardsdottir, *Emotion in Old Norse Literature: Translations, Voices, Contexts* (Cambridge: D.S. Brewer, 2017).

THE FUNCTION OF WRITTEN TEXTILES IN THE *ÍSLENDINGASÖGUR*   111

this approach – rather than prescriptive. Although there are many examples of important written textiles from across the *Íslendingasögur*, I will look at how they enhance and interact with specific narrative moments in only three sagas: *Laxdæla saga*, *Gísla saga súrssonar*, and *Gunnlaugs saga ormstungu*.[9]

The way in which the texts of the *Íslendingasögur* relate to history is not straightforward.[10] The difficulties presented by the hybridity of the sagas do not prevent us from using them to explore the social and cultural realities of early medieval northern Europe, but any approach should be made with caution. Although the saga narratives are set during the Viking Age, they can be more accurately compared to the modern genre of 'historical fiction' than to history. The relationship between individual texts presents a consistent and coherent 'world', which further complicates how they relate to history. Robert Kellog reminds us that the sagas 'present a mental version of a world, not the actuality itself', but that the presentation is so consistent that 'it has not been in the least absurd to apply the point of view and methods of the social sciences – of history, anthropology, sociology – to an understanding of this fictional world'.[11]

The narratives of the *Íslendingasögur* are rich with references to various different types of cloth and clothing. Given the constraints and caveats already discussed, 'written textiles' (as opposed to real, material textiles) are still extremely important to our understanding of early medieval attitudes towards clothing and textiles. While literary approaches to written textiles in the *Íslendingasögur* cannot reveal the specific realities of Viking Age textiles in the way that other, more materially focused disciplines can, they do add texture to our understanding of those material realities. However, this is not all that they are capable of. The study of early medieval textiles has largely been the remit of

---

9   A note on editions: initial research was carried out across both Íslenzk Fornrit and Svart á hvitu editions of the edited texts (Bragi Halldorsson et al., ed., *Islendingasögur og þættir* (Reykjavik: Svart á hvitu, 1987). Manuscript sources are not consistent across the two editions, and certainly the complex way in which manuscripts relate to each other means that the following analysis is far from the final word on the function and significance of written textiles in the *Íslendingasögur*. Due to accessibility and scholarly convention, all references to primary texts will be made to the Íslenzk Fornrit edited editions: Einar Ólafur Sveinsson, ed., *Laxdæla saga*, Íslenzk Fornrit 5 (Reykjavik: Hið Íslenzka Fornritafélag, 1934); Sigurður Nordal and Guðni Jónsson, ed., *Gunnlaugs Saga Ormstungu* in *Borgfirðinga sogur, Hænsa-Þóris Saga, Gunnlaugs Saga Ormstungu, Bjarnar Saga Hítdælakappa, Heiðarvíga Saga, Gísls þáttr Illugasonar*, Íslenzk Fornrit 3 (Reykjavik: Hið Íslenzka Fornritafélag, 1951); Björn K. Þórólfsson and Guðni Jónsson, ed., *Gísla saga Súrssonar* in *Vèstfirðinga sögur, Gísla saga Súrssonar, Fóstbroeðra saga, Þáttr Þormóðar, Hávarðar saga Ísfirðings, Auðunar Þáttr Vèstfirzka*, Íslenzk Fornrit 6 (Reykjavik: Hið Íslenzka Fornritafélag, 1958). All translations are quoted from the multi-volume *The Complete Sagas of Icelanders*: Keneva Kunz, trans., *The Saga of the People of Laxardal*, in *The Complete Sagas of Icelanders*, V, pp. 1–120; Katrina C. Attwood, trans., *The Saga of Gunnlaug Serpent-Tongue*, in *The Complete Sagas of Icelanders*, I., pp. 305–333; Martin S. Regal, trans., *Gisli's Saga*, in *The Complete Sagas of Icelanders*, II, pp. 1–48.

10   Kellog, 'Introduction', pp. xli–xlv.

11   Kellog, 'Introduction', pp. xli–xlii.

more materially focused disciplines, such as archaeology.[12] Little has been done in terms of literary or textual studies, especially for Old Norse language and culture. However, this is not the case in the related field of Old English literary and textual studies. Gale Owen-Crocker and Maren Clegg Hyer, among others, have greatly influenced the interdisciplinary study of textiles in medieval written sources, specifically Old English and Latin.[13] However, with the exception of a few significant shorter studies[14] and Anita Sauckel's monograph, *Die Literarische Funktion von Kleidung in den* Íslendingasögur *und* Íslendingaþættir, textiles in Old Norse sources have been largely ignored.

Sauckel demonstrates how textiles are imbued with a range of different significations, and how those significations can be incorporated into well-known social and cultural parameters. She argues that textiles and clothing in the sagas possess an important literary function, an 'expanded social and psychological characterization' that was purposefully wielded by saga authors and compilers to express their characters' inner states, and enable narrative foreshadowing.[15] In a comparable way, this chapter argues that written textiles in the *Íslendingasögur* function as narrative and emotive devices, and are also sites for – and modes of – negotiation in both interpersonal relationships and individual expressions of identity. A wide range of cultural values and significances are projected on to, and conveyed by, written textiles, which are then interpreted or decoded by characters who inhabit the constructed saga world. These same processes are also enacted by the medieval audiences contemporary to and post the time of composition/compilation. The question remains: how might we best go about decoding written clothing and textiles in the *Íslendingasögur* for ourselves?

[12]   Although the later Middle Ages is often a subject for economic historians, see P.J.P. Goldberg, *Women, Work and Life Cycle in a Medieval Economy: Women in York and Yorkshire, c. 1300–1520* (Oxford: Clarendon, 1992), and John Munro, 'Medieval woollens: textiles, textile technology and industrial organisation, c. 800–1500', in *The Cambridge History of Western Textiles*, ed. by David Jenkins, 2 vols. (Cambridge: Cambridge University Press, 2003), I, pp. 181–227.

[13]   Gale R. Owen-Crocker, *Dress in Anglo-Saxon England: Revised and Enlarged Edition* (Woodbridge: Boydell, 2004); Maren Clegg Hyer, 'Text/textile: "wordweaving" in the literatures of Anglo-Saxon England', *Medieval Clothing and Textiles* 15 (2019), 33–52; Maren Clegg Hyer and Gale R. Owen-Crocker, 'Woven works: making and using textiles', in *The Material Culture of Daily Living in the Anglo-Saxon World*, ed. by Maren Clegg Hyer and Gale R. Owen-Crocker (Exeter: Exeter University Press, 2011), pp. 157–184.

[14]   Including, but not limited to: Sandra Baliff Straubhaar, 'Wrapped in a blue mantle: fashion for Icelandic slayers?' *Medieval Clothing and Textiles* 1 (2005), 53–65; Kirsten Wolf's analysis of *blár* in 'The color blue in Old Norse-Icelandic literature', *Scripta Islandica* 57 (2006), 55–78; Gesa Snell, 'Der höfischen Züge – insbesondere die Kleidungsbescreibung – als Stilmittel in der *Laxdœla saga*', in *Arbeiten zur Skandinavistik: 13. Arbeitstagung der deutschsprachigen Skandinavistik 29.7–3.8.1997 in Lysebu (Oslo)*, ed. by Paul Fritz, Texte und Untersuchungen zur Germanistik und Skandinavistik 45 (Frankfurt am Main: Peter Lang, 2000), pp. 249–257; and Anna Zanchi, '"Melius abundare quam deficere": scarlet clothing in *Laxdœla saga* and *Njáls saga*', *Medieval Clothing and Textiles* 4 (2008), 21–37.

[15]   Sauckel, *Die Literarische Funktion von Kleidung*, p. 5. Translation my own.

Despite the fluid, mercurial relationship between material textile-practices and written words, the cloth and clothing described in the sagas are not real.[16] Rather, they are signs (in the semiotic sense), linguistic markers that draw on, and lend shape to, a collective set of social and cultural abstractions that bear a resemblance to their physical, material counterparts. Material methods and approaches cannot account for this subtle yet significant difference. Fortunately, this problem has already been addressed by Roland Barthes.[17] As I will go on to show, the resulting vestimentary code is an essential critical framework that allows us to examine textiles in the *Íslendingasögur* as wholly written phenomena. Written textiles exist only on the page as a linguistic and semantic sign the chief purpose of which is to signify something.

In the semiology of Fashion, Barthes identifies two different 'sets' of relational meaning, whereby a change in one indicates a shift in meaning for the other. 'Set A' is comprised of 'clothing' and 'world', where the semiological meaning of clothing can be discovered because of its direct connection to something concrete.[18] 'Set B' is comprised of 'clothing' and 'fashion', in which the absence of specification and/or explicit expression of purpose suggests that the primary function of a Set B utterance is to '*transmit* Fashion'.[19] Set B utterances are self-contained and self-sufficient, relying only on what is present within the utterance to generate and communicate meaning. Both sets can be seen to work in the *Íslendingasögur*. However, it is problematic to replicate this approach to the textile terminology of the *Íslendingasögur*. While Barthes does not consider the broader contexts that surround individual textile terms to have any significant impact on their meaning, it is possible to fully appreciate the nuance and complexity of the *Íslendingasögur* only if we take narrative, historical and cultural contexts into consideration. Analysis of the various garment and textile nouns in their narrative contexts will elucidate why certain textiles appear in certain scenes, why those textiles are not interchangeable and, furthermore, what those specific textiles, and the use of textile terms, signify.

In her study of violence in the *Íslendingasögur*, Sandra Baliff Straubhaar analyses the adjectives *blár* ('blue') and *svartr* ('black') in relation to clothing nouns based on their narrative context. She seeks to explore and problematise the common assumption that when a saga character wears 'dark' clothing, they typically mean to kill someone.[20] This, she maintains, does not reflect the conceptual differences between what we think of as 'blue' or 'black' today compared to what was thought of as 'blue' or 'black' during

---

[16] Victoria Mitchell, 'Textiles, text and techne', in *The Textile Reader*, ed. by Jessica Hemmings (New York: Berg, 2012), pp. 7–13. See Rachel Balchin, 'Narrative Threads: Written Textiles in Old Norse Prose and Poetry', Unpublished doctoral thesis (University of Leicester, 2021), pp. 145–148.

[17] Barthes, *The Fashion System*, p. 368 See note 5.

[18] Barthes, *The Fashion System*, pp. 20–21.

[19] Barthes, *The Fashion System*, p. 22, original emphasis.

[20] Straubhaar, 'Wrapped in a blue mantle', p. 53.

the early medieval period.[21] As she later explores, 'black' is more akin to a natural, dark-coloured fleece, what Einar Ólafur Sveinsson has identified as *sauðsvartr* in modern Icelandic, otherwise translated as 'sheep-black'. The colour 'blue' is closer to what we as a contemporary readership might think of as black because it is achieved with dyes which result in a richer, more vibrant colour that could range from blue to black.[22] Straubhaar's concern for the conceptual differences between Old Norse terms and our modern under-standing of colour is not merely an aesthetic one. Through corpus analysis she shows that there is some connection between the colour of a character's garments and the like-lihood that they will commit an act of violence, or at the very least be in the vicinity of violence or drawn weapons. She draws a distinction between *blár* and *svartr* by coding them as 'best' and 'not-best' clothes, respectively: *blár* was considered to be the 'dyed, special-occasion colour', and has a nuanced, ambiguous relationship with violence, while *svartr* was the common, everyday colour and associated more exclusively with violence.[23] It is also excluded from the category of 'best clothing'. Straubhaar recounts a textual example previously identified by Valtýr Guðmundsson, where a character is expected to be dressed in his best, but instead wears a *svartr* ('sheep-black') cloak and is mocked for it.[24] Therefore, while the popular assumption suggests that a saga character donning dark clothing means that they are going to kill someone, in actuality it very much depends on what category of dark clothing is worn, and even then, the association is not as straight-forward as the popular assumption has suggested. As Straubhaar succinctly puts it, 'activi-ties such as wearing one's best clothes, carrying special weapons ostensibly for show only, riding horses, and killing people may occur in quick succession with or without causal relationships among them'.[25]

Both Barthes and Straubhaar have demonstrated that paying more attention to the nuanced, coded meaning of clothing and textile terms can reveal or substantiate certain cultural significations. Straubhaar's linguistic analysis is analogous to Barthes' 'Set A', as there is an overt and specific relationship between clothing (a *blár* cloak) and world (vio-lence). While Barthes is dismissive of the meaning found in the textile terms of literature, Straubhaar demonstrates that, although not straightforward, descriptions of textiles in literature have a recognisable relationship with material and physical culture.[26] She illus-trates this with Guðrún Ósvífsdóttir's garments in *Laxdæla saga* 55.[27] Guðrún's clothing is described in detail a number of times throughout the saga, which is interesting in itself because of the propensity in saga narrative to focus on action – of which there is plenty

---

[21]   See also Wolf, 'The color blue'.

[22]   Einar Ólafur Sveinsson, *Laxdæla saga*, p. 254, as cited in Straubhaar, 'Wrapped in a blue mantle', p. 63.

[23]   Straubhaar, 'Wrapped in a blue mantle', pp. 63–65.

[24]   Straubhaar, 'Wrapped in a blue mantle', p. 65; Valtýr Guðmundsson, *'Litklædi'*, *Arkiv för nordiak filologi* 9 (1893), 171–198.

[25]   Straubhaar, 'Wrapped in a blue mantle', p. 64.

[26]   Straubhaar, 'Wrapped in a blue mantle', p. 54.

[27]   Straubhaar, 'Wrapped in a blue mantle', p. 54.

THE FUNCTION OF WRITTEN TEXTILES IN THE *ÍSLENDINGASÖGUR* 115

in this chapter, as her husband is brutally killed. At this point, Guðrún's outfit consists of a *námkyrtill* ('kirtle made of *nám* cloth'), *vefjarupphlutr* ('woven upper-bodice'), *sveigr* ('headdress'), as well as her *blæja* (discussed below) with *mörk blá og tröf fyrir enda* ('with black "stitches" and fringe(s) at the end').[28] Straubhaar argues that Guðrún's clothes are 'several centuries younger than Guðrún herself, since it [her clothes] seems to resemble the high-medieval gowns worn by various queens on the friezes at the cathedrals of Chartres, Angers, and Nôtre-Dame de Corbeil'.[29] While she considers this anachronism to be a hindrance to the accuracy of her results, I would suggest that it is in keeping with the functionality of Barthes' Set B, and my Old Norse code. A later writer's choice to clothe the saga's heroine in garments usually associated with royalty is indicative of how Guðrún was perceived by an audience contemporaneous with the garments in question, and represents a clear connection between written textiles and material culture.[30]

The Old Norse vestimentary code enables us, as modern readers of the *Íslendingasögur*, to gain a deeper understanding of Guðrún and the importance of clothing as markers (and makers) of identity. Her personality and actions drive a significant portion of *Laxdæla saga*, which is why it is fitting that she wears the 'costume' of a queen.[31] As a modern audience lacking the culturally contingent understanding of such comparisons, however, it is important to recognise the ways in which our understanding of the social and cultural significations of Guðrún's clothes can be deepened through close attention and analysis of the textile terminology. For example, *blæja* is defined as 'fine coloured cloth' which can be variably used as a bed sheet, burial sheet or altar cloth.[32] In one translated edition it is called a 'shawl', which does convey the nature of the garment (in that it wraps, covers, enfolds and is worn on the outside of other garments as a top layer) but omits the nature of the fabric, as well as any material or cultural significance that a thirteenth-century audience may have attributed to it. Furthermore, *Laxdæla saga* 55 is the only instance in which a *blæja* is understood to be a shawl: the majority of records

---

[28] Sveinsson, *Laxdæla saga* 55, p. 168; *The Saga of the People of Laxardal* 55, p. 87.

[29] Straubhaar, 'Wrapped in a blue mantle', p. 54.

[30] Sif Rikhardsdottir offers an alternative perspective on the significance of the description of Guðrún's clothes. She argues that 'the narrative voice directs the reader's (or audience's) attention to her clothing, thus focusing on her body which provides an analogue to the mutilated body of Bolli lying close by [...] The focus on Guðrún's clothes draws attention to the blood remnants that will stain the material; a visceral and mental mnemonic image that lays the groundwork for the later whetting scene where the bloodstained clothes will play a vital role.' *Emotion in Old Norse Literature*, p. 128.

[31] 'Costume' is not the same as 'dress'. See Roland Barthes, 'Language and clothing', in his *The Language of Fashion*, ed. by Michael Carter, trans. by Andy Stafford (London: Bloomsbury, 2006), pp. 21–22, originally published in *Critique* 142 (1959), 243–252.

[32] References to Old Norse definitions derived from Richard Cleasby, Gudbrand Vigfusson and Sir William A. Craigie, *An Icelandic-English Dictionary* 2nd edn (Oxford: Clarendon, 1957), unless otherwise stated. Further references will appear in the main body, abbreviated to 'Cleasby-Vigfusson'.

refer to bed coverings, or as an altar cloth.[33] The characteristic which is shared across all three meanings is that it is considered to be a thin fabric. Due to its association with the church, as well as the above-mentioned sculptural depictions of royal dress, 'thin' could be interpreted as 'fine'. Earlier on in the saga, Guðrún is described as 'the most beautiful woman to have grown up in Iceland'.[34] In her first marriage it is supposedly her demand for fine things that drives her husband to physically assault her.[35] There is also the matter of the headdress, which is gifted to her potential third husband, Kjartan, by the Norwegian king's sister, Ingibjörg. It is intended as a token of her favour and affection, and as a blessing upon his future marriage to Guðrún.[36] However, by the time he returns to Iceland, Guðrún has already married Bolli, his sworn-brother. Kjartan then decides to marry Hrefna and it is she, not Guðrún, who receives Ingibjörg's headdress. There are many narrative reasons for the tension between the two households, but when the headdress goes missing – suspected to have been stolen by Guðrún – it marks the end of their cordial relationship.[37]

The headdress serves as a locus for Guðrún's frustration because it is a physical reminder of what perhaps should have been hers (i.e. both Kjartan as her husband and the headdress), along with the status and power which would have accompanied that marriage:

> Kjartan gaf Hrefnu að línfé moturinn og var sú gjöf allfræg því að engi var þar svo vitur eða stórauðigur að slíka gersemi hefði séð eða átta. En það er hygginna manna frásögn að átta aurum gulls væri ofið í moturinn.

> (Kjartan gave Hrefna the headdress as a wedding present and the gift was renowned throughout the country, as no Icelander was so cultured that he had seen, or so wealthy that he had possessed, such a treasure. According to reliable reports, there were eight ounces of gold woven into the headdress.)[38]

The headdress is clearly valuable, in terms both of the weight of gold woven into it as well as the social and cultural importance it conveys to the one who owns it. While it can be said that garments can be more than just garments to all of the characters in the sagas, this is especially true for Guðrún, who sews a shirt to initiate a divorce, and who presents Bolli's blood-soaked clothes to her teenage sons in order to incite them to vengeance.[39] Therefore, while the attention paid to Guðrún's appearance at

---

33 'blæja', Aldís Sigurðardóttir et al., ed., Ordbog over det norrøne prosaprog (Dictionary of Old Norse Prose); https://onp.ku.dk/onp/onp.php?o9598, accessed 16 February 2023.

34 The Saga of the People of Laxardal 32, p. 43.

35 Sveinsson, Laxdæla saga 34, pp. 93–94.

36 Sveinsson, Laxdæla saga 43, p. 131.

37 Sveinsson, Laxdæla saga 46, p. 143.

38 Sveinsson, Laxdæla saga 45, p. 138; The Saga of the People of Laxardal 45, p. 71.

39 For further detail of the function and significance of bloodied clothing in the incitement ritual, see Balchin, 'Narrative Threads', pp. 159–164.

the moment Bolli is murdered is jarring against the background of graphic violence, it is actually a consistent and significant aspect of her characterisation. Close examination of textile vocabulary reveals implicit, culturally contingent meaning. The association of *blæja* with a luxury fabric used in – among other places – a religious setting, and the similarity of apparel worn by both Guðrún and the friezes of royal women adorning the walls of Chartres, Angers, and Nôtre-Dame de Corbeil, is significant. Sartorially speaking, her *blæja* conveys this queenly association to a later medieval audience in a way that the modern English noun 'shawl' fails to replicate.[40]

In light of the knowledge of Guðrún's personality and social aspirations, the associations between the *blæja* and queenliness are symbolically appropriate. Approaching written textiles in a way that draws on implicit significations that have been inferred through linguistic and cultural analysis is akin to Set B, which operates in a more subtle capacity to 'transmit' meaning. This reflection of material realities can illuminate a number of things, such as how clothing and textiles within the sagas were received by later scribes and audiences. The language used to depict dress and textiles – even adjectives as simple as *svartr* and *blár* – indicates certain codified cultural significances which imbue the sagas with additional layers of meaning that often goes unexplored or unnoticed. For example, a more nuanced understanding of textile terminology reveals the intimate connection between identity and clothing during a key moment in *Gísla saga súrssonar*. In the middle of Iceland during the mid-tenth century, a man gives his cloak to his servant and offers to pull him on their sled for a short while. In return, he would like to wear his servant's cloak.[41] The servant agrees, partly because his lower status means that he has to, but also because his master is renowned for being *vel búin* ('well dressed').[42] This suggests that the cloak swap will benefit the servant because he will obtain a better cloak than his own. Shortly after, however, it is revealed that their swap is intended to confuse his master's pursuers, who are closing in on their location, hunting the man who killed one brother-in-law to avenge the other. This man is Gísli Súrsson, and in the resulting skirmish, the men giving chase kill the servant. They congratulate themselves for slaying Gísli, until they discover the real identity of the dead man, Þórðr the 'coward', who was forced to wear Gísli's cloak and act as a decoy.[43]

This cloak swap might seem straightforward on the surface, but this case of mistaken identity is complicated because Gísli is well known by his pursuers. The differences between Gísli and his servant, Þórðr, are explicitly mentioned by the saga narrator, the most significant of which is that Þórðr is a big man but lacks both courage and wit.[44]

---

[40] For further details regarding the diminishing potential of the modern English noun 'shawl', see Balchin, 'Narrative Threads', ch. 3.

[41] Björn K. Þórólfsson and Guðni Jónsson, *Gísla saga súrssonar* 20, pp. 64–65.

[42] For a discussion on the role of livery and other clothing in the master–servant power dynamic, see Anne Rosalind Jones and Peter Stallybrass, *Renaissance Clothing and the Materials of Memory* (Cambridge: Cambridge University Press, 2000), pp. 17–33.

[43] His name in the text is 'Þórðr inn huglausi'. 'Huglauss' means 'cowardly' or 'faint hearted'.

[44] 'Þórðr var mikill maðr vexti', Björn K. Þórólfsson and Guðni Jónsson, *Gísla saga* 20, p. 65.

Gísli's status as a 'saga hero' is ambiguous and has been discussed in detail by David Clark and Heather O'Donoghue, but it would be a stretch to accuse him of being a coward.[45] In the mythic and heroic texts of the *Poetic Edda*, which are understood to influence the worldviews, personality traits and social and cultural dynamics of the *Íslendingasögur*, heroism can often be conceived of in physiological terms.[46] In the poem *Atlakviða*, for example, the heart of the legendary Högni is ripped out of his body. His brother, Gunnar, successfully identifies it as Högni's heart because it is like a stone (compared to the trembling heart of the cowardly Hjalli, which was offered first in an attempt to trick him).[47] The relationship between the 'heroic past' and saga literature is far from straightforward but it does exist, and highlights certain points of interest in *Gísla saga*. Here there are also two men, one more cowardly than the other, who attempt to avoid detection by swapping cloaks. However, according to the logic of heroic poetry, cowardice manifests itself physically – the heart trembles even after death and separation from its body. It is unusual, then, that the cloak swap is initially successful. Not only is Gísli known to his pursuers, but Þórðr's cowardly heart should manifest and be made visible by his very existence. When Gísli's pursuers do not recognise that he and Þórðr have swapped places, it is evident that *something* is in place that allows the deception to succeed.

That 'something' is their swapped cloaks. The noun 'cloak', however, is perhaps as inaccurate a translation as Guðrún's 'shawl'. Without the specificity of terminology we would not know that Gísli's cloak is a *kápa*, while his servant's cloak is a *kufl*, both Old Norse terms for a cloak with a cowl or hood attached to it (Cleasby-Vigfusson). The material similarity of both garments lends itself to the identity swap, but the fact that Gísli's first recourse is to swap cloaks with his servant to avoid capture, and the fact that his pursuers are successfully deceived by their swap, suggests that within the collective cultural consciousness of saga society is the understanding that a *kápa* and a *kufl* are worn by different people for different reasons, and have different significations. I have explored these differences in detail elsewhere, but to summarise: the meaning attached to Gísli's *kápa* falls within a spectrum that conveys high status and power which is often

---

[45] David Clark, *Gender, Violence and the Past in Edda and Saga* (Oxford: Oxford University Press, 2012), pp. 89–116; Heather O'Donoghue, *Skaldic Verse and the Poetics of Saga Narrative* (Oxford: Oxford University Press, 2005), pp. 136–179. See also Rebecca Merkelbach, *Monsters in Society: Alterity, Transgression, and the Use of the Past in Medieval Iceland* (Kalamazoo, MI: Medieval Institute Publications, 2019), pp. 79–82.

[46] Clark, *Gender, Violence and the Past*.

[47] *Atlakviða* 23, IV–V: 'er mioc bifaz, er á bióði liggr;/ bifðiz hálfo meirr, er í briósti lá' ('It [Hialli's heart] quivers greatly as it lies on the platter;/ it quivered twice as much when it was in the breast'). Primary quotations from *Poetic Edda* searchable electronic text of Gustav Neckel, ed., *Edda: Die Lieder des Codex Regius nebst verwandten Denkmälern*, rev. Hans Kuhn, 5th edn (Heidelberg: Carl Winter, 1983); http://titus.uni-frankfurt.de/texte/etcs/germ/anord/edda/edda.htm, accessed 16 February 2023. Unless otherwise stated, translations by Carolyne Larrington, *The Poetic Edda* (Oxford: Oxford University Press, 2008).

THE FUNCTION OF WRITTEN TEXTILES IN THE *ÍSLENDINGASÖGUR*   119

accompanied by varying levels of threat, violence and murderous intent.[48] Conversely, Þórðr's *kufl* conveys stealth, disguise and survival, attributes which bear a heavy association with the condition of the outlaw, or with an individual involved with morally grey activities.[49] It is no coincidence of description or sartorial whim that the saga narrator dressed Gísli and Þórðr in these particular garments. The allusions which Clark observes between heroic Eddic past and the saga present allow for many parallels, even between the two 'cowardly' decoys, Hjalli in *Atlakviða* and Þórðr in *Gísla saga*. Þórðr's *kufl* is an indication of his weak character, signifying the full range of socially unacceptable behaviours. Within the context of the heroic past this is usually a negative thing. However, as Clark and O'Donoghue have shown, the relationship between heroic ideal and saga reality is both complicated and undermined in the narrative, particularly by Gísli, whose relationship with heroism is ambivalent.[50] This attitude is exemplified when he identifies that the traits associated with the *kufl* – specifically, but not limited to, disguise – are beneficial to him now that he is an outlaw. The moment when Gísli and Þórðr swap cloaks is a liminal space where the function and importance of literary textiles cannot be ignored. Clothing is a material manifestation of an individual's character, and Gísli's choice to draw around him the embodiment of Þórðr's cowardly nature, rather than maintain his heroic status, simply confirms the saga's ambivalent relationship with the heroic past. While the *kápa* and the *kufl* are visually similar, this surface-level trick does not fool Gísli's pursuers beyond a first glance; indeed, they are unaware of the swap until they pull the *kápa* away from Þórðr's corpse. However, when viewed through the lens of the Old Norse vestimentary code, the reason for the success of the swap becomes clear: prior to killing Þorgrím, a man of Gísli's standing would not wear a *kufl* because of the culturally contingent understanding from which we, as a modern audience, are completely removed.

Cloaks and other garments function on more than just the semiotic and symbolic levels that have already been discussed: they also function on a metonymic level. When Gísli and Þórðr swap cloaks they also hand over the very essence of their identity, and when they wear the other man's cloak they 'become' the other. The historic and hybrid literary 'worlds' of Viking Age Iceland are, arguably, what Peter Stallybrass has identified as 'cloth societies', on the basis that 'in its most extreme form, [a cloth society] is a society in which values and exchanges alike take the form of cloth'.[51] He argues that in a cloth society, 'cloth is both a currency and a means of incorporation'.[52] Stallybrass explains that cloth possesses two qualities of materiality which, although contradictory, are simultaneously true. The first is its ability to be permeated and transformed by both maker and wearer alike, as either individual can alter the surface or structure of a garment,

---

[48] Not unlike Straubhaar's spectrum of behaviours associated with *blár* and *svartr*. My own analysis is modelled on – and adapted from – her approach.

[49] Balchin, 'Narrative Threads', pp. 85–100.

[50] Clark, *Gender, Violence and the Past*, pp. 101–102; O'Donoghue, *Skaldic Verse*, pp. 173–174.

[51] Stallybrass, 'Worn worlds', p. 70.

[52] Stallybrass, 'Worn worlds', p. 70.

creating permanent changes that bear the significance of their possession – or embodied experience – of the cloth. The second is that, despite its vulnerability to enforced transformation, cloth has the ability to endure over time.[53]

Owing to its dual nature of permeation/transformation and endurance, Stallybrass suggests that cloth has a powerful association with memory – indeed cloth *is* memory.[54] He illustrates this best when he describes how, after the death of a loved one, their clothes '*are* the pain which the [bereaved] feels. [They] hang there, "waiting", they endure, but only as a residue that recreates absence, darkness, death; things which are not.'[55] Unlike other possessions that the dead leave behind, clothing and textiles maintain the shape of the deceased, such as in the creases at elbows and knees, as well as their smell, such as lingering cologne, stale cigarettes, or bodily secretions.[56] The condition of these garments has the potential to evoke memories of their life or personality – a tear here, a stain there – suggesting that the intimacy, physicality, and visceral reality of clothing provides a material connection between the original wearer and the bereft.[57] Cloth and garments do not replace the deceased, but maintain their shadowy presence, creating an echo of their personality which endures (but eventually fades) over time. In his work with Ann Rosalind Jones, Stallybrass argues that it is in this capacity that cloth and clothing function as material mnemonic. They suggest that 'clothes, like sorrow, inscribe themselves upon a person who comes into being through that inscription'.[58] When a person who has suffered a bereavement wears the garments of the deceased, they clothe themselves in the physical weight of their grief, as well as in the material memory and identity of their lost loved one. For Jones and Stallybrass, clothing is a 'worn world: a world of social relations put upon the wearer's body'.[59] From this it is clear that clothing is not just a matter of practicality or status, but simultaneously a figurative and literal embodiment of identity; cultural, intimate, physical. Clothing in literary texts – including the *Íslendingasögur* – is often valued for its metaphorical potential, as well as a clear indicator of economic wealth and social status.[60] For Jones and Stallybrass, this duality of significance – both economic and metaphoric/mnemonic – is a centre of tension which is 'fertile source of cultural

---

53 Stallybrass, 'Worn worlds', p. 70. A spectacular example of cloth's ability to endure over time is the Norse-Greenlandic textiles, which date from the late tenth to the mid-fifteenth centuries, as detailed in Else Østergård, *Woven into the Earth: Textiles from Norse Greenland* (Aarhus: Aarhus University Press, 2009).

54 Stallybrass, 'Worn worlds', p. 70.

55 Stallybrass, 'Worn worlds', p. 72.

56 Stallybrass, 'Worn worlds', p. 72.

57 Stallybrass, 'Worn worlds', p. 72.

58 Jones and Stallybrass, *Renaissance Clothing*, p. 2.

59 Jones and Stallybrass, *Renaissance Clothing*, p. 3.

60 Jones and Stallybrass, *Renaissance Clothing*, p. 26.

analysis'.[61] Clothes are sources of wealth and value, as well as of identity formation; they are a 'second skin, a skin that names you'.[62]

Cloth can also be a site of emotional expression. Emotion in Old Norse literature has only recently been the subject of focused study.[63] By its very nature, literary emotion must be conceived of as a separate phenomenon compared to its historical, psychological, biological and neurological counterparts.[64] In other words, expressions of 'emotion' – what Sif Rikhardsdottir calls 'emotive signposts' – in Old Norse literature are not reflective of genuine, historical or 'real' emotion.[65] While they may reflect social and cultural realities, 'they nevertheless convey uniquely literary behavioural scripts that are coded to convey interpretative meanings beyond their emotive functionality or their conventional emotional classification in societies'.[66] The literary function of emotion is to act as 'symbolic codes that guide the reader through the signifying network of a text'.[67] The way in which these codes or signposts are expressed depends on generic, social, gendered and other cultural expectations, an intersectional framework that Sif Rikhardsdottir has named the 'horizon of feeling': 'such emotive identities are bound by emotional conventions and generic markers, but must ultimately reflect an emotive framework that is comprehensible and meaningful to its readers'.[68] The combination of generic expectation and cultural convention leads to 'emotive scripts', whereby a character follows a 'blueprint' of performative emotional display that will carry significance for a contemporary medieval audience.[69]

The ability of cloth and clothing to embody an individual, act as a material mnemonic and serve as an emotive signpost can be seen in *Gunnlaugs saga ormstungu*. Gunnlaugr is a 'hero-poet', travelling beyond Iceland in pursuit of his fortune, presenting himself to various kings and lords in Norway, Sweden, Ireland, Orkney and England. Each summer he makes a point of visiting new rulers and reciting his poetry in exchange for material rewards and recognition. Unlike in other poets' sagas, Gunnlaugr's central association is not with a specific king but with Helga, a woman he has known since they were both

---

[61]   Jones and Stallybrass, *Renaissance Clothing*, p. 32.

[62]   Jones and Stallybrass, *Renaissance Clothing*, p. 32.

[63]   Sif Rikhardsdottir, *Emotion in Old Norse Literature*, pp. 14–15.

[64]   Sif Rikhardsdottir, *Emotion in Old Norse Literature*, pp. 6–11.

[65]   Sif Rikhardsdottir, *Emotion in Old Norse Literature*, p. 18. Emotive signposts are different from emotional vocabulary ('emotives').

[66]   Sif Rikhardsdottir, *Emotion in Old Norse Literature*, p. 18.

[67]   Sif Rikhardsdottir, *Emotion in Old Norse Literature*, p. 18.

[68]   Sif Rikhardsdottir, *Emotion in Old Norse Literature*, p. 18.

[69]   Also, to some extent, an audience removed from the immediate temporal and cultural environment from which the text originates, Sif Rikhardsdottir, *Emotion in Old Norse Literature*, p. 11; Sif has adapted the term 'emotive script' from 'emotional script', coined by Sylvan S. Tomkins, 'Script theory: differential magnification of affects', in *Nebraska Symposium on Motivation 1978*, ed. by Herbert E. Howe and Richard A. Dienstbier, Nebraska Symposium on Motivation 26 (Lincoln, NE: University of Nebraska Press, 1979), pp. 201–236.

twelve years old.[70] Before he sets sail from Iceland, he secures an informal agreement with Helga's father to the effect that she will remain unattached for three years while he is away, but if he does not return within that time, Gunnlaugr forfeits their engagement.[71] In London he presents himself to King Aðalráðr and, after reciting his poem, is rewarded by the king with a fur-lined scarlet cloak (*skarlatskikkja*).[72] In the court of Ólafr the Swede he encounters Hrafn, who will become his antagonist and marry Helga before he is able to return to Iceland.[73] This marriage takes place against Helga's wishes, a point which is emphasised at her wedding, where 'flestra manna sögn að brúðurin væri heldur döpur' ('most people say that the bride was rather gloomy'); after hearing about Hrafn's dream in which he is killed by Gunnlaugr, '"það lutis aldrei gráta," segir hún. "Hafið þér illa svikið mig. Mun Gunnlaugur út kominn" og grét Helga þá mjög' ('"I will never weep over that," Helga said. "You have all tricked me wickedly. Gunnlaug must have come back." And then Helga wept bitterly'); and when she learns that Gunnlaugr has, indeed, returned to Iceland, 'Og litlu síðar lutist útkoma Gunnlaugs. Helga gerðist þá svo stirð við Hrafn að hann fékk eigi haldið henni heima þar og fóru þau þá heim aftur til Borgar og nýtti Hrafn lítið af samvistum við hana' ('Indeed, a little while later, news came of Gunnlaug's return. After this, Helga became so intractable towards Hrafn that he could not keep her at home, and so they went back to Borg [her father's home]. Hrafn did not enjoy much intimacy with her').[74]

Helga's explicit and sustained dislike of her husband is exacerbated beyond repair when, in the same chapter, she and Gunnlaugr come face to face at another wedding feast. Gunnlaugr recites a verse expressing his own distress about her marriage before giving her the *skarlatskikkja* from King Aðalráðr, known at this point as *Aðalráðsnaut*.[75] The name denotes the status of the original giver, but, due to the material nature of cloth and clothing and its ability to 'maintain shape', it also *is* King Aðalráðr, or at least some essential part of him that 'haunts' the gift.[76] This *skikkja* is a highly significant emotive signpost and is the site of material embodiment and memory. The emotions that Gunnlaugr vocalises in his verse are inscribed on the *skikkja*, interwoven with the fibres, giving shape to their personal tragedy. In giving it to Helga, Gunnlaugr also gives her part

---

[70] Sigurður Nordal and Guðni Jónsson, *Gunnlaugs saga* 4. Other 'poets' sagas' include *Egils saga Skallagrimssonar*, ed. by Sigurður Nordal, Íslenzk Fornrit 2 (1933), *Hallfreðar saga vandræðaskálds*, in *Vatnsdœla Saga, Hallfreðar Saga, Kormáks Saga, Hrómundar Þáttr Halta, Hrafns Þáttr Guðrúnarsonar*, ed. by Einar Ólafur Sveinsson, Íslenzk Fornrit 8 (1958), pp. 135–200, and *Kormáks saga* in *Vatnsdœla Saga*, Íslenzk Fornrit 8 (1958), pp. 203–302.

[71] Nordal and Jónsson, *Gunnlaugs saga* 5.

[72] Nordal and Jónsson, *Gunnlaugs saga* 7.

[73] Nordal and Jónsson, *Gunnlaugs saga* 9.

[74] *Gunnlaugs saga* 11.

[75] Cf. Sauckel, *Die Literarische Funktion von Kleidung*, p. 47.

[76] See Marcel Mauss, *Essai sur le don: forme archaique de l'echange* (*The Gift: Forms and Functions of Gift Exchange in Archaic Societies*), trans. by Ian Cunnison (London: Cohen and West, 1970) and William Ian Miller, 'Is a gift forever?', *Representations* 100 (2007), 13–22.

of the king as well as of himself.[77] Later on in her second marriage, which takes place after Gunnlaugr and Hrafn kill each other in a *hólmganga* (a ritualised duel), Helga becomes severely ill.[78] It is said that she does not really love her second husband, Þorkell, because she cannot stop thinking about Gunnlaugr. It is also said that 'helst gaman Helgu að hún rekti skikkjuna Gunnlaugsnaut og horfði þar á löngu' ('Helga's greatest pleasure was to unfold the cloak which Gunnlaug had given her and stare at it for a long time').[79] Significantly, *Aðalráðsnaut* is now known as *Gunnlaugsnaut*, which suggests that it is now Gunnlaugr who 'haunts' the cloak. In Helga's final moments, she calls for *Gunnlaugsnaut* to be brought to her. Her last act is to spread the cloak out so that she can look at it, before collapsing, dead, into her husband's arms. In light of cloth's ability to function as both a material mnemonic and an emotive signpost, it is now possible to categorically identify that which a reader might have implicitly understood or – more likely – felt. It is only natural that, in her grief, Helga turns to *Gunnlaugsnaut* for comfort: through the process of identity transference that can occur during gift-exchange, and through cloth's ability to inscribe and be inscribed with emotion and memory, *Gunnlaugsnaut* is Gunnlaugr.[80]

In *Gunnlaugs saga*, the cloak that Gunnlaugr receives in exchange for a poem becomes a signpost for both his and Helga's emotions. Before he gave it to her it was simply a material reward, one among many that he received in purely economic transactions with numerous rulers from numerous lands. Its value was rooted both in the expensive fabrics as well as in the metonymic connection between garment and its giver, King Aðalráðr. This is achieved through cloth's permeability, in which an individual can inscribe themselves on to the fabric, simply through the act of owning or wearing it.[81] Once Gunnlaugr gives it to Helga, however, it forms an additional connection between them and functions as a site of emotional expression and material memory. When Helga looks at *Gunnlaugsnaut*, she does not see a *skikkja* made of scarlet and lined with fur, but rather the material remains – an 'echo' – of the man she loves.

Written textiles are a language in their own right. The Old Norse vestimentary code is an essential theoretical framework and critical tool which can be used to investigate their function and meaning. Just as with any language, however, context is vital to our comprehension. Without such contexts it is easy for inaccurate overgeneralisations to persist, such as the incorrect assumption that when a character wears a 'dark cloak' in the sagas, it means that they are about to kill – an assumption which we have seen Straubhaar complicate.[82] Similarly, important work can be achieved with the Old Norse vestimentary code. Old Norse textile terminology is imbued with culturally contingent meanings

---

77 'It is a standard view in the Maussian vein that the spirit of the giver haunts the gift … the gift comes with the giver imbued in it', Miller, 'Is a gift forever?', p. 17.

78 Nordal and Jónsson, *Gunnlaugs saga* 13.

79 Nordal and Jónsson, *Gunnlaugs saga* 13.

80 As argued by Stallybrass and Jones, the clothes of the dead recreate their presence through their absence; Stallybrass, 'Worn worlds', p. 72; Stallybrass and Jones, *Renaissance Clothing*, p. 2.

81 Stallybrass, 'Worn worlds', p. 72.

82 Straubhaar, 'Wrapped in a blue mantle', pp. 64–65.

that, when used in a narrative, act as signifiers for a variety of significations. It enhances our understanding of the social and literary landscape in which the sagas were produced. For example, the nuances in meaning inferred from the textile terminology to describe Guðrún's clothing in *Laxdæla saga* are directly influenced by a thirteenth-century understanding of what it means to be a woman with status, wealth and socially sanctioned power.[83] Through 'Set A' functionality, the Old Norse vestimentary code reveals the association of a *námkyrtil, vefjarupphlutr, sveigr* and a *blæja* with queenship. This illustrates how Guðrún was perceived by a later medieval audience and alerts us, as a modern readership, to certain nuances of characterisation that might otherwise go unacknowledged.

Furthermore, the Old Norse vestimentary code reveals that in *Gísla saga*, neither Gísli nor his servant possesses a 'cloak' in the way that we understand that word in modern English. Gísli wears a *kápa*, while his servant wears a *kufl*. The use of these two terms is deliberate because each possesses its own spectrum of signification that would have been implicitly understood by an early medieval audience. In addition to this spectrum of signification is the fact that there is an inextricable link between clothing and identity which is enabled by the reciprocal relationship between cloth and body, through the process of permeation and transformation. Cloth *becomes* a person, living or dead, and can serve as a physical manifestation of an individual's qualities, existing independently of the original wearer. Therefore, aside from the fact that there is an explicit connection between *kufl*, survival, practical scenarios and disguise, as well as a more nebulous association between *kápa* and a sliding scale of behaviours ranging from status to intention to kill, there are also additional associations that exist on a more personal level. When Gísli and his servant swap cloaks, they also swap their identities in a process of 'metonymic identity transference'.

The material significance of cloth also adds an extra dimension to our understanding of the *Íslendingasögur*. Cloth is both an embodied, material substitution for, and metonymic symbol of, the original wearer/owner. Furthermore, as cloth is the product of society, both economically valuable and representative of the social web of its inception, it can be argued that it functions as a site of duality and tension between the social and the personal, the economic and intimate. In a genre famous for its emotional brevity, literary emotionality can be expressed only according to culturally contingent horizons of feeling, achieved through the use of signposts that are comprised of generically bound 'emotive scripts'. These signposts can be cloaks and other textile items, as they are inscribed with many layers of cultural, economic, social and personal significance. In *Gunnlaugs saga*, garments can be an affective phenomenon and serve as material mnemonic, forming – as well as taking the form of – the wearer, enduring long after their death.

By examining written textiles it is possible to uncover otherwise unacknowledged depth and sophistication from texts which are deceptively realistic and natural – a style which belies their complexity and literariness. Looking at medieval literature does not necessarily further our understanding of Viking Age material practice, but it does enable

---

[83] As opposed to power without social sanction. See Jóhanna Katrín Friðriksdóttir, *Women in Old Norse Literature: Bodies, Words, and Power* (New York, NY: Palgrave Macmillan, 2013).

us to look closer at the social and cultural landscape of its inception. However, I have demonstrated that written representations of material culture are rich with meaning. Written textiles function paratextually to convey myriad culturally contingent significations that shape our understanding of both the literary sources and their later audiences and co-creators. Written textiles even have the potential to uncover that which has so far been difficult to access, namely the internal and emotional landscapes of saga characters. Through tools like the Old Norse vestimentary code it is possible to begin exploring the full social, cultural, economic, haptic and affective importance of early medieval textiles – both written and real – and begin to gain an understanding of just how valuable cloth was to early medieval society, and how important it can be for our understanding of Old Norse literature in the future.

CHAPTER 7

The Medieval Mantles of Hibernia: Functional Markers of Ethnic Identity

Dolores Kearney

Her Majesty giveth allowance for, an Irish mantle, which costeth but five shillings, will be gained to him in the charge, and be his bed in the night, and a great comfort for him in sickness and health; for the mantle being never so wet, will presently with a little shaking and wringing be presently dry; for the want of which the soldiers lying abroad, marching and keeping watch and ward in cold and wet in the winter time, die in the Irish ague and in flix most pitifully. Therefore it were very meet that present consideration were had hereof against the winter, otherwise it is very like, and so it hath fallen out in experience, that the third part of the English soldiers will die lying abroad the first winter [*marginal note:* 'our difficulty in this article is, that by this means the English shall become in apparel barbarous: which hath hitherto been avoided'].[1]

The soldiers as referenced in the above quotation are those who fought in the Nine Years' War, 1596–1603, between what was termed the Gaelic order of lordships and the rule of the Tudors in Ireland. At the start of this war, Sir Henry Wallop, the English Treasurer at War, had petitioned Sir Robert Cecil, Secretary of State, to request money to buy Hibernia (Irish) mantles to protect their soldiers against the weather and the Irish agues (strains of typhus) as evidenced in detail in the quotation. However, the marginal comment greeted the request with a warning that the wearing of this mantle would function as a mechanism to associate the civilised (England) too closely with the primitiveness of the Irish identity. In fact, by 1600, mantles in the Irish style were issued to the army, possibly in response to the war dispatches that reported more soldiers dying of 'poor food, poor lodgings and the raw, wet Irish climate than through any military

---

[1] *Calendar of the State Papers relating to Ireland of the Reign of Elizabeth, 1598–1599*, ed. by Ernest George Atkinson (London: Eyre and Spottiswoode et al., 1895), p. 251.

engagements'.[2] Wallop was not alone in his observations of the underlying science of how the mantle was used to protect health in that 'raw, wet climate'. Fynes Moryson, secretary to the Tudor Lord Deputy in Ireland Charles Blount, eighth Baron Mountjoy, commented on how the rebels used the mantles at night, firstly wetting them thoroughly on the outside and placing the mantles over their naked bodies as they lay down around a fire in a temporary shelter. Their bodies warmed the wet mantles, and the smoke from the fire served to keep their bodies at an even temperature.[3]

The purpose of this chapter is to explore the cloth type used in the manufacture of these full-length wool mantles/*bratt (gaelige)* of Hibernia (Ireland) (seventh–seventeenth century) through a combination of historical documentary sources, archaeological evidence and aspects of experimental archaeological methodologies, accompanied by two case studies. This cloth style was not exclusive to medieval Ireland (see Hayeur Smith, Chapter 3 this volume) but its usage as a mantle and its connection to economic and political purposes served to confer meaning and interpretation upon it and created for it a distinctive role in the dress of early medieval to early modern Ireland.

HIBERNIA MANTLES/BRATTS: MEANING AND INTERPRETATION THROUGH HISTORICAL DOCUMENTARY EVIDENCE

Fragments of pile or shaggy weaves have been recovered from the site of early medieval Viking Dyflin-Dublin, Ireland.[4] These fragmentary finds resemble those of Denmark, Iceland, and the Hebrides. However, the documentary sources of the early medieval period in Ireland reveal a sense of connectedness between the people and that pile/tufted/curly cloth used to manufacture the mantles.

Unique to early Ireland is the extant corpus of literary sources, which range from cycle tales (*scéla*) to hagiographies, genealogies, law tracts, wisdom texts and annals.[5] These documentary sources demonstrate a strict, hierarchical society comprised of communities which were ordered and structured by laws of personhood involving rank and profession. This society had at its core an affinity and a relationship to the natural landscape. The arrival of Christianity (in the fifth century) to Ireland ushered in change, yet this change was embraced and manipulated in a distinctive manner as these hierarchical communities espoused the opportunities of literacy.[6] Having these documentary sources provides

---

2   Mairead Dunlevy, *Dress in Ireland* (London: Batsford, 1989), p. 41.

3   Fynes Moryson, *The Description of Ireland*, trans. by Charles Hughes 1902–03, p. 232; https://celt.ucc.ie/published/T100071.html, accessed 21 July 2022.

4   Patrick F. Wallace, *Viking Dublin: The Wood Quay Excavations* (Kildare: Irish Academic Press, 2016), p. 263.

5   J.P. Mallory, *In Search of Irish Dreamtime* (London: Thames and Hudson, 2016), pp. 19–24.

6   Kathleen Hughes, *Early Christian Ireland: An Introduction to the Sources* (London: Camelot, 1972), pp. 165–190.

a strong yet complex historical base for investigating and studying the past, and part of the complexity of these sources is how the texts have survived. Many are folio-format manuecripts and are not the originals but, rather, recensions made in about the seventh to ninth centuries; many of the seventh- to ninth-century recensions were further copied into other manuscripts in the fourteenth to sixteenth centuries. Consequently, the original contents were subject to variability in linguistics, possible errors in transcription and/or critical analysis editing. Therefore, using the documentary sources comes with a responsibility to read not what is written but, rather, what may be revealed by this written word. Instances relevant to the mantles crisscross these sources; for example, the cycle tales of Ulster feature the mantles in the famous epic of the *Táin*. These stories are dynamic, extensive genres of storytelling combining heroic biographies, legal structures and historical figures, which results in the entanglement of fact with fiction. In the earliest version of the *Táin*, men are described as wearing tunics and mantles called *bratt* in a variety of colours. Conchobor, a king of Ulster in the tale, is described as wearing a purple fringed *bratt* large enough to wind around him five times and fastened in place with a brooch on his chest.[7] However, the *bratt* was not an exclusively male garment, as there is an account in the Ulster tale *The Destruction of Dá Derga's Hostel* in which a young woman called Étaín is described as wearing a purple, curly *bratt*.[8] This description of the *bratt*/mantle as curly references the woven cloth used to make the mantle.

Apart from the tales, further evidence of mantles from the early medieval period (AD 500–1100) comes from a law tract titled *Lebhor na Cert* (*The Book of Rights*),[9] an account of tributes and stipends paid between the elite of early Ireland, where a cornucopia of clothing descriptions includes many colourful, patterned mantles. Recorded in one stipend are *casbrat cetluaitte, ocht mbruit chorcra bus came-ló* (thirty curly purple cloaks and eight purple fleece cloaks).[10] *Lebhor na Cert* has been the subject of critical scholarship which questioned the dating of the tract and argued that it had an underlying agenda of political endorsement for one group of elites in early medieval Ireland.[11] Therefore, probably, descriptions in *Lebhor na Cert* are hyperbolic; exaggerations may have occurred in how the numbers were recorded.

The incursion of the Vikings into Ireland and their settlement in Dublin (mid-ninth to early tenth centuries) produced archaeological evidence of heavy, pile-woven cloth which is further detailed in the next section of the chapter. After the arrival of

---

7   *The Táin*, trans. by Thomas Kinsella (Dublin: Dolmen Press, 1969), p. 158.

8   *The Destruction of Da Derga's Hostel*, trans. by Whitley Stokes (CELT, Corpus of Electronic Texts, University College, Cork, 2011), p. 14; https://celt.ucc.ie/published/T301017A.html, accessed 22 July 2022.

9   *Lebor na Cert*, trans. by Myles Dillon (CELT, Corpus of Electronic Texts, University College, Cork, 2006); https://celt.ucc.ie/published/T102900.html, accessed 22 July 2022.

10 *Lebor na Cert*, pp. 27, 83.

11 Katherine Simms, 'The O Hanlons, the O Neills and the Anglo-Normans in Thirteenth-century Armagh', *Seanchas Ardmhacha, Journal of the Armagh Diocesan Historical Society* 9.1 (1978), 70–94 (pp. 71–72).

the Anglo-Normans into Ireland in the twelfth century, a cleric called Gerald de Barri (Giraldus Cambrensis or Gerald of Wales) wrote an account titled *Topographia Hibernia*, which contains a passage referencing the wearing of mantles where he wrote 'they [native Irish] used woollen rugs instead of cloaks'.[12] The *Annals of Inisfallen*, Co. Kerry, recorded mantles which counted as part of the wealth of the abbey, and were taken from there in the year AD 1180.[13] In another literary genre, a satirical poem, *Aislinge Meic Conglinne* (*The Vision of MacConglinne*), dated to *c*. 1175–1200, there is a description of the wearing of mantles in a style similar to Conchobor, king of Ulster. Here, the reader is introduced to MacConglinne's white mantle with an iron brooch at the front, which is called a cloak but is evidently a very big one. MacConglinne wraps it in folds around his body and, further into the poem, it is described as a five-folded cloak.[14] A variety of these outer garments appears throughout the poem, with a range of descriptions across colours, textures, sizes, and shapes, being variously described as a dun-coloured soft cloak,[15] a cloak with two peaks about the neck[16] and hairy.[17] Although the poem is satirical, the mention of the cloaks is not, describing the functioning and aesthetic characteristics of the garments. At this time (the late twelfth century), the lordship of Ireland was an office granted by papal fief to Henry II of England, who sought to create a central form of governance in Dublin controlled from London, and from there the colonisation of the island was to begin.[18] These events caused the island to develop into a contested space in opposition to the colonial-imposed changes which ranged across social, political, and economic landscapes. English settlers were planted into the mainly eastern, seaboard area of land which became known as The Pale;[19] but towards the late thirteenth century, a propensity was developing for these settlers to adopt Irish customs, language, and dress. These plantations needed to be built on English laws, language, dress, and habits, as opposed to Irish laws, language, dress, and so forth, so to counteract this development, several laws were put in place. Eventually, the Statute of Drogheda (known as Poynings Law, 1494, a political mechanism for parliamentary control) was enacted and quoted as a baseline for fixed political change. It contained a section on clothing which stated, 'the lords of Ireland should appear in the like parliament robes as the English lords are wont to wear in

---

[12] *The historical works, containing The topography of Ireland and The history of the conquest of Ireland*, tr. by Thomas Forrester; *The itinerary through Wales, and The description of Wales*, tr. by Sir Richard Colt Hoare (London: Bell and Sons, 1905), p. 122.

[13] *Annals of Inisfallen*, trans. by Seán MacAirt, p. 313; https://celt.ucc.ie/published/T100004/, accessed 8 August 2022.

[14] *Aislinge Meic Con Glinne*, trans. by Kuno Meyer, based on William M. Hennessy's translation (*c*. 1891), pp. 8, 42; https://celt.ucc.ie/published/T308002.html, accessed 8 August 2022.

[15] *Aislinge Meic Con Glinne*, p. 52.

[16] *Aislinge Meic Con Glinne*, p. 64.

[17] *Aislinge Meic Con Glinne*, p. 90.

[18] Marie Therese Flanagan, 'Hiberno-papal relations in the late twelfth century', *Archivium Hibernicum* 34 (1977), 55–70 (pp. 56–57).

[19] Steven Ellis, 'The English Pale: a failed entity?', *History Ireland* 19 (2011), 14–17 (p. 14).

the parliaments of England'.[20] The language of dress, in this instance, is communicating the intrinsic link of clothing to English laws and national identity. From this criterion, a range of ordinances, reforming articles, and sumptuary legislation were enacted, in efforts to encourage 'a community of apparel'.[21] However, by 1589, William Herbert, a Munster plantation undertaker,[22] wrote of the inability to implement any clothing control in the ethnic population. He reasoned that the legislation in this area held no meaning and offered no benefit or protection. These political efforts to fix, in particular, the mantle as a negative representation of Irishness had evolved to play an impactful role in the contest of places and persons. On one hand, the English desire was to assimilate the Irish place and person; yet, on the other hand, there existed the fear that Irishness could assimilate Englishness. A visual signifier like the mantle, therefore, needed to be set as a visual cue of opposition to Irish national identity.

Several illustrations of the mantles do exist, such as Albrecht Dürer's watercolour of 1521,[23] John Derricke's woodcuts of c. 1581[24] as featured in this chapter, and the sixteenth-century Flemish artist Lucas de Heere's, whose work was entitled, *Irish as They Stand Accoutred (Attired) Being at the Service of the Late King Henry*.[25] This group includes a woman wearing a full-length, tufted mantle. In another de Heere image, a man is depicted wearing a similar mantle with the top part of it covering his head.[26] For the purpose of this chapter, I have chosen to detail three of the twelve woodcuts from John Derrick's *The Image of Irelande, with a discouerie of Woodkarne*. These woodcuts had a major propaganda agenda for colonising, to which the depiction of the mantles contributed. The woodcuts offered illustrations of the mantles worn regardless of gender and position within Irish society. The mantles were used as symbols to indicate a lack of societal structure, resulting therefore, in a lack of adherence to civilised behaviour according to the coloniser. This was simply not the case. Irish medieval society, as stated in the

---

[20] *The Statutes at Large: From the third year of Edward the Second, A.D. 1310, to the eleventh, twelfth and thirteenth years of James the First, A.D. 1612 inclusive* (Dublin: Boulter Grierson, 1761), Chapter XVI, p. 52.

[21] Margaret Rose Jaster, 'Breeding dissoluteness and disobedience: clothing laws as Tudor colonialist discourse', *Critical Survey* 13.3 (2001), 61–77 (p. 62).

[22] One of the wealthy men who undertook to bring English families across to settle in Ireland.

[23] Albrecht Dürer, *Drawing of Irish Soldiers* (Antwerp: 1521); https://commons.wikimedia.org/wiki/File:Durer-Irish-16thC.jpg, accessed 22 July 2022.

[24] John Derrick, *The Image of Irelande, with a Discoverie of Woodcarne* (London: Daie, 1581); http://www.docs.is.ed.ac.uk/docs/lib-archive/bgallery/Gallery/researchcoll/ireland.html, accessed 8 August 2022.

[25] Lucas de Heere, *Irish as they stand accoutred [attired] being at the service of the late King Henry* (Ghent: c. 1575); https://lib.ugent.be/viewer/archive.ugent.be%3A79D46426-CC9D-11E3-B56B-4FBAD43445F2#?cv=83&c=&m=&s=&xywh=-3631%2C0%2C12670%2C7574, accessed 8 August 2022.

[26] Lucas de Heere, *Irish man and Irish woman* (Ghent: c. 1575); https://lib.ugent.be/viewer/archive.ugent.be%3A79D46426-CC9D-11E3-B56B-4FBAD43445F2#?cv=84&c=&m=&s=&xywh=-3631%2C0%2C12670%2C7574, accessed 8 August 2022.

Fig. 7.1 Irish chieftain wearing a calf-length, smooth mantle. *The Image of Irelande*, by John Derrick (London, 1581 Plates); <http://www.docs.is.ed.ac.uk/docs/lib-archive/bgallery/Gallery/researchcoll/pages/bg0053_jpg.htm>.

Fig. 7.2 Group of people wearing shaggy, 'Waterford rugg' mantle. *The Image of Irelande*, by John Derrick (London, 1581 Plates); <http://www.docs.is.ed.ac.uk/docs/lib-archive/bgallery/Gallery/researchcoll/ireland.html>.

opening paragraphs of this section was a hierarchical network of communities connected to each other through literary structures, craft, trade, religion, art and dress.[27]

Fig. 7.1 depicts an Irish chieftain wearing a calf-length mantle. It is loose in structure, with what appears to be a smooth finish on the outside surface and with a raised collar. The artist has captured the 'fur' resemblance in the mantle.

Fig. 7.2 portrays another chieftain seated and, on either side of him, a woman and a cleric, with a second cleric standing behind. The clerics are identifiable by the 'Celtic tonsure', where the front section of the hair is shaved off. They are wearing mantles similar to that worn by the woman. The collars are identical for all three and the surface is shown in the form of the 'Waterford rugg' (see below, p. 133), shaggy in comparison to Fig 7.1, where a smooth surface is depicted.

Fig. 7.3 depicts, in the foreground, a group of kneeling men. The man at the head of the group is Turlough Lynagh O'Neale, titled as The *Uí Néill*. He is kneeling in submission to Sir Henry Sidney, Lord Deputy of Ireland. The *Uí Néill* had the status of lord of Ireland (under Poynings Law) but kingship status under Native Irish codes of kingship. He is dressed here in a mix of Irish and English fashion: his hand holds a flat-crown hat; his

---

[27] Fergus Kelly, *A Guide to Early Irish Law* (Dublin: Dublin Institute for Advanced Studies 2020), pp. 3–4.

Fig. 7.3 Mixed English/Hibernian dress. *The Image of Irelande*, by John Derrick (London, 1581 Plates); <http://www.docs.is.ed.ac.uk/docs/lib-archive/bgallery/Gallery/researchcoll/pages/bg0064_jpg.htm>.

neck is encircled by a ruff collar and around his body is the Hibernia mantle. His men are dressed in jackets with slashed sleeves and, again, around their body each wears a mantle. Fig. 7.3 depicts how the *Uí Néill* and his men visually encapsulated the complex national identity alignments through the 'the community apparel', and the othering of ethnicity through the Hibernia mantles.

Several scholars have written of versions of the mantle or bratt at this time in Ireland. Ada Longfield (1929) used the customs accounts from a variety of English ports as, unfortunately, many of the Irish records were destroyed during the War of Independence (1922). Longfield devotes a chapter to wool and linen exports, where, from the customs accounts, it is clear that a variety of cloth styles were leaving a number of Irish ports in the sixteenth century. A coarse frieze called 'cheks' was listed, and all of these friezes were described as coarse cloth mantles. The port of Bristol in 1504 imported 2,320 of what were recorded as *Hibernia mantles*.[28]

In Susan Flavin's monograph (2014), there are recorded descriptions of Irish frieze, and dyed frieze mantles.[29] However, a decline in the demand for these frieze-style mantles occurred and they were replaced by another variation on a mantle style called the

---

[28] Ada Longfield, *Anglo-Irish Trade in the 16th century* (London: Routledge and Sons, 1929), p. 84.

[29] Susan Flavin, *Consumption and Culture in Sixteenth Century Ireland: Saffron, Stockings and Silk* (Woodbridge: Boydell, 2014), pp. 14, 20.

'Waterford ruggs', noted for the extreme shagginess of the cloth.[30] This corresponds to the 1581 Derricke images, and the shaggy/fur-style texture of the mantles portrayed in his images. With the Nine Years, War of 1596–1603, Ireland continued as a contested space of political power. John Zeigler notes how the mantle, at this time, was described as a heavy garment with a textured surface of curled, shaggy or fur appearance, in contrast to the English mantle/cloak which was usually of a superior cloth and trimmed and lined.[31] Zeigler, like Dunlevy, observes there were probably a range of mantles/cloaks/bratts worn depending on status and wealth in Ireland in the sixteenth century, yet English writers of the period focused on the larger, curled mantle/bratt as depicted across the John Derricke woodcuts and in the eight mantle-clad figures in the side borders on the John Speed map of 1610.[32]

This concentration on the larger mantles is exemplified in the following extract from a political policy pamphlet published in 1633 titled *A View of the Present State of Ireland*, by Edmund Spenser (author of the famous *Faerie Queene* poem).[33] A discussion takes place between *Irenius* (the voice of the colonial administration) and *Eudoxus* (a citizen of England) regarding the origins of the Hibernia mantle and how it is used by the native Irish. I have provided a shortened version below which outlines the reason for this preoccupation:

Irenius: They have another custome from the Scythians, that is the wearing of manteles and longe glebbes, which is a thicke curled bushe of heare [hair] …

Eudoxus: Doe you think that the mantle cometh from the Scythians I would surely thinke otherwyse, for by that which I have redd, it appeareth that most nacons [nations] in the world auntiently used the mantle. …

Irenius: I cannot deny but aunciently it was common to most … But in this latter age of the world, since the decay of the Romaine empyre, it was renued and brought in againe by those Northerne nacons when, breakinge out of their could [cold] caves and frosen [frozen] habitacons into the sweet soyle of Europe, they brought with them their usuall weedes, fitt to sheild their could, and that continuall frost, to which they had bene at home inured … But still removing from place to place, carryed always with them that weede, as their howse, their Bedde, and their garment. And, cominge lastly into Irelande, they found there more special use therof, by reason of the rawe could clymate …

---

[30] Moryson, *The Description of Ireland*, p. 223.

[31] John R. Zeigler, 'Irish mantles, English nationalism: apparel and national identity in early modern English and Irish texts', *Journal for Early Modern Cultural Studies*, 13.1 (2013), 73–95.

[32] Dunlevy, *Dress in Ireland*, p. 79.

[33] Edmund Spenser, *A View of the Present State of Ireland* (A Veue of The Present State of Ireland Discoursed by way of a Dialogue betwene Eudoxus and Irenius); https://celt.ucc.ie/published/E500000–001/, accessed 22 July 2022.

Eudoxus: Since then the necessitie thereof is so comodious, as ye alegde, that it is insteed of howsinge, Bedding and Clothinge, what reason have you then to wishe so necessary a thinge cast of?

Irenius: Because the commoditie dothe not countervayle against the discomoditie, for the inconveniences that thereby doe aryse are much more many: for it is a fitt howse for an outlawe, a meet Bedd for a Rebell, and apte Cloke for a theef. ... When it raineth it is his penthowse, when it bloweth it is his tente; when it freezeth it is his tabernacle. In Sommer he can weare it loose, in winter he can lappe it close. ... Lykewaise for a Rebell it is as serviceable; for in his warre that he maketh, if at least it deserve the name of warre, when he still flyeth from his foe, and lurketh in the thicke woods and straigt passages, wayting for advantages, it is his Bedd, yea, and almost all his houshold stuffd. For the wood is his howse against all wethers [weathers], and his mantle is his cave to sleepe in ... yea, and often tymes their mantle serveth them, when they are nighe driven, being wrapped about their lefte arme insteed of a Target [shield], for it is hard to cut thorough it with a swoord. ... Lastly, for a theef it is so handsome, as it may seeme it was first invented for him; ... when he goeth abroad in the night in free-booting, it is his best and surest frend; ... Besydes all this, he, or any man eles that is dysposed to any mischeef or villainie, may under his mantle goe privyly armed without suspicon of any: carry his headpeece, his skene [dagger], or pistole if he please, to be alwaies in a readines. Thus necessarye and fytting is a mantle for a Badd man. And surely for a badd huswyfe [housewife] it is no lesse convenient, for some of them that be wandring women ... it is half a Wardrobe, for in Somer ye shall fynd her arayed commonly but in her smocke and mantle; to be more ready for the light services: in Wynter, and in her travill, it is her cloake and safeguard for her lewde exercise. And when she hathe fylled her vessill, under it she can hyde bothe her burden, and her blame; yea, and when her bastard is borne it serves insteed of all her wadling cloutes ... Theis be some of the abuses for which I would thinke it meete to forbidd all mantles.

The mantle is vilified in this account whilst still recognised for its practicalities, utilitarian yet considered with a dual perception as a weapon of war and as an asset for tactical warfare. The section on women casts aspersions on the moral character of women who wore the mantle.

Further to the topic of women wearing the Irish mantle, this chapter offers two case studies detailing the mantle/bratt artefacts from historical and archaeological evidence, starting with the historical artefact.

THE MANTLE OF ST BRIGID

The first case study involves a fragment of a cloth object, now housed in the cathedral of St Sauveur, Bruges, Belgium, with the recognised status of a saint's relic in the Roman Catholic Church. It is believed to be a fragment of the mantle of St Brigid. St Brigid is

THE MEDIEVAL MANTLES OF HIBERNIA

one of the three national saints of Ireland; her feast day is celebrated on 1 February.[34] Several debates surround the reality of this saintly figure. The modern consensus is that a composite figure did exist in early Irish hagiography and Cogitosus Uí Aido (a monk of Ireland) wrote her first life, *Vita Brigitae*, in about the seventh century.[35] The theme of this, and the other lives of Brigid, suggests that she represented a local church perspective striving to adopt and adapt to the wider early church practices and politics, and fostered an agenda of a united church in early medieval Ireland. In the seventh century, Ireland witnessed the emergence of the cult of sainthood, which included many female saints.[36] This cult of saints encompassed practices such as rituals, relics, pilgrimages, and the reading of the saint's *vita*/biography on their feast day. The cult of saints, in modern parlance, could be, albeit reductively, compared to the creation of a brand with content and merchandise. As an early Christian saint, Brigid appears to fit into this holy branding with merchandise, as she has an abundance of holy wells, belts, bells, ribbons, crosses made of rushes and pieces of her supposed mantle known as Brat Bhride (*gaelige*) which translates into English as 'the mantle of Brigid'. It is this Brat Bhride that in folkloric practice[37] is a piece of cloth, traditionally placed outside a house on Brigid's Eve (31 January). It was, and still is, taken in before sunrise, with the belief that this piece of cloth, the Brat Bhride, had taken on healing powers associated with the saint. The cult of St Brigid was well established by the eleventh century, and the saint enjoyed a far-reaching esteem across Scotland, England, Wales, Brittany, Italy, and further north in Norway, Sweden and Denmark.

Technical Analysis 1866[38]

In 1866, a record was made of the examination of St Brigid's mantle in Bruges that was carried out for its authentication as a modern relic in the Roman Catholic Church. When the exhibit case was opened, what was thought to be the mantle was, in fact, found to be a small covering cape of yellow silk crisscrossed with gold thread and edged with gold lace. The material used in the cape dated in style to the fifteenth century.[39] Inside this fifteenth-century covering was the fragment of the supposed wool mantle of the saint.

---

[34] Sean O'Riordan, 'The cult of St Brigid', *The Furrow* 2.2 (1951), 88–93.

[35] Sean Connolly and J.M. Picard, 'Cogitosus's "Life of St Brigit" content and value', *The Journal of the Royal Society of Antiquaries of Ireland* 117 (1987), 5–27.

[36] O'Riordain, 'The cult of St Brigid'.

[37] 'Feast of St Brigid', National Folklore Collection University College Dublin; https://www.duchas.ie/en/tpc/cbes/5285239, accessed 22 July 2022.

[38] H.F. McClintock, 'The "Mantle of St Brigid" at Bruges', *The Journal of the Royal Society of Antiquaries of Ireland* 7th series, 6.1 (1936), 32–40.

[39] McClintock, 'The "Mantle of St Brigid" at Bruges', p. 33.

Table 7.1   Technical details of St Brigid's mantle, materials and construction, observed in 1866.

Fibre: Wool.

Weave: Recorded as a type of shaggy cloth.

Colour: None recorded, but a linen lining was listed as blue and green.

Condition: No comments recorded regarding condition of the 'shaggy cloth', but repairs had been made to the linen lining.

Dimensions: 533 mm x 635 mm recorded.

Twist or spin direction: No comments recorded.

Yarn diameter: No comments recorded.

Selvedges: No comments recorded.

Dye: Blue and green for the linen dye, but no comments recorded for colour of shaggy wool cloth.

Sewing: No comments recorded.

Compiled by Dolores Kearney.

After this examination, the silk cape was not reinstated. Unfortunately, there is no further recorded information on the cape, and it is presumed missing. The wool relic was then placed in a glazed exhibit case and accorded the status of an official relic of the Roman Catholic Church. The examination was only one part of the relic's authentication, as there was also documentary evidence of provenance. The written evidence for this fragment listed it as part of the property of the cathedral of St Donaas in AD 1847.[40] It was purportedly recorded as a gift presented to the cathedral by a historical figure, Princess Gunnhild, a sister of King Harold II of England, who was killed at the Battle of Hastings in 1066. After her brother's death, Gunnhild fled to Flanders and died there in 1087. When a young woman, she had taken a vow of chastity, to which she remained true throughout her life. In 1786 a small engraving was discovered at St Donaas which noted the lineage of Gunnhild, her piety, and her death at Bruges.[41] She may have received the relic from her brothers, after the events of 1051, when Gunnhild's father, Earl Godwine, was exiled from England to Flanders following a quarrel with his son-in-law, Edward the Confessor (who was married to Edith, Gunnhild's sister). At this time Harold and another brother, Leofwine, had travelled to Ireland to seek help for their exiled father from Diarmait Mac Máel na Mbó, king of the Uí Cheinselaig, who held power in the south-eastern region of the province of Leinster, Ireland. There is no secure, direct evidence to connect the brothers with receiving the relic in Ireland, but, as previously mentioned, the cult of St Brigid was well known by the eleventh century. Harold was a pious man, and the brothers might have received the relic in Ireland and passed it to their sister after the family was reunited,

---

[40]   McClintock, 'The "Mantle of St Brigid" at Bruges', p. 33.

[41]   Frank Barlow, *The Godwins: The Rise and Fall of a Noble Dynasty* (London and New York: Routledge, 2002), p. 167.

which occurred in 1052. There is nothing directly to connect the fragmentary relic to the saint herself or to Gunnhild. The cathedral of St Donaas was destroyed in the eighteenth century, but the relic was rescued and transferred to St Sauver. No record was discovered explaining why a fifteenth-century cape of silk was placed over the mantle.

Technical Analysis 1935

In 1935, a request to examine the mantle was made by a Major Henry Foster McClintock. McClintock was a Fellow of the Royal Society of Antiquaries of Ireland, and in 1936 he presented his study on 'The Mantle of St Brigid at Bruges' to the Society.[42] McClintock's aim, in his examination and analysis of the mantle, was to create an understanding of the properties of the cloth fragment and its origins. He conducted the examination in the company of a textile expert, Marguerite Calberg from the Department of Textiles, Royal Museum, Brussels. At the start of the technical analysis, they offered this hypothesis:

> Brigid's cloak seems to be simply a plain bit of woolen stuff, the outside of which is covered with curled tufts of wool made by one of the two threads of the groundwork. The question is whether these thick threads are those of the warp or of the weft.[43]

Their technical analysis is presented in Table 7.2.

Table 7.2   Technical details of St Brigid's mantle, materials and construction, observed in 1935.

Fibre: Wool. Although microscopic work was conducted on samples of the wool fibre it returned inconclusive results.

Weave: Plain weave–tabby weave. 'This woollen fabric is characterised by a thick curly fleece which entirely covers its outer surface'. Calberg records the reverse as 'perfectly smooth'. Both the warp (vertical) and weft (horizontal) threads were spaced at four threads per cm and on the outer surface she recorded a difference between threads as 'one being relatively fine and the other made of thick yarn with hardly any twist'. She records that the tufts or curls are not knotted comparable to carpet design; rather, the tufts or curls were interlocked in a 'free and varied' fashion into the ground weave and are of different lengths across the entire surface.[44]

Colour: Visual analysis conducted. Deep violet colour with red silk/taffeta lining oversewn (to strengthen seam), possibly added after the 1866 analysis as part of the repairs, although no record was found. The green and blue linen lining which was reported in 1866 was not visible and, again, no written record survived of its whereabouts.

Condition: The 'perfectly smooth' reverse surface had darning repairs in some places and evidence existed for the re-insertion of 'curls' into the cloth. No record of these repairs was discovered.

[42]   McClintock, 'The "Mantle of St Brigid" at Bruges', p. 32.

[43]   McClintock, 'The "Mantle of St Brigid" at Bruges', p. 35.

[44]   McClintock, 'The "Mantle of St Brigid" at Bruges'.

Dimensions: 545 mm in width and 640 mm in length. The 1866 examination recorded the measurements as 533 mm x 635 mm.

Twist or spin direction: No comment made on the fibre spin.

Yarn diameter: No comment made concerning the yarn diameter.

Selvedges: No selvedges on the fragment, therefore the warp and weft threads were indistinguishable and therefore the width of the loom was also indistinguishable

Dye: Analysis carried out at the Laboratories of the Royal Museums of Art and History at Brussels. Iron oxide was detected. Iron oxide is used as a pigment, as a colour-changing agent to create shades and hues and as a mordant to assist in colourfastness.

Sewing: No sewing detected on the wool, only on the silk/taffeta lining.

Compiled by Dolores Kearney.

After her analysis, and in discussion with McClintock, Calberg agreed that the weave technique differed from their original assessment of 'a plain bit of woolen stuff' (worsted cloth/frieze). They began to explore evidence for a second hypothesis and McClintock decided to adopt an anthropological approach based on the indigenous contemporary textile skills of Hungarian farmers.[45] These farmers used a technique that produced a style of shaggy coat on small hand looms. This technique involved weaving a cloth in plain weave for four rows of weft, with bundles of unspun fleece yarn inserted in groups of four into the open weave shed, after which the shed was closed. The inserted bundles overlapped each other and the result resembled an unbroken line of curly weft threads. When taken from the loom, the pieces were soaked in water to tighten the cloth, thus making the inserted bundles look almost identical to the ground warp and weft threads, except for some curls of the fleece which hung down. McClintock had purchased a piece of this Hungarian cloth and had taken it apart to investigate the farmers' technique and compare it to the relic. Calberg, as the textile expert, concluded that the relic and the Hungarian cloth were woven in a similar manner but, interestingly, she proposed that perhaps no weft thread was used in the relic. What were originally identified as weft threads she thought might be the lower parts of the curled tufts woven in plain weave. McClintock quoted the 'fixated writers of the 16th century' and their words on the shaggy mantle and the exports of 'Waterford rugg' as evidence for the cloth/mantle weaving technique existing in late medieval and early modern Ireland. He also wrote that evidence for the existence of this technique in the early medieval period was scant; however, he indicated that future archaeological discoveries might reveal evidence of this technique or pile weaving prior to the Viking settlements.[46] That is exactly what occurred in 2005 in the midlands of Ireland, as is outlined in the second case study.

---

45   McClintock, 'The "Mantle of St Brigid" at Bruges', p. 36.

46   McClintock, 'The "Mantle of St Brigid" at Bruges', pp. 38–39.

THE MEDIEVAL MANTLES OF HIBERNIA

Contested Production Techniques of 'the Holy Mantle'

After publication in 1936, the McClintock and Calberg analysis was challenged by Anthony Lucas (director of the National Museum of Ireland 1954–76).[47] Lucas asserted that this relic was indeed a piece of plain stuff, but it was a napped cloth or a frieze cloth with its surfaces raised by steel combs or teasels (*dipsacus fullonum* or, in Irish, *leadán úcaire*), thus creating a surface of small curls.[48] This was the original hypothesis of McClintock and Calberg, subsequently dismissed after full analysis. Lucas, as far as I am aware, did not examine the relic and he based his argument on how cloths were finished using techniques recorded from Irish traditional craft in oral and written history.

He highlighted the finishing cloth work of Martin Lally, a weaver in Galway in the 1950s (Lally was born in the 1880s and had learnt the trade from his father and grandfather, both weavers). Lally used carders to agitate the wool fibres of the woven cloth, tearing them and thus causing them to stand up on the surface of the cloth. He then used honey or golden syrup (a light treacle) to curl these fibres, in conjunction with a sheet of cork.[49] Certainly, the method raises small curls, and Lucas contended 'that the curly cloaks mentioned in the native literature and the shag mantles of the later English commentators were woven, napped and curled in the same way'.[50] He asserted that all of the Hibernian mantles were produced using the carding technique. Lucas appeared to disregard or confuse the evidence from archaeology and history for pile weaving and his focus was entirely on how the cloth was finished. Certainly, all cloth undergoes some finishing processes after it is taken from the loom; but the analysis of the relic by Calberg and McClintock was aligned with pile weaving after their physical examination of the relic, and, as earlier mentioned, the archaeology of the twentieth and twenty-first centuries has supported that analysis and interpretation.

HIBERNIA MANTLES/BRATTS: MEANING AND INTERPRETATION THROUGH ARCHAEOLOGICAL EVIDENCE

As stated already, several fragments of pile weaves or shaggy weaves were discovered at the site of early medieval Viking Dyflin/Dublin.[51] From the mid-ninth century, through the tenth century, the settlement was a mixture of cultural narratives and this is reflected in the material culture.[52] These changes are known as Hiberno-Scandinavian/Norse, a mixing of native and Viking cultures. From the mid-eleventh century, the Hibernian

---

[47] Anthony T. Lucas, 'Cloth finishing in Ireland', *Folk Life* 6.1 (1968), 18–67.

[48] Lucas, 'Cloth finishing', p. 24.

[49] Lucas, 'Cloth finishing', p. 54.

[50] Lucas, 'Cloth finishing', p. 61.

[51] Wallace, *Viking Dublin: The Wood Quay Excavations*, p. 263.

[52] Wallace, *Viking Dublin: The Wood Quay Excavations*, p. 16.

element was in the ascendancy, yet the influences of the Norse did still impact across a range of civic, art, dress and economic practices in the town.[53]

The excavations at the Wood Quay site (a focal point for Viking Dublin) were undertaken from the early 1970s to the early 1980s by the National Museum of Ireland. The site's vast amount of textile evidence was due to the anoxic/anaerobic conditions found at quay-side settlements. The organic materials were sealed into a wet/damp and oxygen deficient environment which prevented decomposition.[54] Frances Pritchard's contribution in Patrick F. Wallace, *Viking Dublin: The Wood Quay Excavations* was in the analysis of several types of heavy weaves, where she proposed that certain tabby-woven, heavy textile fragments were the remains of mantles. She also commented on fragments of a heavy 2/2 twill with warp and weft threads of contrasting colour, spin and thickness with traces of a long, shaggy s-spun pile weave woven into the cloth after every four weft throw/lines of weave.[55] She linked this style of pile weaving to the techniques of south-west Iceland. In medieval Greenland and Iceland, pile-woven cloth used to manufacture mantles acquired the name *Roggvarafeldir*, translated as a 'trade cloak', which would imply a garment constructed for economic gain, an instance of how functionality can gain an additional layer of value.[56] The Icelandic legal text *Grágás*, 'the Gray Goose Laws' (tenth to thirteenth century) contained the standardisation expected of these trade cloaks: 'two ounce-units [monetary value], four thumb-ells [a measurement of length from elbow down to the middle finger], thirteen tufts across the piece [the insertion of the fleece tufts across the lines of weave]'.[57] This production method of adding tufts across the cloth during the weaving process would have added an insulating layer to the cloth. After weaving, these shaggy weft locks of fleece hang downwards on the cloth in the style of fur.[58] Apart from having a fur resemblance, the design and production technique of a pile-weave wool mantle has properties that can be manipulated in response to the environmental conditions, corresponding to Fynes Moryson's observation, 'being never so wet, [the mantles] will presently with a little shaking and wringing be presently dry'.[59]

---

53 Dunlevy, *Dress in Ireland*, p. 27.

54 Wallace, *Viking Dublin: The Wood Quay Excavations*, p. 19.

55 Wallace, *Viking Dublin: The Wood Quay Excavations*, p. 263.

56 Michèle Hayeur Smith, 'Weaving wealth: cloth and trade in Viking Age and medieval Iceland', in *Textiles and the Medieval Economy: Production, Trade, and Consumption of Textiles, 8th–16th Centuries*, ed. by Angela Ling Huang and Carsten Jahnke (Oxford: Oxbow, 2019), pp. 23–40 (p. 23).

57 Hayeur Smith, 'Weaving wealth', p. 23.

58 Nille Viking, 'Experimental archaeology/pile weaving', 2022; https://nilleviking.no/experimental-archaeology/pile-weaving/, accessed 22 July 2022.

59 Atkinson, *Calendar of the State Papers ... 1598–1599*, p. 251.

THE MEDIEVAL MANTLES OF HIBERNIA

THE CLOONSHANNAGH MANTLE

In May 2005, during a turf-cutting operation in a bog situated in the Irish midlands, a bog skeleton with cloth attached was discovered. The skeleton was disturbed by the cutting machinery and the associated clothing was rendered fragmentary. The police were informed, and staff of the National Museum of Ireland (NMI) travelled to the site to commence a recovery exercise. It took three days and was a difficult task due to inclement weather conditions. The initial focus was on the human remains, which were examined on site by an osteoarchaeologist and tentatively identified as those of a young woman, possibly in her early twenties. Elizabeth Wincott Heckett later analysed over 130 pieces of cloth from the burial which included twill and plain-woven cloth.[60] For the purpose of this case study and relevance to the chapter, the largest collection of fragments is presented in Table 7.3.

Table 7.3   Technical details of the Cloonshannagh mantle, materials and construction, presented by Elizabeth Wincott Heckett in 2011.

Fragments: Recovered from Boney Bog, Cloonshannagh, Co. Roscommon, Ireland (2005). Forty-seven fragments.

Fibre: Wool.

Weave: 2 x 1 twill weave decorated with extra thick pile/tassels placed at regular intervals into the weave and identified as a pile-weaving technique. When reversed this cloth was discovered to have still attached a 2 x 2 twill material (lining as it was attached to rib bones).

Colour: Brown.

Condition: Fragmentary.

Dimensions: Approx. one metre in width from the existing fragments and two-thirds of a metre in depth. Too fragmentary to be precise on the original shape.

Weave: z/z spun yarn.

Pile: S twist and s-spun yarn c. 50–70 mm.

Yarn diameter: None recorded.

Folds: Several folds were detected, indicating gathering of the material possibly around the body of the wearer.

Selvedges: One fragment had a strengthened length. Unmeasured.

Piles: Described as extra-thick pile threads or tassels. Various widths detected in the tassels.

Dye: Not analysed for colour.

Sewing: Small hem with some stitching.

Compiled by Dolores Kearney.

---

[60] Elizabeth Wincott Heckett, 'The Lady of Cloonshannagh: An Irish 7th century bog body and the related textiles', in *NESAT XI: The North European Symposium for Archaeological Textiles. 10–13 May 2011 in Esslingen am Neckar*, ed. by Johanna Banck-Burgess and Carla Nubold (Eahden/Westf: VML Verlag Marie Leidorf, 2013), pp. 167–172 (167).

Based on the type and quality of all the textile fragments recovered, an initial date of the seventeenth century was put forward. However, radiocarbon dating of fragments of the pile-woven cloth that had remained attached to both legs, the metatarsal bones, and the rib cage, produced a result of the seventh century.[61] In her interpretation, Wincott Heckett suggested that the young woman from Cloonshannagh was of high status, indicated by this unique variety and type of woven clothing found with her consisting, perhaps, of her bratt/mantle, two *leíne* (tunics), a belt and head covering.[62] The wearing of a mantle might indicate that she died during winter. The clothes indicate that the death was not natural but accidental or foul play, as burials in early medieval Ireland tended to be unfurnished.[63] Also widespread, and intrinsic to Christianity, was the new societal model of an early Church landscape of monasteries and nunneries. Cloonshannagh bog, where the young woman was found, is associated with the monastery and church of St Berach, founded in the sixth century.[64] St Berach had a sister, St Midabaria,[65] who was abbess of a nunnery at the edge of the Cloonshannagh. It is not clear if she was a familial sister of Berach or a sister in religion. St Berach is recorded in the *Martyrology of Donegal*, a calendar of saints, and he is described as a person linked to water and the presence of holy wells. Data from bog surveys recorded dry conditions at Cloonshannagh in the fifth century, followed by exceptionally wet conditions in the sixth century.[66] Possibly these conditions persisted on the bog into the seventh century and the woman suffered a fatal incident as a result. Perhaps the young woman was travelling to the monastery, the church, or the nunnery. Alternatively, she may have been traversing the bog for secular reasons: the hierarchical community of *tuatha* (petty kingdoms)[67] in Ireland is noticeable for its collective architecture of enclosed, circular living settlements. The bog at Cloonshannagh has a large number of these spaces, traditionally called raths or ringforts.

These are speculative comments based partially on landscape archaeology, and on historical sources which did feature, in the cycle tales, a young woman called Étaín who was recorded as wearing a curly mantle (see above, p. 128). Here, archaeology has

---

[61] Wincott Heckett, 'The Lady of Cloonshannagh', p. 168. I can offer no details on average date and the calibrated age intervals.

[62] Wincott Heckett, 'The Lady of Cloonshannagh', p. 168.

[63] Aidan O'Sullivan, Finbar McCormick, Thomas R. Kerr, and Lorcan Harney, *Early Medieval Ireland, AD 400–1100: The Evidence from Archaeological Excavations* (Dublin: Royal Irish Academy, 2021), p. 286.

[64] *Bethada Náem n Érenn: Lives of Irish Saints*, II, ed. by Charles Plummer (Oxford: Clarendon, 1922), pp. 38–40.

[65] Plummer, *Bethada Náem n Érenn*, II, p. 393.

[66] Philip Stastney,'Examining the Relationships between Holocene Climate Change, Hydrology and Human Society in Ireland', Ph.D. thesis (University of Reading, 2014); https://www.researchgate.net/profile/Philip-Stastney/publication/304142116_Examining_the_relationships_between_Holocene_climate_change_hydrology_and_human_society_in_Ireland/links/5767db9f08ae1658e2f89808/Examining-the-relationships-between-Holocene-climate-change-hydrology-and-human-society-in-Ireland.pdf, accessed 22 July 2022.

[67] Kelly, *A Guide to Early Irish Law*, p. 3.

provided the material evidence of a young woman at some time in the seventh century wearing a similar curly mantle/bratt. It also adds credence to the existence of pile-woven style mantles worn in early medieval Ireland as hypothesised by Calberg and McClintock in 1936 (above, p. 137).

HIBERNIA MANTLES/BRATTS: MEANING AND INTERPRETATION THROUGH EXPERIMENTAL ARCHAEOLOGICAL EVIDENCE

Experimental archaeology is a methodology of reconstructing, to test, record and repeat experiments underpinned by archaeological evidence and historical sources. In research for my MSc thesis in experimental archaeology, I wanted to test the waterproof and windproof efficacy of a Hibernian mantle produced in the same style as the mantle of St Brigid.[68] I produced five samples for testing, all woven to the dimensions of the relic, using spun wool and unspun wool from Soay sheep. I used a plain weave for four lines, and on the fifth line I wove in through the warp threads under and over the threads, and then inserted, tassels of unspun wool; I then repeated the action of weaving with the weft thread across four warp threads and again inserted the tassels. In hindsight, I regret not following the interesting theory of Marguerite Calberg of using no weft thread (above p. 138) to produce the samples. When I had all the samples woven and taken off the loom, I followed a description by Thomas Dineley, an English traveller in Ireland (1681): 'the manner of tucking and thickening cloth, without a mill, is thus, they place the cloth double upon a large wicker or twiggen door, called here a hurle, and work it with their hands and feet'.[69]

Archaeological evidence from the early medieval houses at Deer Park Farms, Co. Antrim, supports the use of woven wickerwork in house construction, external and internal,[70] and this style of door continued to be used into the nineteenth century in isolated areas of the west and north coasts of Ireland. My wicker door, which I made, was more hurdle than door, but it did provide me with a strong, firm base from which I worked on finishing off the samples. They were placed on the hurdle, covered in boiling water, 100°C. I waited for it to cool down to 50/55100°C and began to apply constant pressure with hands and feet. I and another person worked on this process over several hours, keeping the samples warm, moist and under pressure. The aim was to consolidate the structure of the samples, thus strengthening and thickening the cloth. I can offer no exact scientific measurements for this process, as it involved a multiplicity of variables.

---

[68] Dolores Kearney, 'The Irish Medieval Shaggy Mantle: Testing Its Functionality and Investigating Its Contexts', Unpublished M.Sc. thesis (University College Dublin, 2017).

[69] Lucas, 'Cloth finishing in Ireland', p. 29.

[70] Chris. J. Lynn and Jacqueline McDowell, *Deer Park Farms: The Excavation of a Raised Rath in the Glenarm Valley, Co. Antrim* (Norwich: Stationery Office, Belfast: Northern Ireland Environment Agency, 2011), p. 145.

From my observations, as I worked the samples with the water I was aware that it did not adversely affect the tassels of wool hanging down from the weave. The tassels underwent a slight felting process like the results of the Hungarian farmers described by McClintock. This resulted in securing the tassels firmly into the weave, but the tassels were not fully felted and could still be manipulated by fanning them out widthwise, where they resembled a fur surface as noted by Dunlevy and Zeigler (above, p. 133) and illustrated in the Derricke woodcuts.

CONCLUSIONS

Clothing reflects life; it has function, aestheticism, is a form of communication and a chronicle of revelatory nuances. Clothing can be used to display status and wealth, and it can be manipulated to stress differences, between genders and ethnicities, positively and negatively.

Documentary sources record the wearing of mantles by both sexes in medieval Ireland. Described as purple, curly, tufted and fringed, the mantle functioned as a warm, protective garment, but it was also visualised as a weapon of war and as a component of 'othering' in colonialism.[71] Several cloth types are attested in the manufacture of mantles in the documentary sources, but the archaeology has revealed pile-woven, shaggy, curled and tufted mantles/bratts. The archaeology of Viking Dublin has revealed the use of pile-woven cloths, and the second case study provides material evidence for the wearing of these mantles in earlier medieval Ireland. The methodologies of experimental archaeology did and can still afford the opportunities to test hypotheses regarding the processes of this cloth production relevant to the Hibernia mantles in all their splendour, a type of mantle worn, in reality, by a young, seventh-century woman and, as attested by a surviving fragment, a mantle fit for a saint.

[71] Zeigler, 'Irish mantles, English nationalism', p. 77.

PART II

Understanding through Replicating

CHAPTER 8

Making the Best of It: Planning Decisions for Reproduction Fabrics

Ruth Gilbert

What seems like half a lifetime ago, a short paper presented at the Early Textiles Study Group conference on the subject of making replicas of historical fabrics was subsequently published in *Archaeological Textiles Newsletter* 40.[1] This chapter is based on the flow diagram of decision making produced for that article, and although much has been learned since then, the basic questions remain the same. These are: why – the purpose of the reconstruction; what – can one establish enough about the source material and are adequate materials and techniques available to produce a reasonable reconstruction; and how – is the method important or can modern tools be used? An additional question that now seems important is 'who is doing the work?' because the level of skill and experience will affect the outcome. These questions will be reviewed first, and then, in order to examine all of the choices made and the reasoning behind them a specific job, the re-creation of a piece of tenth-century woollen cloth from York, will be discussed with reference to the *châine opératoire* for cloth production.

WHY ARE YOU DOING THIS?

The first and most important question is why the work is being undertaken. There are many reasons for reproducing textile artefacts and the concern of this chapter is with the finished product rather than the process. Experimental archaeology has long been a part of the study of textiles and there has been much good work done on the use of

---

[1] Ruth Gilbert, 'Decisions taken in planning a replica artefact', *Archaeological Textiles Newsletter* 40 (2005), 18–19. The present chapter was written before the publication of Anna Nøgård's excellent article, 'Reconstructions revived: a handweaver's personal perspective', *Archaeological Textiles Review* 63 (2021), 90–100. Nøgård draws on her experience of recreating early Bronze Age and early Iron Age textiles from Scandinavia, and of Viking Age sails.

specific tools and the working methods of the past.[2] Replicas for wear and display appear to have taken longer to become established, although improved understanding among museums and costumed interpreters that modern cloth does not adequately demonstrate the properties of pre-industrial fabrics has produced a small but increasing demand for evidence-based reconstructions that do not necessarily have to be produced in a historically accurate way.

It would appear that the work done by Elizabeth Peacock between 1949 and 1951 for the 'People of Britain' display at the Festival of Britain was the first such project, even though Britain lagged behind the Scandinavian countries in the recording and analysis of archaeological textiles. Five groups of figures were made under the guidance of Jacquetta Hawkes, designed to show people from the Stone Age to the Saxons, and suitable cloth was needed for three of these – the Stone Age groups (Mesolithic and Neolithic) being dressed in skins.[3]

The weaving workshop at the research centre at Lejre in Denmark, which produces both specific replicas and cloth for clothing those peopling the site, dates from 1965.[4] Else Østergård says of the garments from Norse settlements in Greenland, 'for the exhibition at Brede ['Clothes Make the Man' in 1971] reconstructions were made',[5] but these were made from commercial cloth.[6] More recently the National Museum in Copenhagen, where the medieval Greenland finds are kept, has had two sets of replica garments made for display, one set for themselves and one for the Greenland National Museum in Nuuk. These 'were made of hand spun Greenlandic wool, the fabric woven on an upright loom, and the garments were hand sewn', which is now the Scandinavian norm but depends both on the existence of skilled craftsmen and the willingness to spend money.[7] Funding may be helped by the understanding that the reproduction of fabrics for display can double as research and publicity: work on the dress from the Hammerum burial in Denmark went further than most, involving fashion students and members of the public

---

[2] Contents listings for *Archaeological Textiles Review* and its predecessor, *Archaeological Textiles Newsletter*, can be found at http://atnfriends.com. A list of published proceedings of the North European Symposium on Archaeological Textiles can be found at http://www.nesat.org/main/history_en.html, both accessed 18 March 2022.

[3] https://www.vads.ac.uk/digital/collection/DCA/id/7420, accessed 18 March 2022, shows the Iron Age group. These are credited as 'South Bank Exhibition. The People of Britain: Designer: James Gardner O.B.E., R.D.I. Family Groups by Phyllis Richards'.

[4] Ida Demant, 'Making a replica of textile 1 – the dress', in Tinna Møbjerg et al., *The Hammerum Burial Site: Customs and Clothing in the Roman Iron Age* (Højbjerg: Jutland Archaeological Society/Museum Midtjylland, 2019), 167–185, p. 167; [Museum handbook], *Lejre Forsøgscenter: Forsøg med Fortiden 5* (Lejre: Historisk Arkæologisk Forsøgscenter 1998), p. 26.

[5] Brede is the location of the open-air section and store of the National Museum of Denmark, north of Copenhagen.

[6] Else Østergård, *Woven Into the Earth: Textiles from Norse Greenland* (Aarhus: Aarhus University Press, 2004), pp. 28–29.

[7] Information from Jette Arneborg, National Museum in Copenhagen. The word 'craftsman' is used as gender neutral, the suffix being of Saxon origin and not implying maleness.

in study days as well as producing an exhibition at the Midtjylland Museum in Herning and a smartphone app to encourage investigation of historical sites.[8]

WHAT ARE YOU MAKING?

A 'reconstruction' or 'replica' presumes the existence of an original, which ideally should be examined, but this is often impractical. Fortunately, the standard of publication of textile finds is now generally high, and a great deal of information may be available. However good the information, what is made is always an interpretation of the evidence, and developments in research techniques may produce revisions, as demonstrated by the most recent reproduction of the man's clothing from Bjerringhøj in Denmark.[9] The new outfit is strikingly different from the previous interpretation, showing changes in assumptions as well as new information.

It is possible to produce entirely hypothetical reconstructions, but modern museum practice requires that this is understood by both the makers and those responsible for offering the result to the public. It is necessary to make clear what is known, what has been deduced and how, and also to be honest, explaining where compromises have been made and what is hypothetical. The conjectural nature may reflect experimental work carried out, particularly where clothing will be worn, as in re-enactment, but it must be borne in mind that it can be seen as factual and may also be reported as such by the press.

The cloths and garments for the Festival of Britain figures were based largely on published work by Margrethe Hald, at the time available only in Danish but with many illustrations and English translations of the picture captions. Audrey Henshall may have contributed information on British archaeological textiles and, while the source for the Saxon garments is as yet unidentified, much of this can probably be attributed to Grace M. Crowfoot, who reported on pre-war excavated textiles, including the Sutton Hoo ship burial.[10]

When Tamworth Castle displayed items from the Staffordshire Hoard, an entire outfit for King Offa of Mercia was commissioned from Sarah Thursfield in the spring of 2011. As nothing survives to indicate how King Offa should be dressed, the choice of fabrics was based on an understanding of the range of likely textiles such a person would have worn. The linen shirt fabric, woollen leg-windings and decorative tablet-woven bands for the cloak were hand woven because suitable cloths are not available commercially. A replica of the birdhead-shaped brooch from the hoard was used to fasten the cloak. The

---

[8] Tinna Møbjerg, 'The Hammerum Girl in the public space', in Møbjerg et al., *The Hammerum Burial Site*, pp. 187–202.

[9] New version: https://www.khm.uio.no/english/visit-us/historical-museum/exhibitions/ fashioning-the-viking-age/index.html. Previous interpretation: https://en.natmus.dk/histori cal-knowledge/denmark/prehistoric-period-until-1050-ad/the-viking-age/the-people/ clothes-and-jewellery/, both accessed 18 March 2022.

[10] Research ongoing into sources. Grace M. Crowfoot certainly knew Ethel Mairet, in whose workshop Elizabeth Peacock had trained (personal comment, Hero Granger-Taylor).

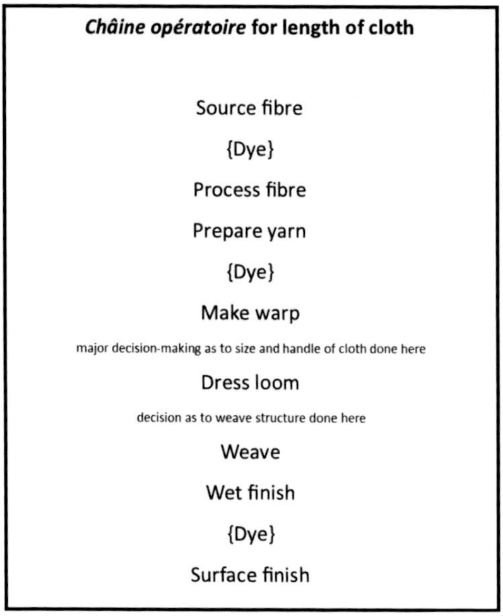

Château opératoire for length of cloth
Source fibre
{Dye}
Process fibre
Prepare yarn
{Dye}
Make warp
major decision-making as to size and handle of cloth done here
Dress loom
decision as to weave structure done here
Weave
Wet finish
{Dye}
Surface finish

Fig. 8.1 A brief diagram showing the *châine opératoire* for length of cloth. © Ruth Gilbert.

breeches and cloak were made from commercial wool cloths. The clothes were worn by a costumed interpreter, a volunteer who 'is' King Offa and interacts with the public. While the garments would not be handled or examined closely by the public, they had to give an impression of the possible appearance of a high-status man who could have owned the kind of items in the hoard that were on display at the castle.

For this outfit, it was planned to make a spin-patterned shirt cloth, with s- and z-spun yarn, but it was impossible to buy s-spun linen, so a broken-lozenge twill based on a cloth from the Sutton Hoo ship burial was chosen as the basis for the reconstruction instead.[11] This original is not identifiable as clothing fabric and probably dates from the first quarter of the seventh century, whereas Offa reigned from 757 to 796, but the patterned linen made it distinctive, not something one could buy at John Lewis.

There are three choices for strips of fabric for leg windings: cut/torn and not hemmed, cut and hemmed, or woven to the correct width with selvedges. The latter is the most suitable alternative for a high-status outfit. The cloth is based on fragments of wool twill which showed traces of lichen purple dye (1306) excavated at 16–22 Coppergate, York[12] that Penelope Walton Rogers suggests 'may well be' leg windings.[13]

---

[11] Elisabeth Crowfoot, 'The textiles', in Rupert L.S. Bruce-Mitford, *The Sutton Hoo Ship Burial* 3, ed. by Angela Care Evans (London: British Museum, 1983) pp. 409–479 (pp. 422–424, SH12 and Fig. 300).

[12] Penelope Walton, *Textiles, Cordage and Raw Fibre from 16–22 Coppergate*, The Archaeology of York The Small Finds 17/5 (York: Council for British Archaeology, 1989), pp. 324–325.

[13] Walton, *Textiles, Cordage*, p. 340.

HOW ARE YOU GOING TO DO IT?

Having decided what is to be made and for what purpose, the next question is how to go about this. The essential *châine opératoire* for a piece of woollen cloth is the same, whatever the detail of the tools and technology, and a brief version is shown in Fig. 8.1. If the published description of the source material is adequate the difficulties arise from external constraints such as the availability of suitable materials and skill as well as time and cost. The decision to commission hand-woven fabric is in itself not to be taken lightly, because the cost is always high. Compromise is inevitable in most situations, however accurate the observation or the published description of the source material, and what is considered here is the extent to which a satisfactory result can be achieved.

The Lejre workshop specify three standards for making replicas, and the degree of accuracy required will depend on the intended use and other outcomes from the work. Cloth to be worn by museum volunteers or in the context of living history re-enactment needs not only to be functional but also within the budget of the organisation or participants. This is Demant's 'C' standard, where 'the processes of production are of no importance'. The 'A' standard 'includes all the original processes and seeks out the best possible raw materials'.[14] As exact a replica as possible may be desirable to test its qualities in use, for example sails made for the reconstructed Viking ships at the museum in Roskilde.[15] These have also provided evidence for the amount of time needed for the work. However, most replicas fall between these two standards due to the constraints already mentioned.

The recent replica Greenland costumes were woven on the appropriate loom for the period, even though this is considerably slower and more demanding than a modern hand loom.[16] The justification would be the slight difference in the structure of the cloth and therefore the way it drapes in use, although it would take a knowledgeable observer to tell, and since we know little of the way cloth was finished during this period, there is an element of 'whistling in the dark'. However, if the project doubles as technical research this is a worthwhile approach.

Hand spinning is also worth mentioning. Certainly it is important to understand the nature of the yarns to be used, but there are gaps in the historical record as regards, for example, fibre preparation and spinning, and archaeological survivals may be seriously degraded. It has only recently become clear that early linens in Europe were made from yarn that was not spun, but spliced, a dying skill now even in rural Korea.[17] To make a piece of linen cloth like that found at Must Farm (Whittlesey, Cambridgeshire) in the way that it

---

[14] Demant, 'Making a replica', p. 167.

[15] https://www.medieval.eu/viking-sails/, accessed 18 March 2022.

[16] Gwendoline Pepper, 'Time looms over us: observations from and experimental comparison of medieval English loom types', *Archaeological Textiles Review* 61 (2019), 71–87.

[17] Margarete Gleba and Susanna Harris, 'The first plant bast fibre technology: identifying splicing in archaeological textiles', *Archaeological and Anthropological Sciences* 11 (2019), 2329–2346.

was made in the Bronze Age is simply not possible now, not just because of the loss of craft skill and knowledge but also because of the relatively poor quality of modern flax.[18]

WHO IS DOING THE WORK?

No matter how good the information, the final product will depend not only on the maker's understanding of that information, but also on their skill. There are very few people who have the necessary hours of practice to make their work anywhere near the standard of the craftsmen who made the original fabrics, and there are specific techniques that can be elusive. A good example is a customer wishing to commission seventeenth-century mockado, a worsted-pile velvet, who came to the conclusion that she had a choice of two weavers, one of whom had never made warp pile fabric and the other a silk weaver, who had no suitable equipment for the job, although compared to most of his work it is simple.[19]

Here the Festival of Britain project is of particular interest, because of the influence that it may have had on the development of craft skills among amateurs in Britain. The figures survive in the store of Leicester Museums, having been on display at the Jewry Wall museum for many years, and a set of cloth samples from the project are in the collection of the Crafts Study Centre at the University for the Creative Arts, Farnham.[20] Hawkes had wanted to show the nature of British textiles. Apart from the lack of British evidence, the real challenge was that the figures were half life-size, meaning that the cloths had to be much finer than the originals to give an accurate impression.

Elizabeth Peacock was a spinner and weaver with an analytical approach to the technical aspects of the work.[21] During World War II she was teaching at Reigate and Redhill School of Art. How she came to be involved in the Festival of Britain project is unclear, but she obviously relished the challenge. The work of sorting, dyeing, carding, combing, spinning and weaving was done by Peacock and her students, working from her understanding of fleece types, historical plant dyes and technical processes. It 'taxed the skill … and proved a tremendously enriching experience … It influenced what she [Peacock] taught'.[22] Thus, while the figures and Peacock herself have slipped into obscurity, the skills that she passed on with such enthusiasm have been spread and continue to be

[18] Must Farm textiles; https://www.youtube.com/watch?v=wNLa_zlosRY, accessed 18 March 2022.

[19] Ultimately the author, the first alternative, took on the job.

[20] https://www.vads.ac.uk/digital/collection/CSC/id/3987/rec/20 (24/06/2021), accessed 1 July 2022.

[21] The only record of Peacock's life and work is a 1979 exhibition catalogue produced by the Crafts Study Centre, then at the Holbourne Museum at Bath and now at the University for the Creative Arts, Farnham, Surrey. The quotation is on p. 12. Morfudd Roberts, who was involved in the Festival project, intended to produce an account of it, but was unable to do so before her untimely death.

[22] Ella McLeod in the catalogue cited above, p. 12.

PLANNING DECISIONS FOR REPRODUCTION FABRICS

taught. She was ahead of her time and it is only relatively recently that the idea of using reconstructions of fabrics has been taken seriously as a way of contributing to the understanding of the past.

A WORKED EXAMPLE:
TENTH CENTURY BROKEN LOZENGE TWILL FROM YORK

In order to explore the necessary decisions, a specific job will be discussed with reference to the *châine opératoire* diagram (Fig. 8.1). Before the production planning can begin, the information must be gathered and considered in the light of intended use and practical constraints. The piece to be discussed is a fragment of tenth-century woollen cloth from 16–22 Coppergate, York, chosen because it is well documented. Care must be taken with published descriptions, as some have been superseded by recent re-assessments of both dates and materials, but in this case the analysis and dating appear to be reliable.[23] The published description is comprehensive and includes a photograph of the fragment itself and a better-preserved close parallel.[24] The intended use of the replica is for costumed re-enactment, and this type of weave appears to have been widely used both in Britain and Europe for clothing over a considerable period of time, making it suitable for this purpose. It is to be made 'on spec', to offer for sale to historical re-enactors at the Viking festival in York, and there is a subtext to the choice of this specific piece, because it is almost certainly a local, Anglian type rather than a Scandinavian one.[25]

Hand-woven cloth is inevitably much dearer than anything produced industrially. The market is small but there are those who know enough about the archaeological finds to want an accurate reconstruction; even so, it is necessary to consider cost when planning the work, and some of the processes will inevitably be 'outsourced'. This is a major factor, because the nature of fibres and their processing is important for the finished quality of the cloth.

The fabric to be reproduced is find 1308 from level 4B, *c.* 930/5–*c.* 975, at 16–22 Coppergate, York. It survives as two tiny scraps, not more than 7 cm in any direction. The technical description is: 'reddish 2 x 2 diamond twill, 14–16/Z/0.4 x 11–13/S/0.7 … Z medium, S hairy medium'.[26] This provides most of the information necessary, given that the diagrams elsewhere make it clear that this is a broken twill in both warp and weft with a small pattern repeat. It appears to be an example of fairly ordinary tenth-century

---

[23] Friederike Hertel and Karina Grömer, 'Project reassessment of iconic textiles at the Halle Museum', *Archaeological Textiles Review* 61 (2019) 128–138; Nigel D. Melton et al., 'On the curious date of the Rylstone log-coffin burial', *Proceedings of the Prehistoric Society* 82 (2016), 383–392.

[24] Walton, *Textiles, Cordage*, Item 1308, p. 435, Fig.137b, Pl. XX.

[25] Walton, *Textiles, Cordage*, p. 339.

[26] Walton, *Textiles, Cordage*, p. 435. This algebraic-looking description gives the information: number of warp threads to the centimetre, their twist and diameter, the same for the weft, and then the fleece type for each.

cloth, a tweed-like, medium-weight wool fabric in a characteristic textured weave and without significant fulling. It tested positive for madder dye, and was probably a strong brownish red when new.

To begin at the beginning: source and prepare fibre, dye, make yarn. This piece will be made from commercially available yarn for reasons of time and cost. To spin the yarn by hand multiplies the cost of the cloth, roughly, by ten, which very few customers are prepared to pay. This means that neither the fleece type, the preparation, nor the spinning are the same as the original. Some years ago, a phone call to a famous worsted spinning firm in Bradford, while disappointing as to outcome, gave an indication of the problem. The manager, whose name is that of the firm, was adamant that one cannot use single worsted yarn for warps and went silent for a moment when told that tenth-century cloths are so made. The differences are several: worsted yarns for modern suiting are spun clean, without oil, from Australian merino wool, and are plied. They are therefore completely unlike pre-industrial, hand-spun, long-staple worsteds of the type described as 'medium'. Fairly hard spun, woollen tweed yarns, while not correct, give a satisfactory cloth, but the original would have been spindle-spun from combed fibre.

Tweed-type yarns are usually available as blended colours, dyed in the wool rather than yarn dyed, which makes them less obviously synthetic although the dyes are 'fast milling acid' type rather than plant roots and clubmoss. It is unclear in general whether an archaeological fragment was dyed as wool, yarn or cloth, although the last is improbable before the high Middle Ages. It is also known that some twills were produced in two colours. Madder dye can produce a range of shades, and it is pleasing to have two slightly different reds to emphasise the pattern. Conventionally the weft yarn should be softer as well as being spun in the opposite direction to the warp, but commercial stock yarns may limit the choice.

What was chosen for the warp of this piece was a blended yarn of white Blue-faced Leicester and black Hebridean fleece, overdyed in a colour described as 'madder', z twist 7.2 Nm and approximately 0.5 mm diameter.[27] Because the intention was to sell garment pieces, several different weft yarns were used. The two pieces shown in Fig. 8.2 used a worsted in very bright pinkish red, S-plied, and a soft z-spun Norfolk Horn yarn dyed coral pink with madder. The spin direction makes no visible difference with the broken lozenge twill, since the direction of the twill line changes.

Having selected the yarn, the next step is to plan the warp. The work was done on my modern horizontal loom. For the plan one must decide on a finished size, and in the absence of any historical evidence, a width suitable for a tunic, a rectangular cloak or a woman's tubular dress was chosen. The aim was for 'single width', 65–70 cm, in roughly two-metre lengths. Textiles that have been worn, washed, buried and retrieved may be hard to interpret, and, particularly with small scraps, the thread count may not be typical of the original piece. In any case the thread count is that of the final, finished cloth and allowance must be made for this in choosing the sett, that is, the number of warp ends to

---

[27] Nm count, now widely used for all types of yarn, is the number of 1 km skeins that weigh 1 kg.

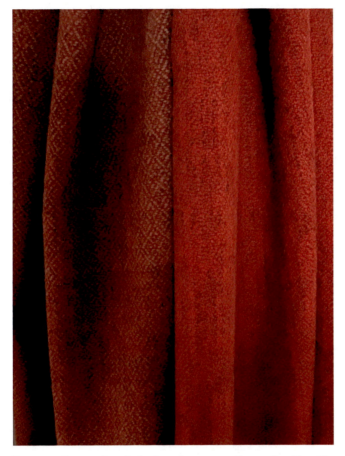

Fig. 8.2   Two replica cloths based on a 2 x 2 diamond twill textile from 10th-century York. Photograph: Ruth Gilbert.

the centimetre, of the replica – sampling may be necessary to establish likely shrinkage. This is more of an issue with wool than with linen but should be taken into account.

The standard calculation for warp yardage is thread/cm x (width + shrinkage) x (length + take-up + waste). In the author's workshop this is done in a random mix of imperial and metric measurements, because some of the equipment is old and many yarn spinners still work in time-honoured systems such as Yorkshire Skeins (256 yards/lb). The stated warp count of the original is 14–16/cm and the reed most suitable for the job was 10/inch, giving 30/inch when threaded three to a dent, approximately 12/cm.[28] The threading is a simple 12-end (warp thread) herringbone, woven in the original with a ten

---

[28] The reed of the horizontal loom controls the width and sett of the cloth. A 10/inch reed has ten dents, spaces, to the inch. Although I work in metric units, much of my equipment is old and much conversion goes on when making calculations.

pick (weft thread) repeat. The break in the twill, an advantage when working on a warp-weighted loom, is awkward to weave on a treadle loom, requiring something more like a polka than the 'left, right, left, right' of a straight twill, and this might be a factor in its decline in popularity with the change in loom type.[29] That said, it is undoubtedly quicker than working in the historically accurate way.

There is no evidence for heavy milling or surface finishing of cloth in the early Middle Ages, although any cloth needs wet finishing of some kind to allow the bedding of the yarns. Commercial yarn is supplied in oil, so an initial hot soak with sodium carbonate is followed by thorough working in soap and a number of rinses in order remove the soap. With most cloths it is better to dry under tension, but this weave is intended to be slightly textured, as its historical designation *haberget* (like a hauberk, that is, a mail shirt) suggests. It is therefore allowed to drip and then hung out in a good Yorkshire breeze. The different weft yarns produced cloths with a noticeably different handle as well as different rates of shrinkage and the finished yarn counts are about 12–13 x 9–11 per cm, so somewhat coarser than the original. One re-enactment trader has an overdress of cloth very similar to these for Viking events, made over twenty years ago, that shows little sign of wear or fading.

CONCLUSION

It is clear that from the point of view of providing good-quality historical information for the public the production of replica cloth is worthwhile. There are significant differences from the tenth-century cloth, but it is far closer to the original than anything commercially available and surprises people when displayed at the fairs; *Textiles, Cordage and Raw Fibre from 16–22 Coppergate* is kept to hand to prove that it is not exceptional.

The main concern is the future of such work. The textile archaeology that provides the information input is a small and relatively undervalued specialism, with no dedicated courses in Britain. Spinning and weaving are both classified as 'currently viable' by the Heritage Crafts Association, but these are largely carried out at a hobby level, with very few practitioners capable of producing cloth by the yard.[30] This is a decline from the situation in the 1960s, and is partly due to the loss of the art school and technical college courses that provided the skill training, which have for the most part been abandoned in favour of fashion, design and 'textile art'. Many modern hand spinners are uninterested in technical challenge, aiming for 'therapeutic' non-engagement. Cloth weaving also requires both large equipment and a considerable commitment of time, and workspace is expensive, even where suitable premises can be found. Recent developments in museums as far apart as Paisley in Scotland, Halifax in West Yorkshire and the Tamar valley in Cornwall are encouraging, however, in that space and equipment are available for the use of suitably trained volunteers. It is to be hoped that such sites may eventually produce cloth for sale, much in the way that the previously mentioned workshop at Lejre does, as part of their educational activity.

[29] Walton, *Textiles, Cordage*, p. 331.
[30] https://heritagecrafts.org.uk/currently-viable-crafts/, accessed 18 March 2022.

CHAPTER 9

The Value of Intangible Knowledge: How Living History Can Aid Experimental Archaeology in Exploring the Past; Iron Age Scandinavian Tablet Weaving and *Nalbinding*

Ann Asplund

STUDY OF HISTORY

There are as many ways of studying history as there are traces left to interpret. Even applying the hypothetico-deductive approach to it,[1] there is still only so much that can be deduced directly from an object before context needs to be evaluated for additional information. For textile fragments especially, the context of the find site, whether it is a burial, or a settlement, is particularly important for the identification and interpretation.[2] Within archaeological contexts with no organic remains, traces left from pro-

---

[1] The making of observations, asking questions, forming hypotheses, making predictions, testing predictions and then repeating the process; William K. Purves, Gordon H. Orians, H. Craig Heller and David Sadava, *Life, the Science of Biology*, 5th edn (Sunderland, MA: Sinauer, 1998), p. 11.

[2] Eva Andersson Strand, Karin Margarita Frei, Margarita Gleba, Ulla Mannering, Marie-Louise Nosch and Irene Skals, 'Old textiles – new possibilities', *European Journal of Archaeology* 13.2 (2010), 149–173 (pp. 151–152).

cessing raw materials into textiles can suggest that textile production took place at a particular location.[3]

Often the best way to test a textile artefact to understand its use and importance in daily life is to use it. Since original artefacts are usually too fragile or fragmentary for people to handle, reconstructions are made and tested. Textiles are a good example of where hard-to-describe qualities such as drape, softness, lustre, stretch, toughness and warmth can form a large part of the interpreted function and status of an object, especially for a costume.[4]

These are all qualities that are subjective to the wearer and their society. Personal preferences and experiences of both the maker and the wearer can have a large impact on the finished object and therefore our interpretation of it.[5] Being able to re-create a textile means that technical properties such as thread count and size, and fibre thickness, suddenly translate into an object that can be evaluated according to its more intangible qualities.

RECONSTRUCTING AND RE-ENACTING HISTORY

There are several different types of textile reconstruction, which are used for different purposes. Experimental archaeologists, textile historians and anthropologists try to collect new information and answer questions, such as what an object is, how it was made, how much time and resources were used in making it, its purpose and what kind of traces are left by production and/or use.[6]

Museums, especially open-air venues such as the Foteviken Viking Museum at Höllviken, Skåne, Sweden,[7] the Plimoth Plantation, Massachusetts, USA[8] and the

---

[3] Andersson Strand et al., 'Old textiles – new possibilities', pp. 160–163; Eva Andersson Strand, 'The textile *chaîne opératoire*: using a multidisciplinary approach to textile archaeology with a focus on the Ancient Near East', *Paléorient* 38.1–2 (2012), 21–40 (p. 22).

[4] Susanna Harris, 'The sensory archaeology of textiles', in *The Routledge Handbook of Sensory Archaeology*, ed. by Robin Skeates and Jo Day (London: Routledge, 2019), pp. 210–132, here citing page 7 in the online version, where pagination is 1–28; https://eprints.gla.ac.uk/206003/7/206003.pdf

[5] Harris, 'The sensory archaeology of textiles', online version, p. 15.

[6] Harris, 'The sensory archaeology of textiles', online version, pp. 12–15; Strand, 'The textile *chaîne opératoire*', pp. 23–37.

[7] 'Foteviken Museum with its Viking town is an archaeological open-air museum, with experimental and living history as the main task.' Their main mission is: 'The Viking ages and the Middle Ages history with the starting point in Scania. Bringing the history to life and conveying our cultural heritage to a wide audience. The passing of our knowledge in an informative and thorough manner, including via modern digital technology'; https://www.fotevikensmuseum.se/d/en/home, accessed 22 March 2022.

[8] 'Plimoth Plantation offers powerful personal encounters with history built on thorough research about the Wampanoag People and the Colonial English Community in the 1600s'; https://plimoth.org/about/who-we-are, accessed 22 March 2022.

THE VALUE OF INTANGIBLE KNOWLEDGE 159

Weald and Downland Living Museum near Chichester, UK,[9] often employ historical re-enactment and reproductions to bring history to life. By using historical or reconstructed buildings and filling them with re-created objects and people wearing historical costumes, the demonstrated daily activities and crafts are made more meaningful for the visitor.[10] There can also be a wider sensory engagement with objects: not just seen, but also touched, smelled, heard and even tasted. This is re-enactment with an educational purpose, transferring information and creating understanding about a historical period or activity with the aid of reconstructions and replicas.

While museums often portray a period of time, other historical re-enactments may re-create a specific episode. Examples include the American Civil War re-enactments where certain battles are acted out,[11] or the Battle of Hastings (UK).[12] These events are huge, both in the number of participants and spectators. The events have a commitment to stay true to the original sources, populating the battle with people role-playing historical figures of note and others demonstrating period activities connected to the event. Participants include historians, historical re-enactors and other volunteers.

Then there is the re-enactment where individuals immerse themselves within different levels of historical accuracy, whether for others' entertainment or education, or for their own enjoyment. There is no specific name for this re-enactment; it may be named for an activity or the group doing it. In the USA, there are options along the entire scale. For example, a Renaissance fair or 'Ren-fair', as it is often abbreviated, is a public event where visitors often dress up to participate. Professional entertainers perform scripted entertainment during the day, and there are vendors and fun is had by all. Local re-enactment groups meet in smaller gatherings, have a small camp, a party or other activities such as crafts. These events are open only to members. Larger groups may invite others to public demonstrations (or 'demos'), where they exhibit period activities and crafts to the public. These groups vary in size, from global to local history guilds, and represent a wide range as regards historical accuracy, level of role-playing (scripted and non-scripted) and purpose. The groups that aim to educate the public often participate at local fairs and history venues, and also work with local museums for special events. Since it is not the purpose of this chapter to list all possible groups, only a few relevant examples will be highlighted here.

---

[9]   'The Museum has an extremely strong commitment to lifelong learning. In addition to 20–25,000 children visiting in school parties every year, the Museum operates as a private sector training provider, selling over 3,600 student-days of adult teaching and training every year, with a broad spectrum of provision from workshop-based skills training to two graduate courses run in association with the University of York'; https://www.wealddown.co.uk/about/corporate-profile/, accessed 22 March 2022. (Click on 'About us', then 'Corporal profile').

[10]   Harris, 'The sensory archaeology of textiles', online version, p. 12.

[11]   Gettysburg Reenactment; https://www.gbpa.org/event/2022-battle-gettysburg, accessed 12 May 2022.

[12]   https://en.wikipedia.org/wiki/Battle_of_Hastings_reenactment, accessed 22 March 2022.

The SCA (Society for Creative Anachronism) is one of the largest global organisations, and has both huge camps, where people from all over the world gather to engage in historical crafts, socialise and practice their variety of historical fighting as a sport, and smaller events involving local groups with or without a public outreach, such as 'demos' at the public library or history-themed days for the local school.[13]

Regia Anglorum (UK) is also a global organisation with a lot of local branch groups. It was the founding member of the NAReS (The National Association of Re-enactment Societies) that represents the interest of the British re-enactor to government bodies, the police and other similar organisations. Regia Anglorum also have a strong media presence, often co-operating in TV and movie projects. Regia Anglorum have many members-only events, but are also often seen at national history events and fairs. They also have their own projects where they build and sail boats, and construct historical buildings for the use of their members.[14]

Common to all these organisations is the presence of the individual re-enactor with a deep commitment to historical accuracy. Such a person is often an independent researcher or a hobbyist and/or historical artisan, with a love of history. These are people who will continue to study and upgrade their re-created costumes and equipment every time they learn something new. These individuals exhibit a deep commitment to obtaining the correct appearance, and can spend years creating items and honing their portrayal of a historical person. With this commitment to historical accuracy, re-enactors face, in many ways, the same kind of choices as any museum or experimental archaeologist does when it comes to creating a reconstruction: time, money, environment, access to information and authenticity versus practicality.

Time can be limited, for finishing a reconstruction project within a specified time frame, or for a specific event. (There is more than one hem that has been finished in the car on the way to an event, and seams on the inside left raw!) Preliminary research may take longer than expected, causing the experiment to miss the historically accurate seasonal time for starting a project. This has implications for things such as wool quality,[15] and plant dyes that use historical recipes, including optimal times to harvest and process the dye plant and for the temperatures needed to run a fermentation vat.[16]

Information about the original object is not always easy to access. It may be unpublished, or published in another language, which takes time to translate; or it may be dependent on old information that has been proven faulty in some way but is still popular and currently accepted by the general public. All this impacts on the time required

---

[13] https://www.sca.org, accessed 22 March 2022.

[14] https://regia.org/about.php, accessed 22 March 2022. Also see Christensen, Chapter 1 in this volume.

[15] Lise Warburg, *Spinnbok* (Stockholm: Wahlström & Widstrand, 1974), p. 19.

[16] Krista Vajanto and M.R. van Bommel, 'Dyed textiles from late Iron Age Finland', *Fennoscandia Archaeologica* 31 (2014), 61–78.

THE VALUE OF INTANGIBLE KNOWLEDGE   161

for the preliminary research needed in order for a re-creation to be made as accurately as possible.[17]

Budget is often a problem and hard-to-find authentic materials may be expensive. There is always a trade-off: depending on whether the focus of a reconstruction is on the process of making or the finished object, different levels of authenticity are sacrificed. Between shearing your own sheep, then spinning and weaving the cloth by hand, or buying wool cloth close to a historical quality, or opting for a wool blend or something that looks and feels like wool, there are a myriad of practical decisions, besides cost, that affect the project.

The environment is another important factor in the re-creating process. For many re-enactors or museum settings, reproducing items from another time, location and even climate can be problematic. The modern geographical location designated for re-creating and using the textile can be colder or warmer than the environment the historical costume was originally made for. A different level of humidity can not only make it harder to wear a historic costume, it can also affect the craft being shown. Textile crafts are a good example, since different types of fibre react differently to humidity in the air: linen actually likes to be sprinkled with water in preparation for weaving in order to strengthen it.

The practicality of an experiment can encompass many things from whether the process is too dangerous, such as the medieval processes for roasting white lead for pigments,[18] or simply too large an undertaking, such as needing several thousand people willing to haul rocks to test how the Pyramids were built.[19] Nevertheless, not all experiments need to be large, complicated or expensive to be effective. The following examples of textile reconstruction experiments, a Viking Age sock and tablet-woven band, both started quite modestly, but required additional research and different levels of skill to fulfil.

THE AUTHOR'S PERSONAL RECONSTRUCTION ADVENTURES

Reconstructing Viking Age (AD 750 to 1050) Nalbound Socks
Any project that reconstructs an item is about focus. When first confronted with an object that you want to make, you focus on the appearance and how to make it look the same; but simply looking the same does not mean that it was constructed in the same

---

[17] An example of a case where older information has been found erroneous, but the update is difficult to access, is the Åsle mitten, a *nalbound* mitten from Sweden. Published in English in Odd Nordland, *Primitive Scandinavian Textiles in Knotless Netting* (Oslo: University Press, 1961), p. 37, it is stated to be from the first century AD. The mitten was subsequently reassigned to AD 1510–1640 by carbon-14 dating, published in Swedish: Margareta Nockert and Göran Possnert, *Att datera textil* (Hedemora: Gidlund, 2002). Unless one is bilingual, that is easily missed, and translation takes time.

[18] *On Divers Arts: The Treatise of Theophilus*, trans. with introduction and notes by John G. Hawthorne and Cyril Stanley Smith (New York: Dover publications, 1963, 1979), p. 14.

[19] For Mark Lehner and Zahi Hawass's excavations and testing of building techniques, see 'Who built the pyramids?'; https://www.pbs.org/wgbh/nova/pyramid/explore/builders. html, accessed 22 March 2022.

way. There are many layers of information in any one object, which contribute to the finished piece.

A reconstruction can require many attempts in order to make it accurately. This is because the material you initially used may not have been quite right, the technique used to make the textile was not accurate or the finished object may have looked right from the front, but when you turned it over the reverse was wrong. By making the object multiple times, its properties and the process of making it become clear. In turn, the maker's knowledge and understanding also develop. To begin any project, learning and mastering the technique used to make it is essential. This helps us understand how this particular technique is different from others and how the process of construction is ordered.

Nalbinding (needle binding) as a technique is quite simple. It does not really require any advanced tools, beyond two hands, a thumb, yarn and a large needle. The technique has many names beyond needle binding and the multiple dialect names in the different countries of Scandinavia, of which several have been adopted into English (*naalbinding, nålbindning, nalebinding*); it is also called single-needle knitting, knotless netting and needle looping. There are several families of stitches, of which the oldest one, 'Coptic stitch', or 'cross knit looping stitch', actually results in the same fabric as knitting, but is made by weaving the needle in and out of the fabric to create each loop, instead of manipulating loops with knitting needles. This makes it hard to distinguish from knitting. However, because it is a single thread pulled completely through each step and loop at each manipulation, *nalbinding* can be identified by looking at a decrease stitch to see if it was worked with a single thread/yarn (as in *nalbinding*) or if the decrease stitch is made by two threads, as in knitting (the loop having two 'legs' passing through whichever stitch is decreased or increased, like sewing with double thread versus single thread, knitting versus *nalbinding*).[20]

Other *nalbinding* stitches create striped or herringbone-patterned surfaces, sometimes with protruding ridges. The front and back can also have different appearances. There are stitches that use only one loop on the thumb, while others use multiple loops, creating another level of complexity. Beyond the basic stitch, which creates a single row, there are also different ways of joining the rows.[21] It is easy to produce a multitude of different *nalbound* textiles, from thick and heavy to light, stretchy and lacy. The technique has been used in many cultures all over the world to make objects such as carrying nets, bags, bracelets, socks and mittens.[22]

---

[20] Anne Marie Decker, 'Nalbinding or not?: some structural differences between nalbinding and other non-woven textile techniques', unpublished conference paper (39th International Medieval Congress, Kalamazoo, 2004); Anne Marie Decker, 'But it looks like… methods of differentiating non-woven looped structures', *NESAT XIV*; https://nalbound. com/2021/09/03/but-it-looks-like/, accessed 10 December 2023.

[21] Nordland, *Primitive Scandinavian Textiles*, pp. 33–39; Berit Westman and Anna Karin Reimerson, *Nålbindning 12 varianter*, revised edn (Västerås: Västmanlands läns hemslöjdsförbund, 2001), p. 17.

[22] Margrethe Hald, *Ancient Danish Textiles from Bogs and Burials: A Comparative Study of Costume and Iron Age Textiles*, trans. Jean Olsen (Copenhagen: National Museum of Denmark, 1980), pp. 285–312.

THE VALUE OF INTANGIBLE KNOWLEDGE 163

The Coppergate sock,[23] which I re-created, was discovered in York, UK, and dates to the tenth century. At this time York was settled by Scandinavians and it has generally been accepted that the Coppergate sock is Scandinavian.[24] It may have been a shoe liner or short sock if the red border was simply a decorative edging, or alternatively it could have been a longer sock if the red part is the surviving trace of a different-coloured leg that is now missing.[25] The *nalbound* stitch is now identified as the 'York' stitch, after its find location.

I chose to re-create this item because I needed socks to wear with my Viking-style leather turnshoes and because this example is similar in date to the pieces that inspired the rest of my costume. But beyond the simple initial need for a sock, there was the desire to get the re-creation right. With each attempt, something new was understood and learned, especially the character of the York stitch and its suitability for socks.

The aim of the first reconstruction was not only to test the stitch and size of the sock, but also to work in a historical material. I therefore used yarn spun with a drop spindle (which, incidentally, was one of my first attempts at spinning in this way). At a glance, this reconstruction looks like the original (without the mending that the original sock displays). However, it was hard to see how the heel was worked on the original, since most of it is missing, and when looking closer at the reconstruction, it is apparent that it does not look 'quite right'. The yarn was also quite obviously not spun to the specifications of the original (Fig. 9.1).

Additional research pointed to an alternative method for joining the rows of stitching, which could change the way the sock looked, and which I incorporated into the second sock (Fig. 9.2) (as a result, the first pair of socks became well-used house slippers, and suffered hard use for over a decade before I had to mend them. With additional mending, that first pair is now in its second decade of use). It was also made from yarn that was closer in thickness to the original, and more attention was paid to how the heel was constructed. This single-sock version looked much better than the first one, but it still did not have the right number of stitch rows per centimetre.

By the time I attempted the third sample, new pictures of the original sock were available for study. It had been remounted and it was now possible to see sections of its interior. Studying these images gave me a new idea: by turning the third reconstruction, which was made with a thinner yarn, inside out, the turning of the rows on the heel side of the sock looked much more like the original. This idea was not quite out of the blue, since this is what may actually have happened to the later medieval mitten from Åsle, Sweden. Reconstructions of this mitten's stitch were made twice, once for each of the sides being considered as the outside. It is proposed that it was probably discovered turned inside out (since one of the stitch reconstructions otherwise is a very complicated

---

23 The Coppergate sock; https://www.jorvikvikingcentre.co.uk/about/jorvik-artefact-gallery/sock/, accessed 16 February 2023.

24 Penelope Walton, *Textiles, Cordage and Raw Fibre from 16–22 Coppergate*, The Archaeology of York The Small Finds, 17/5 (London: the Council for British Archeology for the York Archaeological Trust, 1989) pp. 341–345.

25 Walton, *Textiles, Cordage*, p. 343.

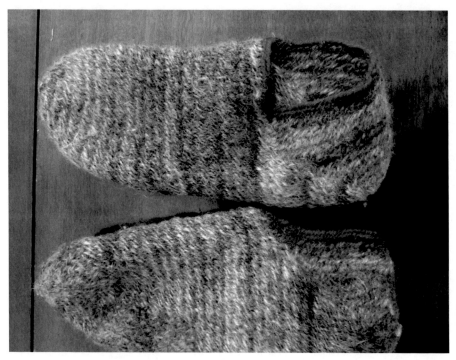

Fig. 9.1 First reconstruction attempt of the 10th-century *nalbound* sock found at Coppergate, York. © Ann Asplund.

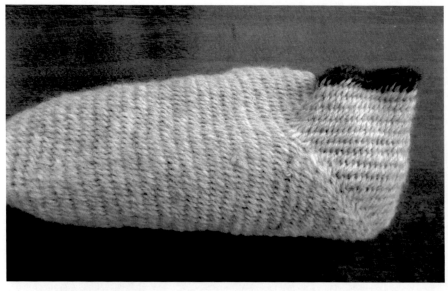

Fig. 9.2 Second reconstruction attempt of the 10th-century *nalbound* sock found at Coppergate, York. © Ann Asplund.

THE VALUE OF INTANGIBLE KNOWLEDGE 165

set of movements), but whether this had occurred on purpose or not, is still to be determined.[26] The next step in the Coppergate sock's re-creation would be to see the original and compare it to the reconstruction directly. In this way, adjustments for the next reconstruction could be worked out.

A Tablet-woven Band from Birka

Originally, I was simply fascinated by the tablet-weaving technique itself, and never thought I would be able to reconstruct any of the bands from Birka; but as the Coppergate sock reproduction was achieved one tweak at a time, mastering of one technique after another, patterns, tools and understanding materials led to the confidence and patience needed to actually finish a brocaded band.

Viking Age examples of tablet-woven items and tablet-weaving tools survive in considerable numbers, comparably speaking. Therefore, it is possible to compare them and see the wide variety of uses to which tablet weaving was put. Tablet-weaving tablets and bands have been found in several Viking Age burials, such as Kaupang, Norway, and Birka, Sweden, and most notably in the Oseberg, Norway, ship burial, where a tablet-weaving loom was discovered with the band set up and prepared for weaving.[27] The bands found at Birka[28] and Oseberg are all of a complex design, using brocading techniques worked, respectively, in silk and metal threads and in linen.

In burials, tablet-woven bands have been found in different positions on the deceased's body and have, as a result, been identified as a number of different dress items. Examples include sleeve cuffs; potential starting borders for the top of apron dresses, hats and, possibly, necklines of tunics; coat decoration; decorations on wrap-around jackets and dresses;[29] and probable ribbons and apron ties;[30] not to mention all the ecclesiastic uses.[31] Plain or simply woven bands were also used as selvedges[32] for woven cloth, and as the starting border on the warp-weighted loom. Tablet-woven finds from Scandinavian countries, both before and during the Viking Age, show a large variety and skill level of

[26]   Hald, *Ancient Danish Textiles*, pp. 285–312 (p. 294).

[27]   Peter Collingwood, *The Techniques of Tablet Weaving* (McMinneville, OR: Faber and Faber, 1982).

[28]   Agnes Geijer, *Birka III, Die Textilfunde Aus Den Gräbern* (Uppsala: Kungl. Vitterhets Historie och Antikvitets Akademien, 1938), pp. 75–98.

[29]   Inga Hägg, 'Mantel och Kjortel i Vikingatidens dräkt', *Fornvännen* 66 (1971), 141–153; https://raa.diva-portal.org/smash/get/diva2:1225059/FULLTEXT01.pdf, accessed 13 May 2022.

[30]   Pirkko-Liisa Lehtosalo-Hilander, *Ancient Finnish Costumes* (Helsinki: The Finnish Archeological Society, 1984), pp. 1–76 (pp. 46–48).

[31]   Nancy Spies, *Ecclesiastical Pomp and Aristocratic Circumstance: a thousand years of Brocaded Tablet Woven Bands* (Jarrettsville, MA: Arelate Studio, 2000).

[32]   Selvedge is the lengthwise edge of the fabric, which is usually firmer than the rest of the cloth.

patterning.[33] As a result, tablet weaving gives plenty of opportunity for a wide variety of patterns to be reconstructed on bands of various uses, sizes and widths.

The tablet-weaving technique is a variation of weaving, where the shed[34] is opened and closed by the manipulation of tablets, instead of heddles.[35] The difference lies in that, while a heddle simply lifts a warp[36] thread straight up or down (or in the case of a vertical loom, in or out), the opening and closing of the shed by turning the tablets in a tablet-woven band introduces twist to the warp threads. Further, where tablet-woven bands are (mostly) warp-faced,[37] since the weft[38] is hidden, a fabric woven on a loom can be warp-faced, balanced[39] or weft-faced,[40] depending on the selection of weaving pattern and materials. This makes tablet-woven bands relatively stiff compared to a weave of the same number of threads in a balanced plain (tabby) weave fabric, especially since the warp is woven around the weft, making it three layers thick, with warp threads both above and below the weft, which is sandwiched in the middle. In a tabby fabric, the fabric is only two threads thick, at the point where the warp and weft cross.

The tablets themselves usually have four holes, but examples have also been found with three, or more than four, holes, increasing the capacity to make a variety of patterns, since each hole can carry a different colour. Other bands seem to have only used two holes, or were woven with threads that have since disintegrated. The simplest way of making patterns is to have different coloured threads in different tablets; the next step is to have different coloured threads in holes of the same tablet. Further, by staggering the position of the colours in the tablet, another level of simple geometric pattern is possible. Added to this is the choice of when the weaver should change the direction of twist, which manipulates the patterns further still.

As a further step the tablets can be turned in different directions individually, creating a brocade-like pattern called 'Icelandic double weave', where the pattern is visible

---

[33] Collingwood, *The Techniques of Tablet Weaving*, pp. 1–3.

[34] The shed is the space made by moving warp threads to make it easier to pass the thread of the weft through in the making of a fabric. This is in contrast with a fabric where the weft is moved around the warp, and no shed is opened.

[35] A heddle is a tool used for moving the warp threads to create the shed, the opening.

[36] Warp is the fixed thread in weaving, the thread going lengthwise through the fabric, and since it is the thread under tension in the different weaving systems, it needs to be stronger than the weft.

[37] Warp-faced means that in the final fabric the weft is not visible, or visible only on the edges; all the colour in the final fabric is from the coloured warp threads.

[38] Weft is the moving thread in weaving, the thread going crosswise over the fabric. It is not under tension, and can be of a different quality from the warp, to create different fabrics.

[39] In a balanced weave, both the warp and the weft are seen. Tabby is a good example, where each warp and weft goes over and under the other.

[40] Weft-faced is opposite to warp-faced, with the weft the only visible thread. Velvet is a good example of a weft-faced fabric.

THE VALUE OF INTANGIBLE KNOWLEDGE 167

in reverse on the back. Beyond this, a supplementary weft[41] for brocading can be introduced. The resulting tablet-woven bands are no longer fully warp-faced, because the pattern is made with the contrasting supplementary wefts. The bands from Birka use metal threads as a supplementary weft.[42]

This brief description of the technical diversity available to tablet weavers demonstrates the variety and complexity of tablet-woven patterns. In turn, this can reflect the weaver's skill and possibly their own aesthetic appreciation of colour and design, or that of the person for whom the tablet-woven band was made.

Silk and metal threads are not easy to handle for a novice tablet-weaver. The materials are also quite expensive, so when I decided to learn the metal-thread brocading technique, by combining different patterns found on the bands from Birka, I approached the project gradually. I began by simply learning how to weave with tablets.

During the first experiment, cotton yarn was used, which was useful in learning the rhythm of turning tablets and how to control the width of the band. This is especially true for human-tensioned weaving in a horizontal system, where one end of the warp bundle is attached to a fixed point, and the other end is attached to the person. The warp threads need to be placed under constant tension in order to beat each weft thread into place properly and keep the tablets in position. With a lack of tension, the tablets may turn, jump a line (warp thread), become tangled or even flip, thus changing the side from which the tablet is threaded and therefore affecting the pattern. However, too much tension makes it harder to turn the tablets. Learning to rock forward slightly when turning the tablets not only makes it easier to turn them, but also relieves some of the wear and tear on the warp threads. Progressing from narrower bands to wider ones, it became even more important to be able to control a larger number of tablets that needed to be turned simultaneously.

When I felt confident enough to weave with authentic materials such as plant-dyed wool, I found that this simple change was like learning to weave anew. Wool threads are more prone than others to bobbling, depending on the quality and spin, and the resulting fluff builds up, causing threads to bind to each other and lock tight. This stops the tablets from turning, which was a new problem for me, as was the inherent stretch of the wool yarns. I had to learn to be more sensitive to the tension of each warp thread and to make sure the tablets did not sit too long in the same position in the warp, which helped solve the problems of bobbling and stretch. Experiments making multiple bands with different qualities and ply of wool further honed the fingertip feel for the tension, and a more distinguished taste in the wool yarn used. Finally, I found I was able to produce a consistent quality of band. I therefore decided it was time to focus on weaving a pattern made by turning the tablets individually and in different directions.

---

[41] A supplementary weft is introduced on top of, and in addition too, the normal warp and weft to create a specific effect. It can include materials such as metal threads, but also horse hair, for shine. Modern supplementary wefts in tablet weaving and tapestry weaving can include anything from VHS tape ribbons, to straw, plastic strips, etc.

[42] Geijer, *Birka III*, pp. 69–98; Spies, *Ecclesiastical Pomp*, pp. 13–14.

This experiment required a completely new skill: I had to learn how to interpret and follow a pattern. Simple geometric patterns are easy to construct because their underlying principle is how the colours present according to the placement in the tablet. Therefore, it is easy to learn how to spot where to switch the turning direction of the tablets in a pattern in order to mirror and produce the pattern.

As soon as a pattern requires individual tablets to be turned in different orders and different directions, the number of possible manipulations for each row of the pattern increases, especially if the tablet contains multiple colours. Today most known tablet-weaving patterns are drawn out on paper and can be followed line by line. However, the historical record on this point is very slim, with a few literary references to buying pattern parchment, and only one medieval notebook from a nun in 1517 notating patterns for a gold-brocaded band, making it rare indeed.[43] Many of the surviving band patterns repeat themselves mathematically, or have recurring lifts of the same number of tablets but with staggered intervals, making it possible to reduce a complex pattern to a smaller pattern repeat. This helps the weaver to remember the geometric patterns but it does not help for figurative patterns, which leaves a question unanswered, concerning how patterns were generally remembered, taught and otherwise passed on.

I have found, trying a brocade pattern worked in metal thread (metal filament wrapped around core) on a wool band, that it became obvious, from a maker's perspective, that a stiff warp, such as silk or linen, was generally used for the original bands, not wool (or at least not a soft spun wool). The elasticity of the wool threads of the quality I had meant that the warp was unable to hold the stiffer, metal threads of the brocading weft in place, and this was with the wrapped metal, not the drawn metal thread, showing a need for a warp that does not stretch. I therefore decided to make the next band with a silk warp and the same modern metal thread substitute. The result confirmed that the properties of silk threads meant the warp was strong enough to hold the metal brocading in place, denting the metal-wrapped thread. I also used this experiment to test the tension and the number of tablets needed to weave the band to the right size.

Size is actually a really important part of the process, especially when reconstructing the metal brocade bands from Birka. All the beautiful pictures of the Birka tablet-woven bands are enlarged and it is easy to overlook their actual size, which is quite narrow (from 6 to 17 mm, 0.2–0.6 inches wide).[44] Holding an accurately made replica band of silk and real silver thread also offers greater insights into their use and how heavy these bands could be.

The stiffness of any band made with metallic threads also makes it impossible to follow a flat curve, for example along a neckline, whereby explaining why it is more commonly suggested that this particularly type of tablet-woven band was attached to hats (or was used as hairbands/headbands) and cuffs, and as the top decorative edge on an apron dress.[45]

---

[43] Spies, *Ecclesiastical Pomp*, p. 92.

[44] Geijer, *Birka III*, p. 88.

[45] Spies, *Ecclesiastical Pomp*, pp. 41–43.

THE VALUE OF INTANGIBLE KNOWLEDGE 169

Any flat tablet-woven band has two dimensions in which it can bend. Firstly, a flat band can bend lengthwise around something, like a cuff, into a tube, without distorting the pattern. The second bend direction is to make it follow a curve while lying flat. To achieve this, it is necessary either to stretch the outer edge of the band, or to fold the inner edge to make a circle, distorting the pattern. A band woven in wool will have some sideways flexibility, depending on how stiff the band has been woven and how wide it is. Therefore, it can be manipulated to follow the shallow curve of a larger neckline. To attach it around a keyhole neckline,[46] which has a sharper curve since it lies closer to the neck than a round neckline, it really needs to be thin and narrow so that it will bend enough to follow the sharper curve. If the band is too wide, the fold at the corners will be bulky and the band can create wrinkles in the fabric it is being attached to. And if the band has a metal supplemental weft, bending and folding it sharply is nigh on impossible. Experimenting with the neckline, the shape and the size of the band caused a diversion where I focused on the discrepancy between the many diverse kinds of necklines present in many later medieval manuscripts, and the relatively narrow variety currently employed by re-enactors, and a review of the necklines and their shape is in progress, which will hopefully add to the knowledge of the mechanics of the neckline construction and the variety in treatments and decoration.

LEARNING THROUGH TEACHING

In my experience I have found that often the best way of learning comes by teaching others. The process of teaching helps the teacher to remember important details that can get lost in the sheer volume of information that is always being mentally assimilated. Going through the basics of the craft being taught refreshes things. This revision can often highlight additional and new information that has come to light since the last time I researched the technique. Teaching can also lead to additional insights, particularly about the passing on of information from one person to another and how an individual learns and uses what they have been taught – for example, the effect that left- versus right-handedness has on a technique, and to what degree a person's previous experience has a bearing on learning something new.

When teaching *nalbinding* in large settings (twenty to thirty people), there are always a certain number of left-handed and ambidextrous people present. When examining items made in the *nalbinding* technique it is not always obvious whether something has been made by a left- or right-handed person, especially if the item is a fragment. Finished objects that are turned inside out will look as if they have been made the opposite way. It also depends on whether the left-handed person learns to *nalbind* right-handed or if the process is mirrored. Mirroring reverses the stitch and it will show on the finished item. It also causes problems in the making, since the working direction of a right-handed person is counter-clockwise, working the stitch around the left thumb, while that of a

---

[46] The additional space needed for the head to go through is created by a slit in the front, creating the appearance of a keyhole.

left-handed person is clockwise, working the stitch around the right thumb. This leads to commercially spun yarn with s twist unwinding and eventually breaking for the left-handed person. These problems can easily be countered by twisting the needle as it is inserted into the thumb loop. Conversely, the working process adds twist to the yarn being used by a right-handed person, which sometimes has to be relieved by letting the needle threaded with the yarn hang free so it can untwist.

Teaching in larger and smaller settings also impacts on how stitches are taught and whether the stitch is actually assimilated. From my experience, the evolution of the information passed on by the teacher can be quite rapid within a larger group, causing quite significant differences in the stitch, as compared to information passed on in smaller settings. Many times it becomes a game of 'telephone': if the teacher is unable to visit each student, the instruction is passed on from student to student, sometimes causing the creation of completely different stitches. When historical *nalbinding* stitches are examined, it can be seen that the stitch has generally remained the same over long periods of time. This points to the stitch being taught person-to-person actively, not mimicked by someone watching the crafter in a passive learning situation, and possibly under societal pressure and practical reasons to conform within geographical areas for specific uses.[47] I would therefore suggest that it is not until quite recently, with the advancement of online information and the availability of different stitches, that it has become more common for people to learn more than one stitch.

PRODUCING RECONSTRUCTIONS AND THEIR VALUE FOR RESEARCH

It soon became obvious for both projects described above that beyond mastering an actual technique, one of the most important considerations for a good reconstruction was being able to source raw materials of the same qualities as the original. The experience of recognising and sourcing the right materials, or recognising the right material and knowing what to make with it and how to adjust the technique, is what Michael Polanyi (1891–1976) calls 'tacit knowledge'.[48] It may seem unnecessary to try to match the fibres in the yarn for a reconstructed sock, but making many different socks with the only difference between them being the fibre demonstrated a clear difference in stretch, warmth and longevity of each sock according to its material. In turn, this leads to bigger questions that affect our interpretation of the original object – was it an everyday sock that needed to last for as long as possible? Was it warm enough to be a winter-wear sock? Did the stretch make it fit like a glove, or would it soon simply bag around the foot? Or was it made of soft, maybe even imported wool, hinting at it being more of a high-end item? Answers to such questions may open up questions about the size of a settlement

---

[47] Nordland, *Primitive Scandinavian Textiles*, pp. 94–96.

[48] Ruth Kotinski, 'Michael Polanyi and tacit knowledge'; https://infed.org/mobi/michael-polanyi-and-tacit-knowledge/, accessed 22 March 2022.

and the status of its inhabitants, possible trade routes and overflow production of items for sale versus self-sufficiency.

Being able to replicate the historical making process can also give insights into what traces the original production system may leave. Neither *nalbinding* nor tablet weaving may seem to be processes that leave much trace beyond the actual needle and tablets, and the remnants of the textile itself. However, expanding the experimental reconstruction to encompass the making of the raw materials highlights some interesting things, such as the trading of silk and metal threads.

The greatest variation in the process of making *nalbinding* is the different stitches. These all have their own characteristics, caused and shaped by the number of coils and crossings that affect how easy it is to work with different-sized and shaped needles, in different qualities of yarn. This tacit knowledge offers insights into which needle sizes and shapes are more likely to have been used for *nalbinding*. Archaeological finds from Viking Age Sweden have yielded a large variety of bone needles, for which the usage of most is unknown.[49] However, a crafter with experience of *nalbinding* is more likely to be able to pick which needles may have been used for this technique, in the same way that an experienced leather crafter was able to identify an ancient antler tool as a leather-working tool, and a medieval book artist being able to identify possible penknives from other knifes, since many tools are dependent on their shape for their function; they have not really changed.

By using the same yarns in both knitted and *nalbound* socks, I discovered that a completed *nalbound* textile survives longer use than a knitted one, because the finished structure of the *nalbound* textile contains a higher density of yarn per square centimetre.

One of the most important factors affecting the tablet-weaving process is the tension of the warp threads, within each tablet and between tablets, especially when using a human tension system with the warp in a bundle. When making narrow bands the effect is not so great, but in wider bands, with more and/or thicker tablets, there is a significant spread of the threads from attachment point of the warp bundle to the tablets. The difference in length of travel (from the point of attachment to the tablet) between the threads in the middle of the band and the edges of the band is large enough to create a difference in the tension of the threads. This can be alleviated by running the warp over and/or round a bar to spread the threads evenly, or by using a warp spreader (a comb, used in many different cultures for tablet weaving).[50]

My experiments have also shown that for more complex patterns, where tablets and groups of tablets are rotated at different times or turned in different directions, the weaving may have been set up on an upright loom, where individual loom weights could be attached to each tablet, allowing any excess twist in the yarn to unwind for each tablet separately, enabling more complex patterns where some tablets will be turned more

---

[49] Märta Lindström, 'Nålar av ben, horn och brons', in *Uppgrävt förflutet för PK-banken i Lund*, ed. by Anders W. Mårtensson, Archaeologica Lundensia 7 (Lund: Kulturhistoriska museet i Lund, 1976), pp. 275–278.

[50] Collingwood, *The Techniques of Tablet Weaving*, p. 41.

often in one direction than others. Alleviating the different amounts of twist also evens out the tension, because warp threads with more twist experience higher tension.[51]

Personal experience also shows that having the band set up in a modern inkle loom makes it easier to weave brocading patterns. As soon as a human-tensioned band contains two sets of tablets (any brocaded pattern or Icelandic double weave, or anything more complex than a basic geometric pattern, such as letters, or animal patterns) that need to be turned individually, there is the risk that when the tension is reduced to turn the first set, the tablets in the second set may move, tangling them, or causing a tablet to be missed and not turned.

Historical tablets are smaller than modern ones (the Oseberg tablets being roughly 43 x 43 mm, 1.7 x 1.7 in, while modern store-bought plastic/cardboard ones are usually around 8.8 cm, 3.5 in, square or larger). My favourite size is formed by squaring off a business card, so slightly larger than the Oseberg ones, but still smaller than most commercially available modern ones. A more significant difference is the thickness of the tablet, where modern cards made of cardboard or thin plastic are so much thinner than wooden ones. The thicker the tablet, the fewer can be comfortably held and turned in one hand.[52] The weight of the tablets is also reflected in the weaving. Wooden tablets are light and easy to use in any setup, be it human tensioned, horizontal or vertical (either attached at a high point or in an upright loom), while heavier tablets, such as ones made from antler or horn, are subject to both line-jumping and flipping as soon as the tension is released, requiring a steady tension and a system to tie them in place if the weave has to be moved.

An additional interesting aspect to the making of a reproduction is the value that the maker personally places on the re-created object simply because of the time spent making it, and how that may translate into monetary value. While this is an important lesson to learn for any reproduced item, it is especially true for fabric. Having turned sheared fleece into yarn for both *nalbinding* and tablet weaving, I can now understand why every little scrap of fabric was used, simply from the amount of time and work put into each piece.

USING RECONSTRUCTIONS

While making reconstructions helps to answer questions about how the tools were used, what traces may be left from the production, to what degree the maker's skill affects the outcome and how the quality of the raw material can change the result, the finished object can reveal much more if it is actually used. Using a textile reconstruction can test the hypothesis of what the item may have been made for, and how efficient it was in its intended purpose. It can also give valuable information about normal wear and tear seen upon regular items versus items that may have been used only for special occasions and for burial.

---

[51] Collingwood, *The Techniques of Tablet Weaving*, p. 65.
[52] Collingwood, *The Techniques of Tablet Weaving*, p. 11.

THE VALUE OF INTANGIBLE KNOWLEDGE173

Whereas experimental archaeologists and living history re-enactors may be well matched in research, mastery of technique and execution of reconstructions, living history re-enactors excel in the wearing and use of re-created items. If my experience from simply mending the amount of medieval garb that my husband and I wear through was not enough, my professional capacity as a maker of historical clothing has given me an extensive amount of experience in mending and remaking historical clothes.

Historically speaking, we know several instances of reused fabrics, where gold work, both embroidered borders and tablet-woven bands, survived (and in some cases still survive) in a secondary function, often going from secular wear to become ecclesiastic wear as decorations on priestly garments or being re-sewn.[53] For the more secular instances, the Coppergate sock is a good example of a clothing item well mended. An extreme case of reuse construction is the seventh- to eighth-century Bernuthsfeld, Germany, tunic, which was made of forty-nine different pieces of fabric, with different weaves and colours (the tunic, and the fabric itself, was noted to not have been noticeably worn). It is speculated that the owner may have been a very poor man or a beggar, it not being a common thing to see a tunic made of so many pieces.[54]

While academic scholars have often discussed aspects of recycling and reusing clothing and textiles, wearing authentically made re-creations of clothing can give further, sometimes unexpected, insights. Having worn a re-created, thirteenth-century, wool dress over a linen underdress for several years, I discovered that the most worn part of the dress was not the hem or sleeves but the upper-shoulder portion, including the neckline. This was because the weight of the wool dress presses down on the underdress, causing friction and wear. This is a relatively simple part of the clothing to replace because the demarcation line between still-good fabric and worn fabric lies quite straight across the dress. Having cut out the piece, I discovered that it is an exact copy of the piece of neckline found wrapped around the foot of the Bocksten man as an additional foot padding.[55] The man from Bocksten was found in 1936 in a bog in Sweden, and all his wool clothing, hose, tunic, hood and cloak was preserved. He had reused several pieces of fabric from worn-out clothing as foot wrap/extra padding. The worn-out piece of my neckline suggested that after the Bocksten neckline had worn out during normal wear and tear, it had been re-purposed as a wrapping. It had not worn out while used in the secondary function of a wrapper.

This is a good example of how living history and historical re-enactors can collaborate in academic research. There are other obvious opportunities for collaboration, such as

---

[53] Maren Clegg Hyer, 'Reduce reuse, recycle: imagined and reimagined textiles in Anglo-Saxon England', *Medieval Clothing and Textiles* 8 (2012), 49–62.

[54] Heidemarie Farke, 'Der Männerkittel aus Bernuthsfeld. Beobachtungen während einer Restaurierung', in *Textiles in European Archaeology. Report from the 6th NESAT Symposium 7–11th May 1996 in Borås*, ed. by Lise Bender Jørgensen and Christina Rinaldo (Göteborg: Göteborg University, Dept. of Archaeology, 1998) pp. 99–106 (p. 100).

[55] Margareta Nockert, *Bockstensmannen och hans dräkt* (Halmstad och Varberg: Stiftelsen Hallands Länsmuseer, 1997), pp. 7–158, p. 67.

offering the possibility of huge sample sizes for different kinds of craft experiments. For example, clothing can be monitored over time, linking archaeological finds to the reality of wear and use. There has long been a gap between people simply researching history for the sake of knowing, and people researching for the sake of experiencing history. I believe both groups would benefit by learning from each other. By doing so, in order to create a greater understanding of history 'as a whole', both the small and the larger questions can be explored.

EXAMPLES OF COOPERATION BETWEEN LIVING HISTORY RE-ENACTORS, MUSEUMS AND ACADEMIA

There are many good examples of cooperation between re-enactors, museums and academia. Projects range from the large to the small, and the general to the specific. I have found that smaller museums are often more willing to welcome local craftsmen and historical re-enactors for specific events, such as the Midwest Viking Festival at the Hjemkomst museum (Moorhead, Minnesota, USA),[56] and to make items for special exhibits. Larger museums, on the other hand, often have more resources to make a larger involvement possible, such as making it an annual event or a more permanent part of an exhibit.[57] There is no registry for craftspeople or historical re-enactors and word of mouth plays an important role in connecting people for projects and collaborations. Even despite a prominent online presence of both individual re-enactors and living history in general, it can be hard to connect, if people do not know that the resources they are seeking actually exist and are out there. This requires a willingness of institutions, museums etc. to have an open mind, and besides recruiting within an organisation, to also look beyond.

Another good example of cooperation can be found at the Foteviken Viking museum in Skåne, Sweden.[58] The Foteviken museum is a municipal archaeological open-air museum with reconstructed buildings. Its aim is to recreate the Foteviken Viking Age settlement, with several houses surrounded by an earthwork wall. It employs several museum educators and researchers and has participated in a number of international research projects. The unique aspect of this museum is the Byalag, an organisation that participates in different activities within the village, such as growing vegetables and maintaining the houses. The members meet every week at the village. They belong to different households that 'live' in the reconstructed houses, and they have permanent free access to the 'Viking reserve', as they call it. During the museum's annual summer Viking market, members of the Byalag live in the houses and work in the village, interacting with visitors.

---

[56] Historical and Cultural Society of Clay County – Home, hcscconline.org, accessed 23 March 2022.

[57] For instance, the 'Viking Summer' annual event that the Historiska museet in Stockholm sets up every year, where re-enactors and museum staff lead different activities; www.historiska.se/events-and-programmes-spring-2022/, accessed 21 May 2022.

[58] See note 7.

This is a successful form of cooperation, where the re-enactors help with museum maintenance, do research together to improve and expand the museum and become part of the experience for visitors. Many members are also proficient in different crafts, such as coin striking, blacksmithing, tablet weaving, loom weaving and bread baking, and they demonstrate these skills to visitors. During the Foteviken Viking market, this is also a good and economical way for the museum to man all the houses with fully dressed and equipped 'Vikings' at no extra cost, and for visitors to see a spectrum of a Viking population and their crafts.

Not all museums or research centres have a suitable village that re-enactors can populate, or even space for experimental archaeology. However, it is amazing what can be achieved with an empty field and historical re-enactors willing to camp.

Days of Knights 'is a public educational event that strives to bring you a historically accurate re-creation of several time periods from the era known as the Middle Ages. Visitors will be able to walk through a time line encampment featuring living history enthusiasts re-creating the Norman invaders of Britain in 1066, crusaders from the 1200s, archers and knights from the 100 Years War, and many others'.[59] Re-enactors gather from across the USA to present a time line of encampments, where each camp has different ongoing activities or displays, presenting a variety of activities from the period represented. This event was first held in Kentucky, USA, in 2012. The founder was involved with the county's historical organisation and reached out to friends in the re-enactment world to help him present this event. It was so popular that it became an annual event, currently based in Lancaster, Ohio.

At the other end of the spectrum are academic conferences. One such example was the 'From Fibres to Decorative Textiles' sessions held at the 2019 IONA conference in Vancouver, Canada, which gave rise to this volume. Artisans were invited to teach several different techniques alongside more conventional academic presentations. Not all conferences are able to combine practical and traditional sessions. There can be several reasons for this, such as the need for specialist and large equipment, or access to fire, water or similar requirements. However, there are already some living-history museums that offer combinations of classes and workshops, such as the Weald and Downland Living Museum. Maybe they could expand their mission beyond having normal visitors to hosting conferences as well. Other possible venues include those that have the equipment and space to host hands-on teaching. There are several countries that have historical trade schools and cultural projects that aim to maintain and teach traditional crafts, which often already have a strong background in history with a degree of research. Maybe these could expand into the cross-over field of experimental archaeology and reconstruction.

However, the largest barrier for a historical re-enactor or historical craft person in attending academic conferences is cost. As a result, independent researchers and historical re-enactors with no institutional backing often find it impossible to attend a conference. I argue that there need to be alternatives to in-person attendance for makers who want to partake in the academic lectures, such as the online options that have flourished

---

[59] https://thedaysofknights.com, accessed 23 March 2022.

due to the pandemic of the early 2020s. Likewise, since it is harder to teach practical hands-on crafts through remote learning, there should be budgets for guest artisans as well. Then it could become more common to have practical tracks running alongside traditional sessions.

There is also little opportunity for those working in academia, independent researchers, crafters and re-enactors to come together regularly to share knowledge. However, EXARC, the Experimental Archaeology organisation based in The Netherlands, is an exciting and innovative exception. Its mission is to share and facilitate both research and education. 'It does this through creating opportunities for researchers and practitioners to collaborate, exchange information, and share best practices in archaeological open-air museums, experimental archaeology research, educational and presentational tools and demonstrations of cultural heritage.' Their goal is to bring people together and make them more professional. Their platform is worldwide and therefore brings people from different cultures together to explore how things were made and used, sharing their knowledge freely.[60]

CONCLUSION

Exploring history through experimental archaeology, by reconstructing items, processes and activities, can be approached in several forms, depending on the purpose of the reconstruction. Reconstruction also goes hand in hand with historical re-enactment, both for educational purposes and for entertainment and enjoyment. Historical re-enactment comes in many forms, but the common denominator is a genuine interest in history, prompting re-enactors to create their own accurate reproduction items for their own personal use, often reaching a high level of skill.

Textiles are particularly suited for reconstructions, since the original artefacts are usually too fragmentary and fragile to handle. We are surrounded by textiles and they form tactile objects that define us, both directly and indirectly, as clothing and furnishings. By making reconstructions of historical textiles we can learn about the people who made and used the original pieces, from how a technique was worked and how a tool was used, to recognising and understanding the correct materials for each textile and the social contexts in which the textiles were made and used. This is very true for tablet weaving, where the underlying principle is quite simple, but with the increasing complexity of patterns, more experience is required. The effort and value of each piece increases, but the usage within a costume is also connected to its size and width, which is not always obvious in a quick comparison of different bands without the knowledge and experience of construction.

From studying a reconstruction, we can measure tensile strength, moisture absorption, thread count and so on, but from using a reconstruction, we can also appreciate the more intangible qualities such as softness, colour and warmth, which is what are more commonly used to actually describe a textile, both historically speaking and today. With

---

[60] https://exarc.net/about-us/2020-vision, accessed 23 March 2022.

wear and tear, it is even possible to understand what secondary use may be possible, as in recycling and reusing, but also in mending items, giving a further insight into the entire life span of a textile. Mending my socks, I was faced with the same questions as the maker and/or mender of the Coppergate sock. As the maker, I would be more likely have access to yarn of the same quality to mend with, or I could choose a different quality on purpose. As a mender, owner or secondary owner, I might simply use whatever was at hand. Evaluating the possibility of what choices have been made, and the quality or difference in the hand between makers, owners and menders, the life span and possible transition of ownership can be speculated, in short affecting the perceived value of the item.

It is hard for anyone to be an expert in all historical crafts, and to have the time to spend creating and maintaining the skills to make items. With the increased interest and knowledge of historical re-enactors all over the world, there is now a huge resource for academic scholars to access, to collaborate with as research partners and sounding boards. Knowledge freely shared leads to more knowledge and greater understanding.

The study of history is like any other science, ever changing, with new and better technologies giving us new and insightful data. As a result, our perception of the past widens and changes, and records are re-written. Working collaboratively, academics, independent researchers, crafters and re-enactors have the power to rewrite history seen through the use and making of textiles.

As with any research, it cannot be done in a vacuum, and it does not matter if you are a professor or a re-enactor, the research will only be stronger together. As a botanist by profession, I am all for cross-pollination.

CHAPTER 10

Collaborative Working Practices: Creating and Theorising Sprang

Carol James

This chapter presents a reflection on the important contribution skilled artisans offer towards a better understanding of historic textiles and their manufacture, by focusing on a discussion about the braiding textile technique known today as sprang. Briefly put, scholars who research and write about textiles benefit significantly when they interact with people who create textiles. Avoiding this step can result in misrecognition, and a less-than-robust understanding of the textile and its context, if key aspects of construction and identification, details that are not always apparent through inspection, are missed. By exploring the reconstruction, and therefore the construction of a textile, researchers may gain insights into new diagnostic markers, as, for instance, aspects that might seem merely decorative to the non-specialist may be revealed, by the reconstruction, to be structural devices of shaping, short cuts, repairs, or mistakes by the maker. Going beyond these essential technical details of textile construction, reconstruction can reveal diverse aspects of daily life, particularly the necessary skills, space and equipment required to construct a certain textile. In short, collaboration between historical textile researchers and skilled textile reconstruction artisans, in this case in the study of sprang-construction textiles, opens doors to insights not always available through the inspection and study of textile samples alone.

The chapter begins with a brief overview of the techniques, history and geographical distribution of sprang-created textiles. It then moves on to discuss some of the insights I have gained through the act of creating replicas of historic textile items in conjunction with American and European museums, based on items from their collections that have been identified as having been produced using the sprang technique. In doing this, I will give examples of where my understanding of decorative options and structure changed dramatically as my work on a particular piece progressed, suggesting some of the insights that textile reproduction can offer to textile studies. Finally, I will discuss the importance

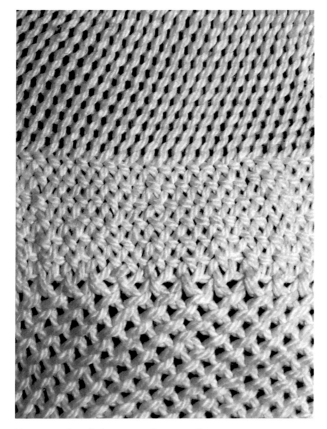

Fig. 10.1 Interlinking, interlacing and intertwining structures that can be produced when making sprang textiles. Photograph Carol James.

of delivering workshops and lectures, the opportunities for collegiality these offer and the benefit some textile professionals might derive from attending them.

OVERVIEW OF THE SPRANG TECHNIQUE

At its most basic level, sprang can be understood as a textile method where threads, stretched on a frame, are manipulated to form two joined sections of cloth, one section at either end of the frame, mirror-images of one another. In his book *The Techniques of Sprang: Plaiting on Stretched Threads*, Peter Collingwood describes sprang as 'a method of making fabric by manipulating the parallel threads of a warp that is fixed at both ends'. Essentially, sprang produces a fabric from warp threads alone. Because sprang is worked on a frame that fixes the warp at both ends, another characteristic of sprang is that, by manipulating the threads at one end of the loom, the weaver is simultaneously producing a mirrored piece at the other end of the frame. The movements the weaver

Fig. 10.2 Detail of sprang textile missing its selvedge. It could be mis-interpreted as a loom-woven fabric. Photograph Carol James.

Fig. 10.3 Left, diagram of a loom-woven twill textile. The warp and weft threads are distinct. Right, diagram of sprang twill. All the threads are warp threads. © Carol James.

uses to manipulate the threads on the frame 'can take the form of interlinking, interlacing or intertwining of adjacent threads or groups of threads'.[1] These three structures are featured in Fig. 10.1.

While the sprang technique can vary significantly from loom-weaving techniques that employ both warp and weft threads, some structures amenable to sprang, such as interlacing structures, can appear to be identical to woven cloth. For instance, a fragment of twill fabric missing its selvedge could either have been constructed using the sprang method or been produced by a conventional loom using warp and weft (Figs 10.2, 10.3). The piece of cloth in Fig 10.2 features an over-2, under-2 structure. Was it loom-woven or created using the sprang technique? The question can be resolved only by looking at the edges of the cloth. If the edges of the cloth have disappeared over time, then the method of construction cannot be definitively determined.

GEOGRAPHIC RANGE AND TIME FRAME

The footprint of textiles created using the technique today known as sprang is enormous. Collingwood gives examples of sprang-constructed fabric that reach back to the Neolithic age, through nineteenth-century military sashes, and into the twentieth century. Evidence of sprang-worked garments, bags, and accessories, notes Collingwood, ranges from Rome to Peru; while some of the oldest extant examples of this technique have been found in Scandinavia and the North Atlantic, dating to times before, and extending into, the Viking era. Ian Jenkins and Dyfri Williams, in studying sprang hairnets manufactured in ancient Greece, note their similarity to Coptic versions, while David Meyer and Thomas R. Smith write about the sprang bags used in ceramic production, their likeness preserved in the impressions they have left in clay pottery that was made in North America long before European contact in the Saskatchewan River region of what is today Canada.[2]

Evidence of sprang during the Viking era includes a rectangular piece of cloth from Mickelgate Bar in York, UK, with ends that were cut and knotted on only one of the four sides. Finished on three sides of the piece of cloth, it is assumed the manner of

---

[1] Peter Collingwood, *The Techniques of Sprang: Plaiting on Stretched Threads* (London: Faber and Faber, 1974), p. 31.

[2] Collingwood, *The Techniques of Sprang*, pp. 37–44; Margarethe Hald, *Ancient Danish Textiles from Bogs and Burials: A Comparative Study of Costumes and Iron Age Textiles* (Copenhagen: The National Museum of Denmark, 1980), pp. 28–32, 58–60; Louise Clark, 'Notes on small textile frames pictured on Greek vases', *American Journal of Archaeology* 87.1 (1983), 91–96, DOI: 10.2307/504671, accessed 16 February 2023; Ian Jenkins and Dyfri Williams, 'Sprang hair nets: their manufacture and use in ancient Greece', *American Journal of Archaeology* 89.3 (1985), 411–418, DOI: 10.2307/504357, accessed 16 February 2023; David Meyer and Thomas R. Smith, 'The Mudrick Site: Selkirk in the Saskatchewan Parklands', *Canadian Journal of Archaeology/Journal Canadien D'Archéologie* 34.2 (2010), 174–211 (p. 185); http://www.jstor.org/stable/41103697, accessed 16 February 2023.

construction was sprang. Sewn into a tube, it is assumed it was used as a stocking. In her report, Audrey Henshall also noted:

> An early 10th century Viking brooch from Unst, Shetland, in the National Museum, Edinburgh (IL, 223) (Shetelig, II, 1840, 104; P.S.A.S. XVII, 17) which bears a positive impression of some fabric. The mesh forms slender diamond shapes, and a fine plain 'sprang' seems to be the only technique which would leave such an impression.[3]

The ship found at Oseberg in Norway, and dating to AD 850, contained a free-standing frame that has been called a sprang frame.[4] The Oseberg frame is currently housed in the Viking Ship Museum in Oslo, Norway.

There is evidence of the continued use of the sprang technique in Europe. Peter Collingwood lists a number of European sprang items dating from the fifteenth century to 1850.[5] He also lists images of sprang on vases, dishes, frescoes, woodcuts and engravings, as well as references in the written record.[6] Recent renovations to a Tyrolean castle at Nikolsdorf, in Austria, yielded a cache of textiles, sealed into the space around the year 1480, and examined by textile expert Beatrix Nutz.[7] The cache included items of sprang construction, further confirming the presence of the technique in Europe at that time.

RESEARCHING AND TEACHING SPRANG TECHNIQUES

In a broad sense, the techniques of researching textiles through reproduction can be thought of as a branch of experimental archaeology, which, writes Alan K. Outram, can allow researchers to take 'what has been learned in the lab' and test their theories and ideas in ways that 'reflect more accurately "real life" or "actualistic" scenarios'.[8] In the case of sprang, the potential value of integrating experimental or actualistic reproduction techniques into other forms of textile research becomes apparent when considering the fact that not only have, as Collingwood writes, 'only a small number of sprang fabrics ... chanced to survive', but the technique itself had continued into the twentieth century in only a few small pockets globally, as had, as Louise Clark writes, even the tools used to make sprang, often made of organic materials such as wool.[9] In this context, the reproduction of examples of textiles identified by historic textile professionals as having

---

3   A.S. Henshall, 'Early textiles found in Scotland', *Proceedings of the Society of Antiquaries of Scotland* 86 (1951–2), p. 23.

4   Collingwood, *The Techniques of Sprang*, p. 38.

5   Collingwood, *The Techniques of Sprang*, pp. 43–44.

6   Collingwood, *The Techniques of sprang*, pp. 44–45.

7   Rachel Case, Beatrix Nutz and Carol James, *Enigmatic Beauty, Headwear of Lengberg Castle* (2018), p. 5; https://www.academia.edu/38136973/Enigmatic_Beauty_Headwear_of_Lengberg_Castle_pdf, accessed 16 February 2023.

8   Alan K. Outram, 'Introduction to experimental archaeology', *World Archaeology* 40.1 (2008), 1–6, 2; http://www.jstor.org/stable/40025310, accessed 16 February 2023.

9   Collingwood, *The Techniques of Sprang*, p. 35, 37; Clark, 'Notes on small textile frames', p. 91.

CREATING AND THEORISING SPRANG

been made using the sprang technique can significantly expand the information that can be gleaned from a tiny swatch of surviving fabric or the illustration of a loom on a piece of pottery.

It is from this position of the value of reproduction for teasing out the stories that some artefacts may only hint at that I enter the field of textile studies. I am a self-taught textile practitioner who has been exploring sprang since the mid-1990s. I began in this field by replicating military sashes, at the request of historic re-enactors working at a site near my home in Winnipeg, Canada. Through my exploration of the technique of sprang, and my research into these sashes, my path has led me to find that sprang goes far beyond military sashes from the 1800s. This, in turn, led to connections with a number of museums, curators, and textile historians, and to an examination of sprang items in collections across North America and Europe. Through making replicas of many of these pieces I have learnt a great deal and have developed my own pattern-writing method to accommodate the variety of structures it is possible to produce with sprang, and I have been working to expand awareness of the techniques by teaching the sprang technique to others since 2008.

As an experienced practitioner of sprang, I have often been surprised when speaking with academicians and curators, individuals who have studied sprang textiles at great depth but in a context that has been restricted to a theoretical perspective. For example, attending the Textiles of the Nile Valley conference, held biennially in Antwerp, Belgium, individuals who have curated Egyptian sprang bonnets for years, and those who have published detailed information on sprang bonnets, marvelled at my reproductions. Holding the bonnets in their hands they expressed surprise at details such as the manner in which certain thread groups can easily detach from the others, the difference in stretch and resistance to stretch of the various structures. These are details that would have been obvious, even important, to the original wearers of the bonnets, but had not been identified by individuals curating and diagramming the bonnets, restricted as they were to visual examination only. Through these and similar experiences, I have learnt that while training/learning from textbooks and visually surveying items in collections can yield considerable insight into a textile, this type of study cannot detect certain characteristics which would have been obvious and important to the original wearer.

These gaps between theory and understanding the information that is encoded in the physical properties of the garment can be overcome only through the actual practice of making and examining replica pieces. I have, more than once, found myself having to regroup when replicating a sprang textile to meet unanticipated challenges and technical difficulties not predicted by my paper calculations. More than once I have found that the resulting cloth has had unanticipated qualities; qualities that would go undetected if examination was limited to the visual only. There are aspects to a textile: its stretchiness, its firmness, details that make it easy or difficult to adjust to the body, characteristics undetectable to the observer but keenly present to the wearer. Sometimes, recreating a textile is the only way to elucidate the reason why a particular item was produced and worn in the past.

I have also come to realise that there are different levels of understanding textile structures. The researcher's eye for certain details and their consequences develops over time and with experience. The details noted will vary with the type of training. People of diverse backgrounds will describe the same object through different lenses, noting divergent aspects. Because of this, a comprehensive study of any object will necessarily be more rigorous when the study design engages individuals from varying disciplines, allowing the results of the work to include as many aspects of the textile as possible.

My own experiences support these observations. As examples, I will discuss some of my experiences where the re-creation of historic textiles led to surprising discoveries. My initial desire for undertaking re-creation projects was to improve my level of skill in understanding the sprang technique. I had sought out advanced sprang classes, but, finding none available anywhere, set out to educate myself. To do this, I reverse-engineered motifs I saw on historic pieces. I decided that these ancient pieces would be my instructors and, by making copies of what I saw, I would improve my skills, knowledge, and understanding of sprang while learning new techniques. Creating copies of sprang pieces from online images and from museum collections, working to replicate the surface designs, I was sometimes struck by the functional role these designs played in the behaviour of the cloth.

LARGE LOOP SOLUTION: COPTIC EGYPT

Sprang-made headwear, often referred to as 'bonnets' in curated collections, has been associated with Coptic Egyptian archaeological sites, dating to between 100 and 600 CE. These beautiful pieces have been my source for researching a wide variety of surface designs. These bonnets have been described at length by numerous researchers and authors. The detailed discussions by Petra Linscheid and Anne Kwaspen have been particularly useful.[10] I have personally studied examples of these bonnets in collections such as the German Textile Museum in Krefeld, Germany,[11] the Petrie Museum[12] and

---

[10] Petra Linscheid, *Frühbyzantinische textile Kopfbedeckungen: Typologie, Verbreitung, Chronologie und soziologischer Kontext nach Originalfunden* (Wiesbaden: Reichert, 2011); Anne Kwaspen, 'Sprang hairnets in the Katoen Natie Collection', in *Dress Accessories of the 1st Millennium AD from Egypt: Proceedings of the 6th Conference of the Research Group 'Textiles from the Nile Valley', Antwerp, 2–3 October 2009*, ed. by Antoine de Moor (Tielt, Belgium: Lannoo, 2011), pp. 71–95.

[11] Textile Museum, Krefeld, Germany, collection numbers 00202, 00203, 00204, 12729, 12773, 12774, 15202, 15203, 15204, discussed in Carol James, 'Sprang bonnets from Late Antique Egypt: producer knowledge and exchange through experimental reconstruction', in *Textile Society of America Proceedings* (2018); https://digitalcommons.unl.edu/cgi/viewcontent.cgi?article=2093&context=tsaconf, accessed 16 February 2023.

[12] Petrie Museum of Egyptian Archaeology, University College, London, UK, collection numbers UC 28073, UC 28009.

CREATING AND THEORISING SPRANG

British Museum in London, UK,[13] the Guimet Museum in Lyon, France,[14] and the Kelsey Museum in Ann Arbor, Michigan, USA.[15]

Certain design elements in some of these bonnets strike me as having a structural function as well as decorative. One particularly interesting example is an apparent surface design feature that also plays a structural role. As mentioned earlier, sprang can be understood as work that is performed on a set of threads set on a frame.[16] To make a sprang textile, one begins with a warp, consisting of one continuous thread arranged between the two ends of a frame. The thread is tied to one end piece, and then wound, back and forth between the two ends. Some wind the warp around and around, others will set on a 'figure-of-8' warp, which automatically includes a cross. In either case the warp set-up is complete when the other end of the thread is secured. Work begins near the loops formed in this way at one end of the warp. Because of this arrangement, the manipulation of threads to create the sprang textile at one end of the frame results in a mirror-image of the threads' movement at the other end of the frame. Twisting neighbouring threads at one end of the frame will result in the same threads twisting, but in the opposite direction, at the other end of the frame. The mirror-image quality, however, fails along the upper and lower margins of the cloth: each thread is continuous with the neighbouring threads, connecting to the thread to the right at one end of the frame and to the thread at the left at the other end of the frame. Because of this slight lack of symmetry in the set-up, the resulting cloth will similarly lack in symmetry along the edges, where each thread connects to the neighbouring thread.

Many Coptic bonnets are formed from a single rectangular piece of sprang cloth. As the worker creates the upper half of the cloth, the lower half of the cloth also forms. When the two portions of cloth meet in the middle, they are sometimes secured with a chain line,[17] worked in loops over the warp threads similarly to the way chain stitch may

[13] London, The British Museum, London, collection numbers, EA53911, EA21633, EA21640, EA21634, EA72475, EA21632, EA37352, EA37352, AS3371, AM1954.05.605, 21632, 18292, 21633, 12544, EA72475, 12544, 53911.

[14] Lyon, Musée national des arts asiatiques-Guimet, now part of the Musée des Confluences, Lyon, bonnet worn by the mummy of a young girl, inventory number 900.12.60; Carol James and Fabienne Médard, 'Appreciation of the ancient craftsmen through the recreation of a 1st century sprang turban from the Antinoë necropolis', in *Excavating, Analysing, Reconstructing Textiles of the 1st Millennium AD from Egypt and Neighbouring Countries: The Proceedings of the 'Textiles of the Nile Valley' Conference in Antwerp, Belgium, November 27–29, 2015*, ed. by A de Moor, Cäcilia Fluck and Petra Linscheid (Tielt, Belgium: Lannoo, 2017), pp. 148–161.

[15] Kelsey Museum of Archaeology, Ann Arbor, Michigan, 22610, 22618, 10330b, 11971, 13355, 13393, 13401, 13409, 13667, 14000, 10320, 10429, 11350, 11666, 11911, 12090, 13416, 13532, 13819; Julia Galliker and Carol James, 'Textile interrelationships: Karanis sprang hairnets in daily life,' in *Egypt As a Textile Hub: textile interrelationships in the 1st millennium AD: Proceedings of the 10th Conference of the Research Group 'Textiles from the Nile Valley', Antwerp, 27–29 October 2017*, ed. by A. de Moor, Cäcilia Fluck and Petra Linscheid (Tielt: Lannoo, 2019), 258–75.

[16] Collingwood, *Techniques of Sprang*, p. 31. Carol James, *Sprang Unsprung: An Illustrated Guide to Interlinking, Interlacing and Intertwining* (Winnipeg: SashWeaver Press, 2016), p. 6.

[17] James, *Sprang Unsprung*, p. 32.

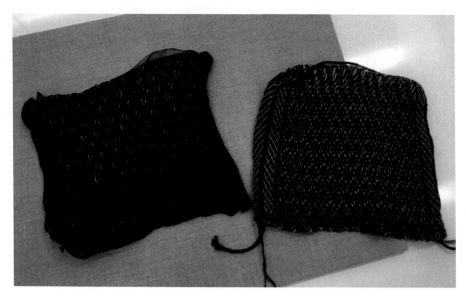

Fig. 10.4 Krefeld 15204 (left) and author's replica (right), a bonnet featuring a chain line near the brim of the bonnet. Photograph: Carol James.

be worked in tapestry weaving, which stabilises the work, preventing its unravelling and maintaining stretchiness.[18] A drawstring, inserted into the loops formed at the bottom of the loom forms the back of the head, allowing for the bonnet to be adjusted for different head sizes, while securely attaching it to the head. A firm band, sometimes woven, sometimes braided,[19] is often stitched across the portion that will form the forehead edge of the bonnet. The worker then folds the initial rectangle along the central chain line and sews up the sides to finish the bonnet.

While it may be possible for an experienced textile researcher to detect the structures and processes described this far by looking at a surviving bonnet, there are subtleties that underscore the skill and process of the original bonnet makers that show themselves only in the actual process of re-creation. Although working the threads at one end of the frame produces the same but opposite arrangement of threads at the other end of the frame, there will always be a slight difference in the structure at the top and the bottom of the cloth. Because of the mechanics of the system, regardless of whether one winds all the way around the frame or if one sets up the figure-of-8 warp as described, loops at one end will always have at least a half-twist more length than those at the other end of the frame. Coptic bonnet makers took advantage of this by choosing to use the longer loops for the part of the bonnet that would sit at the back of the head. This, in turn, meant that

---

[18] This chain structure is often used at the place where the two pieces of mirror-image cloth meet. The role of the chain line at the centre is clear, as it stabilizes the work, preventing the cloth from unravelling. I was initially perplexed to see this same looped structure near the brim of a number of these bonnets.

[19] Linscheid, *Frühbyzantinische textile Kopfbedeckungen*, p. 70.

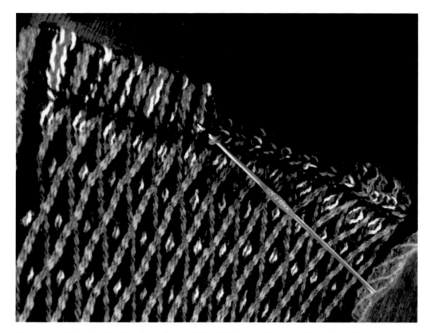

Fig. 10.5 Detail of author's replica of Krefeld 15204 showing how the chain structure shrinks and tightens the stitches at the rim of the cloth. Photograph Carol James.

the small loops would be located at the front of the bonnet, along the edge to which the browband was attached, lying across the forehead.

When studying Coptic bonnets, Anne Kwaspen noted a curious feature near the brim of some bonnets,[20] and includes this feature in her diagram depicting elements of a sprang hairnet. She calls it a chained ridge. During a meeting of the Textiles of the Nile Valley conference in Antwerp in 2015, she asked me to speculate about its role. While the chain clearly serves to stabilise the work when it is located at the centre of a piece, she asked me whether I thought there is a particular reason for the similar structure near the brim of some bonnets (Fig. 10.4).

When I set out to imitate this chain line structure near the brim of a replica bonnet, based on one identified as Krefeld 15204, after having completed the cloth for the bonnet I inserted a chain line a few rows in from the edge, and found a surprising thing happened. As I worked to create the chain line, pulling threads one by one, the initial few rows of cloth shrank in size and I realised that the insertion of the chain line would result in a much firmer edge. I suspect that this could be the reason for inserting a chain line near the front edge where the binding was applied, as it reduces the size of the loops and allows for a tighter seam join between the sprang bonnet and the woven brow band to which it is stitched. It is a useful trick that delights modern workers (Fig. 10.5).

[20] Kwaspen, 'Sprang hairnets', p. 71.

ELASTICITY/RESISTANCE OF THE CLOTH: COPTIC EGYPT

The weaving process to create a dotted fabric used to make another type of Coptic bonnet (Krefeld 15203) led me to another unexpected discovery, this time regarding the elasticity and resistance of sprang textiles.[21] Krefeld 15203 features a motif of red dots on a green background, forming the central pattern similar to other bonnets.[22] When viewed from the inside of the bonnet, you have green dots on a background of red. The inside and outside of the cloth involved in this pattern therefore form a reversed colour order (Fig. 10.6).

Initially, I thought this pattern would be easy to understand, the bonnet structure being a double cloth technique. In double cloth technique, two sets of warp threads (in this case one red and one green) are used, wound onto the loom in parallel. When creating the fabric, the worker brings the desired colour of thread to the front of the cloth and takes the other colour to the back as needed to create the design.

To test this theory, I made a sample. While I did get the desired motif of dots, which reversed the pattern on the inside, I found that the number of dots did not accurately correspond to the number of coloured stripes at the brim of the original bonnet (Fig. 10.7).

Reflecting on this difference, I searched for a way to reconcile the ratio between the number of dots and coloured stripes, and eventually came to understand that the structure of this bonnet is not a double layer cloth structure but, rather, a pattern that alternates between double- and single-layer cloth. The result of these alternations also produces the dots.

When I set up a new warp and created a piece using this alternating technique, the number of dots relative to the number of colour stripes at the brim matched the original piece. On one row, all threads are present, alternating sets of different colours of stitches over four rows. Then the worker separates the threads by colour into two layers. One colour of thread forms stitches sitting on the outside of the hat, and the other forms stitches that sit on the inside of the hat. This segregation continues for four rows, and then all threads once again sit side by side on the same row. The result is a cloth that has a series of horizontal channels which run between the two layers of fabric. These are areas of double cloth. In between the horizontal channels we see horizontal stripes of single-layer cloth.

If the discovery of this complex technique was a surprise, what surprised me even more was the almost contrary behaviour of the resulting cloth. When held in the hand, the cloth is quite stretchy and yet at the same time seems to resist being stretched. This is a result of the number of threads in the walls of the channels in the fabric being fewer than in the walls of the cloth between the channels, producing a difference in the horizontal stretch of the cloth. I now believe that the most obvious visual quality of the cloth, the dots, was probably not the primary interest of the weaver. Rather, their goal had probably been to control the behaviour of the fabric. That said, the contrasting colours used in the

---

[21]   For more information on this project see James, 'Sprang bonnets'.

[22]   Katoen Natie Collection 997-28 and the Fribourg Musée d'Art et d'Histoire Inv. Nr S 446.

Fig. 10.6 Krefeld 15203: pattern inside is the reverse of the outside pattern. Photograph: Carol James.

Fig. 10.7 Author's replica samples of bonnet Krefeld 15203. Left, has twice the number of stripes as dots in the lowest row. Right, has the correct number of stripes and dots and features fabric alternating between double- and single-layer cloths. Photograph Carol James.

warp help the worker to separate the threads into two layers, and to re-integrate them in a manner that creates this reinforced, stretchy fabric efficiently. In the end, I concluded that the coloured pattern of dots was probably a by-product of the process rather than the intent. The stretchy quality of the cloth would mean that it would expand to accommodate a large amount of hair on the head. While other sprang techniques would easily spread horizontally, indeed sag, this structure would spread horizontally and at the same time hold firm. The difference can be likened to a girdle, a 'control' garment for the hair.

ACCOMMODATION FOR AN INCREASE IN WIDTH:
RENAISSANCE ITALY

Like the contrasting dots in the previous example, coloured motifs can hide surprising clues about constructing and using sprang cloth. A particular motif in a pair of sprang leggings offers a case in point.[23] I have been intrigued by depictions of individuals wearing skin-tight legwear in artworks from the late 1400s to the early 1500s ever since Dagmar Drinkler, Textile Conservator at the Bavarian National Museum in Munich, Germany, directed my attention to them.[24] These all feature individuals wearing a tight-fitting garment with vertical stripes over the legs, and another pattern over the hips. In all cases the design over the hips aligns with the stripes in the legs. The colour seen in the leg stripes continues into the hips, where other colours are added. Ms Drinkler and I have interpreted these images as sprang leggings made of a single layer of sprang from ankles to hip, and a two-layered cloth over the top of the thighs to the waist. To test this theory, I decided to recreate these leggings and see if I could work out the technical aspects of their construction. Since starting on this project, I have experimented with the creation of several pairs of leggings and some of the results have been surprising.

When creating a pair of sprang leggings, both legs are made at the same time, taking advantage of the fact that the sprang technique produces a mirror image of the work done at one end of the loom at the other end of the loom. That is, if the work begins at the right ankle at the top of the loom, the left ankle is also created as the mirror-image piece of cloth at the bottom of the loom. From the ankle, work progresses up the legs. When at approximately the mid-thigh position, the worker introduces supplemental warp threads into the work. This supplemental warp is far shorter than the original warp, extending

[23] See Dagmar Drinkler and Carol James, 'Tight-fitting clothes in Antiquity and the Renaissance: research and experimental reconstruction', in *Crafting Textiles: Tablet Weaving, Sprang, Lace and Other Techniques from the Bronze Age to the Early 17th century*, ed. by Frances Pritchard (Oxford and Philadelphia: Oxbow, 2021), pp. 103–128.

[24] These include *San Paolo fuori le mura* by Hans Holbein from 1504 in the Augsburg Staatsgalerie; the *Martyrdom of St Katharine* by Lucas Cranach, 1506, in the Dresden Gemäldegalerie; the *Crucifixion Triptych* by Jean Bellegambe, 1520, in the Leipzig Gemälldegalerie; the *Beheading of St John* on the Gerolzhofen Altar, by Tilman Riemenschneider, c. 1515, Munich, Bayerisches Nationalmuseum, acc. no. MA 1963.

CREATING AND THEORISING SPRANG

from the mid-thigh on the right leg, through the waistline and only as far as mid-thigh on the left leg.[25]

Creating this second introduced warp of exactly the correct length can be tricky, and experience has shown that it is best to calculate the length ahead of time, then set it up beside the original warp several rows before it is needed.[26] Work on the original warp continues until the supplemental warp thread length matches the unworked lengths of thread in the original warp. Combining the two warps to transition from a single-layer cloth to working on a two-layer cloth is a tricky operation requiring skill, experience and judgement. The new threads must be placed between the threads of the single layer in the correct order, without crossing over one another. This requires a great deal of attention to detail on the part of the worker.

The change in the width of the cloth when it transitions from a single-layer cloth to a double-layer cloth also requires experience and judgement to get it right. I confronted this in my first attempts to create a pair of leggings; the change introduced an undesired looseness into the cloth at the point of transition. The single-layered cloth of the legs sat comfortably at a narrower width compared to the patterned double cloth of the upper leg. This is actually a desirable outcome, as it means the larger circumference around the hips is comfortably accommodated, but to the weaver this is a problem: the double-layer cloth requires more width space in which to weave. Until I learnt how to deal with the change of width, the effect was a loosening of the already worked single-layer cloth; to manipulate the two separate layers, the worker holds all the threads in the same plane, and twice the number of threads requires twice the width. Patterns worked in the two-layer cloth involve threads which switch places between the layers, and these threads require space in which to exchange position. This means that the double cloth will sit wider than the single-layered cloth. The place where the cloth transitions from single-layered cloth to double-layered is the place where the cloth widens, and the worker's skill in keeping the tension is critical.

Viewing the variety of designs which I saw when reviewing the leggings in the paintings, my attention was drawn to a gondolier in a late fifteenth-century scene of Venice.[27] In the painting, the gondolier is wearing a garment with vertical stripes over the calf, tumbling blocks around the hips and a diamond motif that bridges the stripes and blocks. I was intrigued by this design and speculated on techniques to recreate it, then set up my equipment to experiment, trying to replicate this motif.[28]

The design of the gondolier's leggings suggests a gradual addition of threads instead of the all-at-once addition described above. Adding threads a few at a time creates the

---

[25] For images of this technique, see Drinkler and James, 'Tight-fitting clothes'.

[26] For more information on this technique, see Drinkler and James, 'Tight-fitting clothes'.

[27] This gondolier appears in the foreground of the painting titled *Miracle of the Cross at the Ponte di Rialto*, also known as *The Healing of the Madman*, by Vittore Carpaccio, *c.* 1496, now in the Gallerie dell'Accademia, Venice; https://www.bl.uk/collection-items/carpaccios-miracle-of-the-relic-of-the-true-cross-on-the-rialto-bridge, accessed 16 February 2023.

[28] For an image of the result, see Drinkler and James, 'Tight-fitting clothes', fig. 7.24.

Fig. 10.8 The author's recreation of the Arizona Openwork Shirt. Photograph Carol James.

lower portion of the diamond motif on the gondolier's thigh. It also allows for the gradual increase in the width of the cloth, easing the task of maintaining tension throughout the transition. This discovery was quite unexpected and would not have occurred to me, had I not set the threads on my frame and sought to reproduce the motif for myself.

COMPLEX DESIGN AND HOW IT WAS ACHIEVED: PRE-COLUMBIAN SOUTH AMERICA

The Arizona Openwork Cotton Shirt, now in the Arizona State Museum collection in Tucson, which has been radiocarbon dated to between 'the late thirteenth century until as late as AD 1475',[29] features three motifs which appear repeatedly across the shirt: swirls, meanders, and wedges (Fig.10.8).

At first glance the designs in the shirt seem highly regular. Mapping them out, however, I discovered a number of irregularities. The meander path, sometimes called a Greek Key, is a thin line composed of three stitches near the shoulders, and elsewhere the meander path is a thicker line that is five stitches wide. The swirl appears at the centre of the shirt with an openwork path that is two holes wide. Near the hem there are two swirls with openwork paths that are three holes wide. Most remarkable are the irregularities in the wedges. The wedges were mainly triangular and evenly spaced. In charting some forty-two wedges, I noted that fourteen of them (30 per cent) have some irregularity. These irregularities have to do with the point of the triangle being blunted or wandering off, and sometimes the irregularity has to do with the lines between the holes that define the wedges. The quantity of the irregularities in the wedges led me to suspect that at least some of them were intentional. Perhaps the intention was to transform very regular wedges or triangles into something more like a 'dancing flame' motif.

I charted the patterns onto graph paper, mapping out the motifs in careful detail, stitch by stitch. As there are multiple motifs in play on any given horizontal row, I also used the chart as a guide for creating the reconstruction, working across the graph paper, forming the cloth row by row as it had been charted. As I progressed in my work to recreate the shirt, I marvelled at the skill of the original worker, who would not have had the benefit of pencil, eraser and graph paper. How did the worker manage the numerous designs encountered in each horizontal row of work?

A possible answer came through a suggestion made by an Arizona weaver whom I met as I toured the state, giving talks and workshops between sessions of work on the shirt. This weaver suggested that when Navaho weavers create complex patterns on their rugs, they do not always work in even horizontal rows, traversing all motifs, and crossing the entire width of the piece. They sometimes work individual patterns in a diagonal line across the piece, working only a small number of the threads at a time, and connecting previously woven sections to the portion currently under construction in every row. The suggestion was that this sprang shirt may have been similarly constructed, motif by motif,

---

[29] Lynn Teague, *Textiles in Southwestern Prehistory* (Albuquerque, NM: University of New Mexico Press, 1998, p. 80, also phone conversation with the author.

Fig. 10.9 Motifs on the Arizona Openwork Shirt outlined and numbered in the order they might be worked. Photograph Carol James.

not row by row. Considering this suggestion, I mapped out the motifs and the order in which they could be worked (Fig. 10.9).

While there are numerous irregularities in the wedge design, by contrast, there is only one break in the meandering path on the entire shirt. This break occurs in zone 12 and at a location to the right of the place where the worker would pause mid-motif in order to work on zone 13. Interestingly enough, there is a corresponding irregularity in the wedge motif of zone 11, along the same latitude line. The irregularity in zone 11 is a type that occurs in only one other place on the shirt. This suggests to me that these two irregularities could be considered as confirmation that the worker created the shirt by working in zones, not row by row, as suggested by the plan in Fig. 10.9. I can imagine myself working in this manner, and pausing mid-motif in zones 11 and 12. After completing zone 13, I can see myself focusing on taking up the threads again, sorting them into their proper position, and, briefly distracted from the pattern, creating these errors: ending too soon the holes defining the wedges, and off-setting the path of the meander. The errors at this place in zone 11 and 12 can be interpreted as evidence concerning the manner in which the patterns on the shirt were created. I cannot imagine coming to this potential insight without having gone through the process of making the replica shirt.

DEVELOPING AN UNDERSTANDING FOR SPRANG STRUCTURE

As can be seen in the discussions above, while the work of recreating a piece can yield important and fascinating insights into the creation and use of sprang garments and techniques, it is never something that happens in isolation. From the suggestions of Dagmar Drinkler to the input of the Arizona weaver, collegial cooperation and shared insights form an important part of the process of investigation and problem solving that lies at the heart of recreating textiles. Even the process of developing a workshop or lecture can sometimes, in itself, help to untangle a line of thinking or shed light on a problem. I have often been invited to give talks and short instructional sessions on sprang and sprang techniques to individuals involved in academic textile research. I can present the essentials of the technique in fewer than five minutes; many of my audience members have reported to me that they listened, observed, and felt the technique was well explained. And then they went home to try it. At home they encountered challenges and were unable to achieve what they had viewed as the easy results they had seen in my demonstration. A brief explanation of sprang can give the general idea of what the technique involves, and what it can be used to produce. But a brief explanation will not be able to even touch on the many details involved in setting up and working sprang pieces, and cannot allow for the complex learning required in order for a person to successfully create or recreate a textile.

I have taught sprang for more than ten years at institutions and to handweaver guilds where I have been invited. Due to travel costs and modern time commitments, these classes are generally compressed into a single weekend. Most organisers suggest six-hour days with an hour for lunch, and perhaps coffee breaks. I have taught many two- and three-day classes, meeting six hours per day. In these twelve- and eighteen-hour courses, I cover a great deal of information, explaining diverse aspects of the technique, helping students to warp, work and finish several pieces based on examples of diverse historic pieces. Frequently, while in class, students express an expectation that understanding and skill will develop immediately. They expect that at the end of a one-day class they will be comfortable with the technique. In my experience this is generally not the case.

There has been much scientific research into the process of learning. Indeed it seems there are a variety of different types of learning, including declarative memory and procedural memory.[30] These need to be considered when thinking about the process of learning to work using the sprang technique. Research results suggest that procedural memory requires a certain amount of brain processing, called 'consolidation', for a person to advance, or gain in skill level, and that this happens during REM (Rapid Eye Movement) sleep.[31] I interpret current thinking in brain science to imply that the mastery of sprang falls into the area of procedural memory, and that repeated practice and REM sleep are required for success; this is impossible to achieve in a twenty-minute demonstration or even a half-day class.

As an instructor, it is clear to me that the student's learning process is not so much an exercise of fine motor movement, 'pick up this thread, and move it over here', as it is a matter of coming to understand the structure to be created. The student needs to learn to

---

[30]   M.G. Packard, 'Neurobiology of procedural learning in animals', in *Concise Learning and Memory: The Editor's Selection*, ed. by J.H. Byrne (London: Elsevier Science & Technology Books 2008), pp. 341–156.

[31]   Robert Stickgold and his colleagues at Harvard Medical School at Boston, Massachusetts conducted a clever set of experiments in which they used the game Tetris to guide the content of people's dreams. Among seventeen subjects they trained to play Tetris, more than 60 per cent reported dreaming of images associated with the game. In addition, the researchers found that when and how the study's sleeping participants saw these images helped to confirm the idea that the brain uses dreaming to reinforce learning; Kristin Leutwyler, 'Tetris dreams', *Scientific American*, 16 October 2000 [no page numbers]; https://www.scientificamerican.com/article/tetris-dreams/, accessed 16 February 2023.

'see' the structure in order to properly identify and reposition the threads. The skill is not as much a matter of finger dexterity as it is an organisational understanding that occurs in the brain. This applies to textile professionals and avocational practitioners alike. My observation is that students are able to consciously attend to the intricacies of their finger movements for only a certain length of time. Then it seems to me that a kind of mental fatigue sets in. In my experience, students follow instructions and within the first half hour most can execute the stitch correctly. Then, as they continue to work, students often start making mistakes, and experience frustration.

I interpret this as the moment when the brain, reacting to newly encoded information, is attempting memory consolidation. Not yet properly assimilated and consolidated, some bits of information are missing, thus mistakes are made. I tell students that mistakes now, after having worked several rows correctly, is really good news as it implies that their brains are beginning to assimilate and consolidate information. I have come to recount to students at this point some of the sleep research data cited above. Hearing of this, I notice that many students seem reassured. That the report of this brain research gives such reassurance to students suggests that at some level it is acknowledged as true. Several have told me subsequently that they dismissed the information as far fetched. Nevertheless, a few days later, picking up the work again, they found their perception of the task had indeed shifted, as predicted by Stickgold's research.

Students engaged in courses that vary from three to five days in length report that the technical learning 'clicks' for them on the third day. They often report a new, clearer understanding that seems to develop after a few days of work and after a number of nights of sleep. Asked to describe this change, the student reports that he/she now 'sees' the structure during the process of creation. The diverse and detailed individual instructions for each finger movement and the adjustment of threads are now replaced with a simple 'work the stitch'. While this shift is reassuring and no doubt satisfying to anyone trying to learn a technique such as sprang, it has particular value for professionals working with textiles that they may not be able to touch. Being able to visualise common textile structures through a process of learning how to produce them offers a unique window into understanding fragile fragments of ancient sprang work.

Since the onset of COVID in 2020, I have begun to teach sprang online. Online classes are not time limited in the same way as the face-to-face classes which I am accustomed to leading. Given the freedom to design my own class, I have reached back into previous experiences of teaching a beginner's knitting class. That was always a six-week class, of two hours per week. The multi-week formula allowed time for students to repeat the movements many more times, to reflect on the movements, and to have a number of nights of regular sleep between sessions. My first online classes were organised and moderated by former sprang students. In every case, the moderator's report highlighted the observation that students attending the six-week class of two hours per week gained a better understanding of the subject, and greater ease at mastery in creating the structures than in the (eighteen-hour contact time) intensive face-to-face classes previously attended by the moderator. The six-week plan, twelve-hour contact time, for teaching sprang generally results in better mastery of the technique by the students.

CONCLUSIONS

In these few examples, I have set out to show how collaborative work between various textile professionals and artisans skilled in textile reproduction can significantly expand our understandings of the stories that even tiny fragments of textiles, such as the sprang-worked examples cited here, have to tell. Located within the area of experimental archaeology, the deliberate reconstruction of textiles and the tools used to make them provides a broader lens into the textiles themselves and the workers who made them. At the same time, these collaborations can work both ways, and can inspire insights that derive from the creation and delivery of lectures and workshops. Finally, while it is probably unrealistic to expect many professionals to be able to find the time to devote to a focused, hands-on study of the techniques of sprang and sprang re-creation, the skills that can be learned and shared at short workshops can enhance the work of professionals, allowing them to view ancient textiles with new eyes and, if the workshop is long enough to allow time to digest and consolidate the learning, so much the better. In total, collaborations between skilled textile recreators and textile professionals offer benefits to the field of historic textiles that cannot be realised in any other way.

Asked to describe cars on the road, many will talk about red cars, and blue cars, and big trucks. Others will talk about Mercedes and Lamborghinis and GLEs and 590GTBs. The eye sees what it has been trained, over years, to acknowledge. As for cars, so for textiles. I therefore advocate for textile researchers to include practitioners on their team if they want a comprehensive understanding of an ancient piece.

DISCUSSION

Q: When you co-present a paper, or co-write an article with a curator or other 'theorist', how does the collaboration work? What do they bring to you? What do you bring to them? How much actual hands-on study is an outsider allowed to do on these presumably fragile objects?

A: The collaboration works like this: I meet someone at a conference. I met Fabienne Médard at a CIETA conference. I met Julia Galliker at a Textiles of the Nile Valley conference. We talk, and she invites me to help out with a project of research on which she has already been working. Sometimes I view the sprang object in person, sometimes only through photographs. I *never* manipulate it, only look and take photos. Sometimes the curator will agree to turn the piece over so I can see the back side. I take notes and sketches, and write up a proposed plan to recreate. Sometimes I return with my sprang pieces to compare and improve on my pattern. The sprang pieces I make allow handling in a manner that cannot be done with the originals.

Q: Accustomed as I am to the brown-stained fragments of textile that archaeologists recover from the soils of north-west Europe, I find the colours of the Egyptian and southern American sprang examples stunning; but from what you have found, the colours are more than decorative, they are a guide to the weaver in creating a range of textures and thicknesses. Is this always the case or just in the few special cases you have picked out for us? And does it work the other way? Are monochrome examples of sprang technically simpler?

A: The colours are sometimes more than decorative … not always. I have *sometimes* found the colours in the patterns to guide the division of threads, the division necessary to create the desired structure. This is not always the case. Some colourful designs do not much affect the behaviour of the cloth.

There are some monochrome pieces, for example Krefeld 15202, which has an area of monochrome work that is very sophisticated indeed.

Q: Does the sprang technique develop/become more sophisticated over time or does it stay relatively similar, just used differently to create the effects you discuss in the examples? Is this something that can be seen in surviving examples through technical analysis by textile archaeologists or re-creations or a combination of the two?

A: I cannot answer this. My expertise is in re-creating specific pieces presented to me. I leave the larger historic context to others with a background in history, dating, analysing, and such-like education.

A sad fact is that most bonnets from Egypt were not properly catalogued but, rather, acquired through informal trade. Most collections (such as the British Museum, the Victoria and Albert, the Krefeld Museum) list the person from whom the bonnet was acquired, and not the location within the find site, key to identifying time, place, and social status of the original wearer.

Many pieces of sprang done today are a great step backwards from what was done in the past.

CHAPTER 11

From Wool to Mitten: When History Comes to Life in Your Hands

Liselotte Öhrling and Anna Josefsson

L
ödöse museum is situated on the west coast of Sweden, a few miles north of Gothenburg. During the twelfth century Lödöse was the site of one of the first medieval towns in Sweden. Archaeologists have uncovered more than half a million objects during the past century, making Lödöse one of the richest sites in Sweden when it comes to medieval finds. Most of the finds are common items from everyday life, but after nearly a millennium in the muddy soil, they are not so common anymore. They now tell the story of the people who lived before us. Runic messages with warnings, promises of friendship and love, give life to the past. Names carved into tools tell us who once used and cherished the items a long time ago (Fig. 11.1).

Lödöse Museum also holds a vast collection of organic materials from medieval Sweden, dating from AD 1000 to 1350. In this collection there are approximately 1,700 registered textile finds, ranging from coarse packing textile to the finest cloth and silk lining. One of those finds is a *nalbound*[1] mitten from the thirteenth century (Fig. 11.2).[2] The mitten was found in 1972 alongside a house wall in the centre of Lödöse, approximately two metres underground. It is made in two different stitches, one of which is not certainly identified, and the other identified as the Åsle stitch.[3] The mitten is very well preserved, with only minor damage.

---

[1] For a description of *nalbinding* and the different ways of spelling the term in different languages see Ulrike Claßen-Büttner, *Nalbinding. What in the world is that? History and Technique of an Almost-forgotten Handicraft* (Norderstedt: Books on demand, 2015), pp. 7–9.

[2] Rune Ekre, Carl Hylander and Rolf Sundberg, *Lödösefynd: ting från en medeltidsstad* (Lödöse: Stödföreningen för Lödöse museum, 1994), p. 40.

[3] Claßen-Büttner, *Nalbinding*, p. 16; Sanna-Mari Pihlajapiha, 'The Åsle stitch', *Nalbinding – Nålbindning – Nålebinding*; https://www.en.neulakintaat.fi/49, accessed 30 May 2022.

Fig. 11.1   A runic message written in old Swedish from medieval Lödöse saying,"Mun Þu mik man Þik un Þu mer an ÞRr". This translates as 'Remember me, I remember you, love me, I love you'. Dated to the eleventh century. Photograph: Liselotte Öhrling.

This *nalbound* mitten was the centre of attention and the starting point for a course called 'From wool to mitten', carried out at Lödöse museum during 2017. The course was open to the public and arranged by Lödöse museum in collaboration with 'Vinterverkstan', a small Swedish handicraft supply company. Liselotte Öhrling holds a Master's degree in archaeology and works as a museum teacher at Lödöse museum. She teaches skills such as medieval dancing, spinning and *nalbinding*. 'Vinterverkstan' is run by Anna Josefsson. Through 'Vinterverkstan', she supplies craft materials and training courses in *nalbinding*, spinning and other crafts.

A few successful *nalbinding* courses and *nalbinding* cafés had been held at the museum during 2015 and 2016. Participants came in good numbers, and the museum offered an interesting and inspiring environment in which we could teach and learn together. During these meetings we noticed an interest from the participants in learning more about medieval society, the history of *nalbinding* and the work preceding the technique, such as preparing and spinning wool. At the time there were several courses in carding and spinning wool at different locations in West Sweden, but none of them combining it with *nalbinding* and history. We wanted to fill this void and decided to offer a course including the history of sheep breeds, choice of wool and preparation, *nalbinding*, plant dyeing and decoration. Furthermore, we would include the medieval history of Lödöse and a hands-on appreciation of the archaeological artefacts at the museum. This part was important, since our aim was to offer more than a *nalbinding* course. We wanted to offer an experience, a sensation of the craft and the past through the museum collection. Much

Fig. 11.2 *Nalbound* mitten from Lödöse, Sweden, early thirteenth century. Photograph: Ian Schemper for Lödöse museum.

as we wished for the participants to connect to the craft through history, we also wished for them to be able to develop a personal relationship to the *nalbinding* technique, finding their own way to use it. To realise our aims for the course, we added the most important ingredient, time for reflection. Most courses available at the time were in the form of a one- or two-day workshop. We decided to arrange four workshops with several weeks in between. It is when one gets time to reflect and process new skills and information that one can gain new insights – and raise new questions.

METHOD AND THEORY

'From wool to mitten' was held on four occasions, extending over January, March, May and September. Each session lasted between three and five hours, with a limit of twelve participants. Based on our earlier experiences of teaching *nalbinding*, we agreed that twelve was a reasonable number of participants for two teachers to handle. To maintain a good quality of instruction, five to six learners per teacher is a maximum, regardless of the participants' level of knowledge. Each occasion started with a theoretical introduction, followed by hands-on practical activities. During the practical learning sessions, we formed two groups. This is necessary for everyone to be able to see the techniques being demonstrated, and for you to be able to guide and instruct each participant step by step if needed. At the end of each session there was time for reflection as a group to discuss what we had been doing.

Expecting participants with different skills and backgrounds, we planned our sessions accordingly. We arranged to cater for different levels of knowledge and preconceptions about each theme, so that everyone could develop their skills and get something out of the course.

'From wool to mitten' was based on the theory of experiential learning, combined with theoretical introductions in lecture format. This framework aims to be interdisciplinary and inclusive of as many senses as possible with regard to the participants.[4] The famous method of 'learning by doing' is an important part of experiential learning.[5] The theory of affective history can also be applied, through the participants' close encounter with the medieval objects.[6] This is an interesting theory that has not been researched to a great extent in our field. When holding an archaeological find, something is realised, whether you are a scholar or a layman. We must question what drives us in our search for human history and why many of us are thrilled when getting close to the artefacts. It is of value to investigate the sensory experience of history, since it can offer an extra dimension that cannot be attained through books or theories.

THE PARTICIPANTS

Twelve participants with various backgrounds and interests were signed up for the course. Focusing on the participants and their interests, questions and expectations from the course, everyone had the chance to introduce themselves to the rest of the group in our first meeting. There were nine women and three men, ranging in age from eighteen to sixty-five. The participants were both local and from cities or communities within a distance of about fifty kilometres from the museum. One family participated: mother, father, daughter and son, though the daughter attended only the first session, realising that the course was not for her. The family was planning to get their own sheep and wanted to learn how to use the wool. The daughter had no previous experience of handicrafts, the mother was a knitter, while the father and son were more inclined to engineering. The father and son later built their own electric spinning machine, and the family are now producers of 3D-printed spindles which they sell in their Etsy shop. Three women were a group of friends who signed up together. All three were experienced knitters and spinners and had taken a *nalbinding* course many years ago. They attended the course to freshen up their *nalbinding* skills. One young woman was a local resident in

4   David A. Kolb, *Experiential Learning: Experience as the Source of Learning and Development* (Englewood Cliffs, NJ: Prentice-Hall, 1984), pp. 21–38.

5   John Dewey, Sven Hartman and Ulf P. Lundgren, *Individ, skola och samhälle: pedagogiska texter*, trans. by Ros Mari Hartman, Sven Hartman and Alf Ahlberg, 4th edn (Stockholm: Natur och kultur, 2004).

6   Emily Robinson, 'Touching the void: affective history and the impossible', in *Rethinking History* 14.4 (2010), pp. 503–520; https://doi.org/10.1080/13642529.2010.515806, accessed 6 July 2022.

Lödöse, with her own sheep. She was an archaeologist and osteologist as well as a knitter and wanted to learn *nalbinding*. Another woman was a skilled *nalbinder* who had taken many courses in the past. She wanted to join because 'there is always more to learn'. She was also a weaver and active within the re-enactment and living history community, focusing on the Viking period. One man had no previous experience of textile crafts and wanted to learn out of an interest in history. Two more women were friends, one being a spinner and a knitter. The final one was a knitter.

Some of the aims and questions brought up by the participants during the introduction were:

- How to *nalbind*
- How to spin wool
- How old is *nalbinding*?
- What kinds of sheep were there?
- Have the techniques of spinning and *nalbinding* changed since the Middle Ages?

THE COURSE

Learning the Principles of Spinning and Nalbinding
Through the museum artefacts, we wanted the participants to understand the craft from a historical perspective. Furthermore, our aim was to enable the participants to use *nalbinding* as their own technique. When you discover the flow in the stitches and know the technique, you can choose different yarns and stitches for different purposes and constructions. We also wanted to lower the threshold by highlighting the simplicity of the crafts. To spin a thread, all you need is fibre and a rotating object to suspend and use as a weight. *Nalbinding* requires a needle and piece of yarn to work with. During the course we wanted to show the participants the medieval finds of textile-related tools, and also modern and traditional tools and methods for preparing wool, spinning and *nalbinding*. By discussing the development of methods and tools, we wanted to give participants an understanding of which to choose so as to get the desired result for a crafted object.

The following is a summary of the course content:

History
- Sheep breeds and wool types in history.
- The history of preparing and spinning wool.
- The history of *nalbinding*.
- The tools that were used in the past (and are still used).
- An overview of the history of medieval society, Lödöse museum and its artefacts.

Handicraft
- What to keep in mind when choosing the right wool for your purpose.
- How to prepare the wool and how to spin it on a spindle.

- How to *nalbind*.
- How to use plant dyes.
- How to decorate mittens, if required.

Time for reflection

Many handicraft courses are held as a workshop for a few hours, or maybe a day or two. We wanted 'From wool to mitten' to stretch over a longer period. That would give the participants a chance to obtain a wider picture of medieval society in which the practical skills they were learning would have been used, but also time to develop their own use and expression of the technique.

Session #1

Getting the Context

Our starting point on the first session was to go back in history and investigate what we know about wool, sheep breeds in history, *nalbinding* and the tools that were used. We also presented the history of Lödöse, introducing the museum's collection of medieval textiles and textile-related tools. We looked at medieval art, discussing the symbolism and meaning of spinning wool and producing fabrics during the Middle Ages, in relation to being a woman in medieval society. We also put this in relation to what the craft means to today's practitioners in Scandinavia. The driving forces of craftspeople then and now differ significantly. Most spinners and *nalbinders* in Scandinavia today do it for the joy of it, not out of necessity. There is research showing the positive impact that practising handicrafts can have for our mental health and relief of stress in today's society.[7] We imagine that spinning was not a way to unwind and recover in the Middle Ages! Of course, it is impossible for us to know what psychological effects carding, spinning and *nalbinding* had on a medieval person. However, we do know that they were necessary skills for many members of medieval society in order to clothe themselves and their families.[8]

---

[7]   Lyndsay W. Andersson and Christina U. Gustavson, 'The impact of a knitting intervention on compassion fatigue in oncology nurses', *Clinical Journal of Oncology Nursing*, 20.1 (2016), 102–104, doi:10.1188/16.cjon.102–104, accessed 6 July 2022; M. Clave-Brule, A. Mazloum, R.J. Park, E.J. Harbottle and C.L. Birmingham, 'Managing anxiety in eating disorders with knitting', *Eating and Weight Disorders – Studies on Anorexia, Bulimia and Obesity*, 14.1 (2009), e1–e5, doi: 10.1007/bf03354620, accessed 6 July 2022; Ann Dolling, Hanna Nilsson and Ylva Lundell, 'Stress recovery in forest or handicraft environments – an intervention study', *Urban Forestry & Urban Greening* 27 (2017), 162–172; https://doi.org/10.1016/j.ufug.2017.07.006, accessed 6 July 2022; Rosemary Kingston, 'Loose ends: unravelling the benefits of knitting', *Psychology Postgraduate Affairs Group Quarterly* 85 (2012), 18–20; Jill Riley, Betsan Corkhill and Clare Morris, 'The benefits of knitting for personal and social wellbeing in adulthood: findings from an international survey', *British Journal of Occupational Therapy* 76.2 (2013), 50–57; https://doi.org/10.4276/030802213X13603244419077, accessed 6 July 2022.

[8]   See Eva I. Andersson, *Kläderna och människan i medeltidens Sverige och Norge* (Gothenburg, Sweden: University of Gothenburg, 2006), p. 37.

Acknowledgement that we do not know everything was also an important part of the course and was brought up early in the first session. Even though there are over half a million finds in medieval Lödöse, it is still just a fraction of what was once there. Most items are lost and gone forever, and the information retrieved from the items that have survived differs through time. History is not something fixed in the past, but very much alive and dynamic, changing with society. It changes through new research and new analytical methods, depending on who is doing the research and the questions asked concerning the material. Some things we may never be able to answer, but it is still of value to explore those questions.

Even though the main focus on this course was to learn how to *nalbind*, those existential questions added a further dimension to the process.

Getting Practical

During the introduction we showed several examples of preparing wool and spinning in medieval art. Looking at medieval depictions gives us a good clue as to the methods that were used.[9] Wool carders occur in art, probably introduced to Europe in the thirteenth century and preceded by wool combs.[10] Both tools are used in a similar way, in pairs, but give different results in the prepared wool.[11] Medieval pictures also show that it was common to use hand-held spindles in combination with a distaff, which requires a different technique from spinning on a drop spindle without a distaff.[12] We discussed the different methods and tools used in the past, comparing them to what today's spinners use. For example, the use of wool combs and the distaff is recurrent in medieval pictures, but these were unknown to the spinning participants on the course, except for the woman active in Viking re-enactment and living history. The other spinners exclusively used modern drop spindles. On modern drop spindles, the rod and whorl (the weight attached to the spindle rod to allow rotation) are commonly fixed together as a single piece.[13] Thus, today's spinners often have several spindles for spinning different kinds of thread – lighter spindles for spinning thinner thread, and heavier spindles for thicker thread or for plying. Medieval spindles, however, consisted of a separate rod and whorl,

---

[9] For more information about interpreting wool preparation and spinning methods from medieval art, see Mary Ann Megan Cleaton, Alice Rose Evans, Jane Hunt and Cathelina di Alessandri, 'Recreating historic European spindle spinning', *EXARC Journal* 2021/2 (2021); https://exarc.net/issue-2021-2/at/recreating-historic-european-spindle-spinning, accessed 30 May 2022.

[10] See John H. Munro, 'Medieval woollens: textiles, textile technology and industrial organisation, *c.* 800–1500', in *The Cambridge History of Western Textiles*, ed. by David Jenkins (Cambridge and New York: Cambridge University Press, 2003), pp. 181–227 (198).

[11] For more information about using the different tools, see Munro, 'Medieval woollens', pp. 197–198.

[12] See Cleaton et al., 'Recreating historic European spindle spinning'.

[13] See Lise Warburg, *Spinnbok. En praktisk vägledning i handspinning* (Uddevalla: Bohusläningens Boktryckeri AB, 1974), p. 77.

Fig. 11.3 Spindles and whorls from Lödöse, Sweden. Dated between 1050–1350. Photograph: David Jeffrey.

offering more flexibility to the spindle (Fig. 11.3).[14] For example, if you want to spin a thin thread you would use a lighter whorl than if you were to spin a thicker thread. Choosing the right weight of whorl, you could use the same rod for spinning thread of different qualities. Also, the whorl could be exchanged or removed during the process. For example, you want a heavier whorl when you start spinning, but as more thread goes on the rod and adds weight, you might want to change the whorl to a lighter one or take it off, so as to obtain an evenly spun thread.[15] During the course we used modern drop spindles with fixed whorls, since it is easier to learn the spinning technique without using a distaff.

When concerned with passing on practical skills such as combing and carding wool, spinning and *nalbinding*, learning by doing is the recommended method. Theoretical knowledge, though, is also required, such as how to choose the right wool for your purpose. Before you start spinning you also need to know what kind of yarn you want to make, which depends on what you intend to use it for. If you were to spin a weaving yarn, you would want to add more twist to it than would be needed for a yarn intended for *nalbinding*. We had a wide range of wool from domestic sheep breeds that the participants could choose from. Some of the wool was washed but not combed or carded, but we also offered washed and carded wool. The participants were free to choose whether they wanted to do the whole process of preparing and spinning the wool for their mittens, or just try the elements and then use purchased yarn for their *nalbinding* project. Every participant tried all the elements, and six of them spun enough yarn to make at least one pair of mittens.

After demonstration of the basics of preparing the wool and spinning on the modern drop spindles, the participants began the practical process. We discussed the difference between the wool types provided, and what to keep in mind when choosing material and spinning the thread. The participants got started under our guidance during the session, to continue the process at home. After trying carding, combing and spinning, we shifted focus towards *nalbinding*. We had a joint introduction explaining the structure of *nalbinding* technique and terminology.[16] It is not easy to explain *nalbinding*, since there are thousands of variations of stitches, with no standardised terminology. Ulrike Claßen-Büttner explains in her book:

> These names [of the stitches] derive from places where archaeological finds were made, or where historical pieces are on display (e.g., Oslo stitch), from regions where special stitches are traditional (e.g., Dalby stitch), or from people who have published instructions (e.g., Brodén stitch).[17]

Several attempts have been made to standardise the terminology for the stitches, but still there is no consensus, neither among *nalbinders* nor textile researchers. However,

---

[14] For more information on how the spindles work etc., see Warburg, *Spinnbok*, p. 89.

[15] Cleaton et al., 'Recreating historic European spindle spinning'.

[16] See Claßen-Büttner, *Nalbinding*, pp. 9–18.

[17] Claßen-Büttner, *Nalbinding*, p. 12.

in 1990 Egon Hansen developed a notation for describing how the stitches are made.[18] This system, called Hansen's notation, is now widely used when describing how a stitch is made. As the system is not easy to understand for beginners, we did not use it in our teaching session. Instead, we used the most common names for the stitches taught: Oslo, Mammen and Brodén.[19] These three stitches are similar and provide a useful stepping-stone to learning more.

The group was split into two, with the beginners in one sub-group and the more experienced participants in the other. At the end of the session, we reconnected to the archaeological finds of *nalbound* items that we had introduced at the beginning of the session, and identified the items made in the same three stitches. For example, two medieval mittens, one from Arnheiðarstaðir, Iceland, and one from Lund, Sweden, were made in Oslo stitch.[20] Two woven textile fragments from medieval Mammen, Denmark, were connected by a *nalbound* insertion made in Mammen stitch.[21]

It became clear that time between sessions was important because it enabled the participants to process the information and new skills obtained. The participants took their craftwork home to continue working on it, and some of them came back to the next session with finished mittens and socks, and had already bought or made more yarn. They were eager to learn more stiches, and more about the wool and yarn.

Session #2

Feedback from Previous Session
When meeting for the second session, held in March, new thoughts and questions were raised. Participants brought their ongoing work and finished items, and reflections regarding the techniques, materials and methods were discussed. Some of the participants asked questions in relation to textile production in medieval Lödöse; for example, how much wool was imported and how much was domestically produced? The participants had also experienced the time required for the craft, although they understood that a medieval person worked much faster since they were introduced to the task as children. We got back to these reflections during the practical part of the session, developing our *nalbinding* skills.

Holding History
During this second session we wanted to get closer to history through the finds. The participants, under the supervision of museum staff, examined some of the artefacts in Lödöse Museum's store. Usually, due to the fragility of the finds, they cannot be touched. However, there are items in our collections that withstand being handled. The spindle whorl is one example. The whorls made of soapstone or ceramics suffer no damage from being held. In our collection we have a whorl made of amber, which

---

[18] Claßen-Büttner, *Nalbinding*, pp. 13–18.

[19] Claßen-Büttner, *Nalbinding*, pp. 64–69, 73–75, 79.

[20] Claßen-Büttner, *Nalbinding*, p. 44.

[21] Claßen-Büttner, *Nalbinding*, pp. 46–47.

benefits from being held (Fig. 11.4). Amber tends to turn brittle over time, so the grease from our hands actually contributes to its longevity. Being able to hold these items in one's hand was an important part of this course, since there is a tangible difference from just viewing them through a pane of glass. With the whorls we could examine the traces left on the inside of the hole from being put onto and taken off a spindle many times. Perhaps most importantly, the participants gained a sensory and emotional link that it is not often possible to offer. To actually feel the weight of the whorl and the material is an experience that is difficult to describe in words. In a way, this is as close as we can get to the people living back then – holding the same items as they did. It is like fingertips touching fingertips through time. This sensation is usually the privilege only of archaeologists, researchers and others working in the field.[22] It is rare that the public receive a close encounter like this with such objects. Therefore, this part of the course provided an extra dimension to the learning process, creating an emotional bond to the items and the handicraft.

The participants were allowed to hold some items while wearing gloves. This does not provide the same closeness and experience as holding an artefact in your hand, but it is the next best thing. A *nalbinding* needle made of bone was one such item (Fig. 11.5). The participants could study the needle up close and see that it looked no different from the modern bone needles provided on the course. The needle, being the simplest of tools, has had the same construction for thousands of years![23]

The participants were not allowed to hold the *nalbound* mitten or other medieval textiles as they are too fragile to be handled. However, it was still an exclusive opportunity to see items that are not usually on display. Extra attention was naturally paid to the *nalbound* mitten, which almost became the centrepiece of the course that everything else was connected to.

The Lödöse mitten (Fig. 11.2) is different from other *nalbound* archaeological finds as it is made of two different stitches. Other medieval mittens or socks that have been found are made using one type of stitch. One question discussed was why the mitten is made with two different stitches. Has it been mended? Was there a practical reason for the difference? Was it only design? We returned to those questions during the making process, when the participants had gained a little more experience of *nalbinding* and started to obtain a feeling for the craft. Other questions that arose throughout this process were 'Was it made top-down or the other way around?' 'Was it a child's mitten, or maybe a woman's?' 'Was it well used or almost new?'. The upper part of the Lödöse mitten is made using the Åsle stitch.[24] An unanswered question remained concerning which stitch the bottom part of the mitten is made of. This was a good example of gaps in our knowledge about the items and the past. There are still things to 'investigate and to discover'.

---

[22] Compare Robinson, 'Touching the void', pp. 503–520.

[23] Claßen-Büttner, *Nalbinding*, p. 28.

[24] Pihlajapiha, 'The Åsle stitch'.

Fig. 11.4 Spindle whorl made of amber from Lödöse, Sweden. Dated between the twelfth and the fourteenth century. Photograph: Liselotte Öhrling.

Fig. 11.5 *Nalbinding* needle from Lödöse. Dated to 1050–1350. Photograph: Liselotte Öhrling.

Moving on with Nalbinding

After our close encounter with the finds, we continued to develop our *nalbinding*. We learned more ways to start a project, more stitches and how to shape our mittens in different ways. Again, we worked in two groups, adapting to the different skills of the participants. For example, some of the participants had already figured out how to insert a thumb into their mittens, while others required guidance.

While working with our projects the participants constantly reconnected to the items just experienced, discussing the construction of the mitten and their fascination over the needles looking just the same, 1,000 years later. During the session it became clear that the experience of seeing the mitten up close and holding the whorls contributed to a 'special' feeling, not experienced by the participants before. Perceiving the effect on the participants, our theory was confirmed; something does happen when you are allowed to experience an artefact, and not just view it though a glass. Although we cannot explain what the effect is, we are convinced that getting close to the artefacts contributes to an embodied connection and understanding of history.

Session # 3 – Colouring and Decoration

The third session was held in May and coincided with a theme day at the museum. The theme was textile crafts in history. With a packed schedule, our session started with a guided tour of the museum exhibition and a wider introduction to medieval everyday life. Finds such as personal messages carved into pieces of wood, children's shoes, locks that once kept someone's valuables safe and other daily items that once were the belongings of someone real contributed to bringing the medieval citizens of Lödöse to life.

After the guided tour it was time for plant dyeing. Discussing what colourants were used in the Middle Ages and how it can be done today, the group used birch leaves, brazilwood,[25] beetroot and yellow onion peel for this session.

While the yarn got coloured, the group participated in the theme day, called *Hantverk och historia*, meaning 'Handicraft and history'. There were demonstrators from the living history society, dressed in medieval clothes. The participants had the chance to meet a re-enactor who stood by the open fire outside, plant-dyeing fabrics. She shared her experiences and knowledge about medieval plant dyeing. The plant used during the demonstration was madder, but she also showed already dyed yarns coloured with buckthorn, woad and walnut, amongst other things. The next stop was the weaving demonstration at the *opstadgogn*, which is a warp-weighted loom, followed by a wool-shearing session with wool shears, medieval style.

When back inside the museum, we sat down to look at how the mittens can be decorated. No decorated *nalbound* mittens from the Middle Ages have been found, but there was a tradition of decorating *nalbound* mittens in Scandinavia from the eighteenth and

---

[25] Brazilwood, a red dye obtained from the sappanwood tree, was imported from India and the Far East. First references to this dye date from the early fourteenth century; http://www.wildcolours.co.uk/html/brazilwood.html (accessed 28 October 2023).

Fig. 11.6 A pair of mittens made by one of the participants on the course. Photograph: Liselotte Öhrling.

nineteenth centuries.[26] This gave us a chance to connect through the centuries, combining historical *nalbinding* with more recent history and the participants' contemporary ways of expressing themselves (Fig. 11.6).

Session #4 – Reflection and Moving Forward
During this fourth and last session, in September, we gathered and finished our mittens. Unfortunately, not all participants were able to attend, due to various personal reasons.

We reflected on our experiences, and what we take with us into the future. Some of the participants had already made several items since the course started, experimenting with different stitches and decorations. Everyone had learned *nalbinding* (Fig. 11.7) and the techniques of preparing and spinning wool, and expressed that they had reached their aims of the course.

MOVING FORWARD WITH THE PAST

We must ask ourselves what is required for the next generation to continue the tradition of *nalbinding*. For the skill itself to survive, it is important for it to evolve. Like other traditions, it is those that develop along with society that stay relevant. According to the Swedish Institute of Language and Folklore, if a tradition is not perceived as important or relevant, or if it does not fulfil any function for those who practise it, it will simply be re-created, or cease altogether.[27] In medieval Scandinavia *nalbinding* was used for

[26] Elisabeth Jacks Svantesson, *Vinterblomster: nålbundna vantar från Dalby i Värmland* (Säffle: Algusta 2011).
[27] 'Vad är en tradition?', *Institutet för språk och folkminnen*; https://www.isof.se/lar-dig-mer/kunskapsbanker/lar-dig-mer-om-traditioner/vad-ar-en-tradition, accessed 30 May 2022.

Fig. 11.7 Anna Josefsson and Liselotte Öhrling, happy *nalbinders*. Photograph: Jessica Randén.

making mittens, hats and socks. When knitting was introduced, *nalbinding* lost out, due to the benefits of knitting, which was faster and offered more possibilities in terms of elasticity and shaping, as well as colour-work. The *nalbinding* tradition survived in a few remote areas of Sweden, Finland and Norway where women could earn a small income from *nalbinding* mittens for weddings and such during the eighteenth to twentieth centuries.[28] For *nalbinding* to survive, it is important for it to evolve, and it is doing just that, adapting and evolving in several ways. For example, amongst archaeologists and members of the living history movement, *nalbinding* has become a method used to understand how historical *nalbound* items were made: the technique has a purpose beyond making warm clothes – it is used in the research field. But that is not enough for the technique to survive in a wider sense. Traditions continuously adapt and evolve with society in order to survive; meaning that we should not pass *nalbinding* on as a historical skill only to be used to re-create historical finds. In addition, we need to encourage people to use the technique in their own way. As mentioned earlier, we have had *nalbinding* cafés at the museum. The concept of meeting for a coffee whilst doing a handicraft is common in Sweden, especially in the knitting community. The tradition has its origin in the eighteenth century, when women had *kafferep*, meaning 'coffee scratch':[29] upper-

[28] Svantesson, *Vinterblomster*.
[29] Eva Thelin, 'Raffel, lumptråd och räckgarn – att återanvända ylle', *Institutet för språk och folkminnen*; https://www.isof.se/lar-dig-mer/bloggar/dialektbloggen/inlagg/2022-03-02-raffel-lumptrad-och-rackgarn---att-ateranvanda-ylle, accessed 30 May 2022.

class women gathered to unravel pieces of silk for re-use as upholstery or new yarn. This later developed into *syjunta* during the early twentieth century.[30] Knitting cafés became a phenomenon during the late twentieth century, increasing in the early twenty-first century. When arranging the *nalbinding* cafés at Lödöse museum, our intention was to develop the tradition of knitting cafés and integrate *nalbinding* into the concept. This was also a way to attract people who might be intimidated or discouraged by a course format but were interested in learning the technique. Many Swedes are more comfortable with socialising in the relaxed, informal format of 'fika',[31] meaning having a coffee, rather than taking a course. Thus, the *nalbinding* cafés were a success in many ways, one being the wide range of people who came – from the re-enactor who was well-versed with the Middle Ages and *nalbinding*, to beginners and happy knitters who just wanted to learn a new craft for the joy of it. There must be room for everyone. A further development of 'From wool to mitten' might be to include *nalbinding* cafés in between sessions. This could provide a natural meeting point for those in need of support, but also an opportunity for *nalbinders* to come together. Having a course like 'From wool to mitten' run parallel to *nalbinding* cafés would contribute to reaching a wider audience, including those more comfortable with a more informal learning environment.

Moving forward is a natural development. Following fellow *nalbinders* on social media, one can see that it is common to make not only traditional items such as mittens or socks, but also wrist warmers, pouches for mobile phones and even jumpers. But it is important not to lose the historical connection. It is imperative for the public to have access to the archaeological finds. The combination of the items, the theoretical knowledge of medieval society and the practical skills increase the chances of *nalbinding* surviving.

QUESTIONS AND OBSERVATIONS

Our aim was to have a course in *nalbinding*, putting it into the context of medieval history and the museum collection. But we wanted to offer more than a *nalbinding* course. We wanted to offer an experience, a sensation of the craft and the past through the museum collection. Time between the sessions was important, since it enabled the participants to process the information and new skills obtained. The participants took their craftwork home to continue work in between sessions, some returning with completed items ready to learn more. New thoughts and questions were raised each time, and everything became linked. It was not 'just' *nalbinding* as a practical skill that was passed on. Together, we experienced the history that is integral to this craft and Lödöse. The participants also developed their own relationship to and expression of the technique. We created a wider view and a deeper relationship to the craft and the people that had been doing it before us, through the artefacts. While we were working on the practical

---

[30] 'Stickning', *Institutet för språk och folkminnen*; https://www.isof.se/lar-dig-mer/levande-traditioner/forslag/2021-03-09-stickning, accessed 30 May 2022.

[31] 'Fika', *Institutet för språk och folkminnen*; https://www.isof.se/other-languages/english/living-traditions/submissions/2016-01-26-fika, accessed 30 May 2022.

tasks, we also created our own vision of medieval society through discussions and conversations. These became more vibrant as the participants gained more practical experience. Through these new practical skills and the theory, participants reached a deeper understanding of wool, *nalbinding* and its use and practice. That in turn led to a higher awareness of material choice and technique for their own creating.

Working with wool today continues a long tradition. Modern research shows that handicrafts have a positive influence on our mental health and and for many modern practitioners are a way to unwind. When encountering the artefacts up close, something happened with the participants on the course. Although we cannot explain why, many of us feel a need and a thrill when getting close to history. Maybe that is part of the reason why some of us feel drawn to spinning thread and making new items that keep us warm – to feel connected to those who came before us, but also to leave something behind.

Glossary

band   1. A narrow textile with a weft used separately or as the decorative or functional border of a larger garment piece of cloth. 2. A stripe on cloth in the weft direction.

braid   A narrow textile without a weft made by a non-loom technique such as plaiting.

brocaded tablet weave   A tablet-woven band with a supplementary weft, usually of gold thread, added during the weaving process for decorative effect.

broken diamond twill   A diamond twill in which the diagonal lines are deliberately interrupted.

chevron twill   Any form of twill weave in which the direction of the diagonal lines is reversed over groups of *warp* or *weft* threads to make a chevron pattern.

diamond twill   A weave in which the direction of the diagonal lines is reversed over groups of warps, and also over groups of wefts, to produce a diamond pattern.

embroidery   Ornamental stitching on a ground fabric worked with a needle after the textile has been removed from the loom.

end   In weaving, an individual warp thread.

fibre   Any substance of animal or vegetable origin that can be spun into thread or used unspun in textile production.

flax   1. A plant of the family *Linaceae, genus Linum*, particularly *Linum usitatissimum*. 2. A bast fibre obtained from the stem of the flax plant, from which linen is most commonly made.

fleece   The unspun *wool* sheared from a sheep.

ground weave   The base textile to which decoration such as pile weave, brocading or embroidery is applied.

kemp   Short, hair-like *fibre* from the outer layer of a sheep's fleece.

linen   A cloth made from spun bast fibre, flax.

mantle   A large cloak.

GLOSSARY

nalbinding (also called *nålebinding*, looped needle netting, Coptic knitting) A Danish term for a technique using a needle and a length of yarn. The yarn is passed through at least two finished thread-loops, producing a series of loops working out from the starting point into a spiral.

pick In weaving, an individual weft thread.

pile weave A weave in which a pile or raised surface is produced above the ground weave by the introduction or insertion of extra short threads, sometimes knotted around the warp, or by pulling threads from the ground weave up into loops.

ply Two or more previously spun yarns twisted together, normally in the opposite direction to the original spinning. The direction of the ply is denoted by either a capital S for an anti-clockwise twist, or a capital Z for a clockwise twist.

shed In weaving, a space between the warp threads through which the weft passes.

sprang A textile-making technique that intertwines warp threads stretched on a frame.

s-spun / twist Yarn spun in an anti-clockwise direction, creating a twist in the shape of the letter S.

system In weaving, either the warp or the weft.

tabby (plain weave) A simple weave, in which each warp passes over one and under one weft.

tablet weave A method of non-loom weaving in which warp threads are threaded through holes in small tablets, usually square, which are turned to change the shed, producing thick, narrow bands.

twill A weave in which each weft passes over two or more adjacent warps and under the next one or more, or under two or more adjacent warps and over the next one or more. In each row this pattern moves to right or left by a regular number of warps. In 2 x 2 twill, the weft passes under two, over two warp threads; in 2 x 1 twill it passes under one, over two or under two, over one. Twill weave produces an effect of diagonal lines.

warp The fixed threads in weaving, which are kept under tension.

warp-chevron twill In weaving, a type of chevron twill where the diagonal patterns are reversed over groups of wefts

warp-weighted loom A vertical loom consisting of two uprights joined near the top by a cloth beam. The uprights are usually placed at an angle against a wall. The warp threads hang vertically and are tensioned by weights, made of clay or stone.

weft The movable threads in weaving, which are inserted during the weaving process into the shed between the warp threads.

wool   1. The fleece of the sheep and certain other animals. 2. Textile fibres from domesticated sheep.

yarn   A continuous strand, made from filaments of fibre, spun together.

z-spun / twist   Yarn spun in a clockwise direction, creating a twist in the shape of a letter Z.

Index

Aðalráðr (Æthelred II), king of the English, in
  Gunnlaugs saga ormstungu 122–123
Africa 2
Ålesund, Norway 62, 65
Alþingisreitur, Reykjavik, Iceland 57–59
America
  North 1, 181, 183
  South 8, 193, *see also* Peru
Andersson Strand, Eva 5, 101
Angers, France, cathedral, frieze 115, 117
Ann Arbor, MI, USA, Kelsey Museum of
  Archaeology 185
Anonymous texts
  Aislinge Meic Conglinne (*The Vision of
    MacConglinne*) 129
  Annals of Inisfallen 129
  Atlakviða 118–119
  Bárðar Saga [*Bárðarsaga
    Snæfellsáss*] 103
  Eyrbyggja Saga 99
  Gísla saga súrssonar 111, 117
  Gunnlaugs saga ormstungu 111, 121
  Historia Norwegiae 104
  Íslendingasögur 7, 109–125
  Laxdæla Saga 99, 111, 114–115, 124
  Lebhor na Cert 128
  Martyrology of Donegal 142
  Nibelungenlied 100
  Poetic Edda 118
  The Destruction of Da Derga's Hostel 128
  the *Táin* 128
  Volsunga Saga 100
Antwerp, Belgium, Textiles of the Nile Valley
  conference 183, 187
Aristotle, Ancient Greek philosopher,
  4th-century BC 91
Armagh, Northern Ireland 67
Árnadóttir, Lilja 51n.1
Arneborg, Jette 51n.1, 148n.7
Arnheiðarstaðir, Iceland 208

Asia 16
Asia Minor, now Turkey 70
Åsle, Sweden, mitten 161n.17, 163
  Åsle stitch 199, 209
Asplund, Ann xii, 7–8
Augsburg, Germany, Staatsgalerie,
    Hans Holbein *San Paolo fuori le
    mura* 190n.24
Austria 62, *see also* Hallstatt, Nikolsdorf

Balchin, Rachel xii, 7
Ballinderry crannóg, Co. Westmeath,
    Ireland 76
Baltic Sea region 1, 16, 62, 79
Barthes, Roland 110, 113–115
Bath, Somerset, England, Holbourne
    Museum 152n.21
Bayeux, France, Bayeux Tapestry 110
Belgium 72, *see also* Antwerp, Bruges,
    Brussels
Bellegambe, Jean, *Crucifixion
    Triptych* 190n.24
Bender Jørgensen, Lise 5, 76, 95
Berach, St, monastery and church of 142
Bergen, Norway 29, 62, 65, 68–69
    Bergen University 62
    see also Bryggen
Bernuthsfeld, Germany, tunic 173
Bessastaðir, Iceland 57, 59
Bielenberg, Alsiosha 51n.1
Birka, Sweden 3, 8, 71, 75, 82–83, 103–104,
    165, 167–168
Bjerringhøj, Mammen, Jutland, Denmark 5,
    75, 80, 83, 86, 149
Blount, Charles, Baron Mountjoy 127
Blue-faced Leicester, sheep breed 154
Bocksten, Sweden, bog burial, probably
    14th-century 173
Bohusläns, Sweden, Bohusläns Museum (in
    Uddevalla) 48n.61

220 INDEX

Bolender, Doug 51n.1
Bolli Bollason in *Laxdœla Saga* 99
Bolli Þorleiksson in *Laxdœla saga* 115n.30–116
Boolabaun, Tipperary, Ireland 59
Borgund, Alesund, Norway 51n.1, 54, 62–69, 71–73
Boston, MA, USA, Harvard Medical School 195n.31
Bradford, West Yorkshire, England, spinning mill 154
Braithwaite, Naomi 96
Brede, Denmark, store and outdoor section of National Museum of Denmark 148
Breniquet, Catherine 70
Brigid, St, mantle of *see* Bruges
Bringetofta, Småland, Sweden, foetal burial 49
Bristol, England 79, 132
British Isles, Festival of Britain 1951 148, 152
Brittany, France 135
Bruges, Belgium
  cathedral of St Donaas [Donatius] 136–137
  cathedral of St Sauveur, mantle of St Brigid 134–139, 143
Brussels, Belgium, Royal Museum, Department of Textiles 137–138
Bryggen, Bergen, Norway 3
  Bryggen Museum 51n.1, 65, 72
Byzantine Empire 1
Byzantium (now Istanbul, Turkey) 1, 99

Calberg, Marguerite, textile specialist 137–139, 143
Cambrensis, Giraldus/Gerald of Wales/ Gerald de Barri *Topographia Hibernia* 129
Canada *see* Saskatchewan, Vancouver, Winnipeg
Carpaccio, Vittore, *Miracle of the Cross at the Ponte di Rialto/The Healing of the Madman* 191n.27
Cecil, Sir Robert 126
Chartres, France, cathedral, frieze 115, 117
Cherblanc, Emile 70
Chester, England 79
  Chester University, *Archaeology Theoretical Group (TAG)* conference 94
Chichester, England, Weald and Downland Living Museum 159
China 2

Christiansen, Carol xii, 6
CIETA *see* Lyon
Clark, David 118–119
Clark, Louise 182
Cloonshannagh, Co. Roscommon, Ireland, mantle 141–142
Cnip/Kneep, Isle of Lewis, Scotland 80
Cogitosus Uí Aido, *Vita Brigitae* 135
Collingwood, Peter, *The Techniques of Sprang: Plaiting on Stretched Threads* 5n.20, 179, 181–182
Conchobor, king of Ulster in the *Táin* 128–129
Coogan, Alan 51n.1
Copenhagen, Denmark
  Centre for Textile Research at the Saxo Institute 75
  National Museum of Denmark 5, 75, 102, 148
  University of Copenhagen 5
Coppergate *see* York
Corbeil-Essonne, France, Nôtre-Dame de Corbeil, cathedral, frieze 115, 117
Crowfoot, Grace M., archaeological textile specialist 149
Cumbria, England 75, *see also* St Bee's Priory

D'Ettore, Kate 99
Davidson, Hilary 96
de Heere, Lucas, *Irish as they stand accoutred* 130
Deer Park Farms, Co. Antrim, Northern Ireland 143
Delong, Marilyn 93
Demant Hatt, Emilie 103
Denmark 1, 127, 135, *see also* Bjerringhøj, Brede, Copenhagen, Faroe Islands, Hammerum, Herning, Huldremose, Hvilehøj, Lejre, Roskilde
Derricke, John, *The Image of Irelande, with a Discoverie of Woodcarne* 130, 133, 144
Diarmait Mac Máel na Mbó, King of the Uí Cheinselaig, Leinster, Ireland 136
Dineley, Thomas, traveller 143
Dnieper, river 90
Dresden, Germany, Gemäldegalerie, Lucas Cranach, *The Martyrdom of St. Katharine* 190n.24
Drinkler, Dagmar 190, 194
Dublin, Ireland 3, 7, 67, 70–71, 74–90, 127–129, 139–140, 144
  Finglas 75–76

INDEX

Fishamble Street   75
High Street   87
Kilmainham   84
National Museum of Ireland   74n.1, 75
Trinity College Library, MS A. I. [58] (*Codex Cennanensis, Book of Kells*)   83
Wood Quay   90, 140
Dürer, Albrecht, *Drawing of Irish Soldiers*   130

Edinburgh, Scotland, National Museum of Scotland   182
University of Edinburgh *First Millennia Studies Group*   94n.10
Edith, queen of Edward the Confessor of England   136
Egypt   69
Coptic culture   8, 70, 181, 184–188, 198
'Coptic stitch'   162
'Coptic knitting'   217
Eigg, Isle of, Scotland   71, 78
England   1, 8, 47, 62, 74, 79, 85, 96, 98, 121, 126, 130, 135–136
Area Museum Service Textile Conservation Laboratory   60
English laws   129
see also Bath, Bristol, Chester, Chichester, Cumbria, Farnham, Halifax, Hastings, Ingleby, Must Farm, Redhill, Leicester, Lincoln, London, Quernmore, Reigate, St Bee's Priory, Staffordshire, Tamar valley, Tamworth Castle, York
Étaín in *The Destruction of Dá Derga's Hostel*   128
Etsy, online shopping community   202
Eudoxus in Spenser's *A View of the Present State of Ireland*   133–134
EXARC, Experimental Archaeology and cultural heritage network (The Netherlands)   176

Farnham, Surrey, England, University for the Creative Arts, Crafts Study Centre   152
Faroe Islands, Denmark, Faroese culture   1, 15–17, 19, 21, 26, 28–29, 62, 67, 69
Finland   1–2, 213
Flanders   136
Flavin, Susan   132
Florence, Italy, Bargello Museum   70
Fortney, Sharon M.   108
France   62, 72, *see also* Angers, Bayeux, Brittany, Chartres, Corbeil-Essonne, Lyon, Paris, Vaudreuil

Frankfort, KY, USA, 'Days of Knights'   175
Frei, Karin   64
Fristad, Rogaland, Norway   75

Gabra-Sanders, Thea   6n.22
Gällared, Halland, Sweden, foetal burial   48–49
Galliker, Julia   197
Garðar, Iceland   57, 59
Garðarsdóttir, Vala   51n.1
Gården under Sandet (GUS), 'The Farm beneath the Sand', Greenland   58, 61
Geijer, Agnes, textile specialist   3, 103
Gelsinger, Bruce   53, 62–63, 68
Germany   62, *see also* Augsburg, Bernuthsfeld, Dresden, Hedeby, Krefeld, Leipzig, Munich
Gilbert, Ruth   xii, 7
Gísladóttir, Guðrún Alda   51n.1
Gísli Súrsson in *Gísla saga súrssonar*   117–119, 124
Gnëzdovo, Russia   90
Godwine, earl of Wessex   136
Gortmahonoge, Co. Tipperary, Ireland   59
Gothenburg, Sweden   199
University of Gothenburg   48
Granger-Taylor, Hero   149n.10
Greece   70, 72, 181
Greenland   1, 6–7, 17, 19, 27, 53, 57–58, 61, 67, 140, 148
Greenland National Museum and Archives, Nuuk, Greenland   51n.1, 148
see also Gården under Sandet, Herjólfsnes, Narsaq, Narsarssuaq
Guckelsberger, Marianne   101
Guðjónsson, Else E., textile specialist   6, 53–54, 56, 57n.24, 61, 68–69, 70, 72
Guðmundsson, Ármann   51n.1
Guðmundsson, Valtýr   114
Guðrun Ósvifrsdóttir in *Laxdæla Saga*   99, 114–117
Gunnar in *Atlakviða*   118
Gunnhild, sister of King Harold II of England and Edith, queen of England   136–137
Gunnlaugr in *Gunnlaugs saga ormstungu*   121–123

Hägg, Inga   83
Hald, Margrethe, textile specialist   149
Halifax, West Yorkshire, England, Museum   156

INDEX

Halland, Sweden, Kulturmiljö Halland
(Halland Museum of Cultural
History) 48
Hallstatt, Austria, period 95
    salt mines 33n.10
Hamilakis, Yannis 93
Hammarlund, Lena 36
Hammerum, Denmark 148
Hansen, Egon, weaver 208
Hansen, Gitte 51n.1, 62
Harðangr, Norway 51
Harald 'Greycloak'/Haraldr 'gráfeldr', king of
Norway 51–53, 66, 73
Harold II, Godwinesson, king of the
English 136
Harris, Susanna 91n.1, 92–95
Harrison, Ramona 51n.1
Harvey, Paula 77n.20
Hastings, England, Battle of 136, 159
Hawkes, Jacquetta, archaeologist 148, 152
Hayeur Smith, Michèle xii, 4, 6, 127
Hebrides, Scotland 99, 127
    Hebridean sheep breed 154
Hedeby, formerly Denmark now Schleswig-
Holstein, Germany 75, 80, 83
Helga in Gunnlaugs saga ormstungu 121–123
Helle, Knut 62, 68–69
Henry II, king of England 129
Henshall, Audrey, textile specialist 149, 182
Herbert, William 130
Heritage Crafts, formerly Heritage Crafts
Association, United Kingdom
charity 156
Herjólfsnes, Greenland 101
Herning, Denmark, Midtjylland
Museum 149
Heuzey, Léon 70
Heynes, Iceland 54, 57–59, 71
Hjalli in Atlakviða 118–119
Högni in Atlakviða 118
Hólar, Iceland, bishopric 72
Höllviken, Skåne, Sweden, Foteviken Viking
Museum 158
Hǫrðaland, Norway 51
Hrafn in Gunnlaugs saga ormstungu 122–123
Hrefna in Laxdæla saga 116
Huldremose, Denmark 102
Hungary, Hungarian cloth 138, 144
Hvammur, Iceland 57, 59
Hvilehøj, Jutland, Denmark 5, 79, 83
Hyer, Maren Clegg 112

Iberian Peninsula 2
Iceland 1–2, 6–7, 16–17, 19, 29, 51–63, 65–69,
71, 73, 99, 101, 109, 116–117, 119, 121–122,
127, 140
    Icelandic Law Codes 53, 55n.17, 56, 140
    National Museum of Iceland,
Reykjavik 51n.1, 57n.24
    see also Alþingisreitur, Arnheiðarstaðir,
Bessastaðir, Garðar, Heynes,
Hólar, Hvammur, Ketilsstaðir,
Meðalheimur, Reykjavik, Skálholt,
Stóraborg, Þingeyrar
Ingibjörg in Laxdæla saga 116
Ingleby, Derbyshire, England 103
Ingstad, Anne Stine 34
Ireland (Eire) 1–2, 7, 16–17, 57, 64, 66–67,
70–73, 79, 87, 97, 121, 126–144
    Irish Laws 74n.5, 127, 129
    Statute of Drogheda (Poynings Law) 129
    see also Ballinderry, Boolabaun,
Cloonshannagh, Dublin, Finglas,
Gortmahonoge, Leinster, Liffey,
Munster, Waterford
Irenius in Spenser's A View of the Present State
of Ireland 133–134
Irish Sea 74
Italy 8, 135, 190, see also Venice

James VI, king of Scotland 23
James, Carol xiii, 8
Jenkins, Ian 181
Jense, Nicolina 6n.22
Jóhannesson, Jón 53
John Lewis, British department store
chain 150
Jones, Ann Rosalind 120
Jönköping, Sweden, Jönköping County
Museum 49
Josefsson, Anna xiii, 8, 200

Kapp Wijk, Svalbard, Norway 46–47
Kaupang, Norway 51n.1, 62–66, 165
Kearney, Dolores xiii, 7
Kellog, Robert 111
Ketilsstaðir, Iceland 2–3, 100
Kjartan in Laxdæla saga 116
Kola Peninsula, Russia 102
Korea 151
Krefeld, Germany, German Textile
Museum 184, 198
Kwaspen, Anne 184, 187

INDEX

Lally, Martin, weaver 139
Lancaster, OH, USA, 'Days of Knights' 175
Långön Island, Ångermanland, Sweden 104
Legrain, Leon 70
Leicester, England, Leicester Museums
    store 152
    Jewry Wall museum 152
Leinster, Ireland 136
Leipzig, Germany, Gemälldegalerie,
    Jean Bellegambe, Crucifixion
    Triptych 190n.24
Lejre, Denmark, Land of Legends Centre for
    Historical–Archaeological Research
    and Communication 75
    weaving workshop 148, 151, 156
Leofwine Godwinesson, earl 136
Lester-Makin, Alexandra xiii, 7
Liffey, river 75
Lincoln, England 85
Linscheid, Petra 184
Lödöse, Sweden 199–200, 202, 204–205,
    208, 211, 214
    mitten 8, 199–200, 209
    Museum 8, 199–200, 203–204, 208, 214
London, England 122, 129
    British Museum 185
    Fuller Brooch 97
    Petrie Museum of Egyptian
      Archaeology 184
    Victoria and Albert Museum 198
Longfield, Ada 132
Lucas, Anthony 72, 139
Lucas, Gavin 51n.1
Lund, Julie 4–5
Lund, Sweden 71, 208
Lyon, France
    CIETA/Centre International d'Etude des
      Textiles Anciens 197
    Musée d'Art Industriel 70
    Musée national des arts asiatiques-
      Guimet, now part of the Musée
      des Confluences 185

MacConglinne in *Aislinge Meic
Conglinne* 129
Madsen, Christian Koch 51n.1
Magnus III 'Barelegs', king of Norway 90
Mairet, Ethel, weaver 149n.10
Mallick, Soumen 51n.1
Maltin, Emma 48n.61
Mammen stitch 208
    for Mammen *see* Bjerringhøj

Man, Isle of, British Crown Dependency 71, 78
Mannering, Ulla 5, 83
McClintock, Henry Foster 137–139, 143–144
Médard, Fabienne 197
Mediterranean Sea region 2, 69–70, 72
Meðalheimur, Iceland 59
Meyer, David 181
Miami, Florida, USA, Isobar
    Laboratories 64
Midabaria, St, abbess 142
Moorhead, MN, USA, Hjemkomst
    Museum 174
Moriuth, fictional Irish poet, 11th-century 76
Moryson, Fynes 127, 140
Mundal, Else 105
Munich, Germany
    Bavarian National Museum (Bayerisches
      Nationalmuseum), textiles 190
    Tilman Riemenschneider *The Beheading
      of St John on the Gerolzhofen
      Altar* 190 n.24
Munster, Ireland 130
Must Farm, Whittlesey, Cambridgeshire,
    England 151

Narsaq, Greenland 58, 61
Narsarssuaq, Greenland 61
National Association of Re-enactment
    Societies/NAReS (UK) 160
Navaho, Native American people,
    weavers 193
Nidaros [Trondheim], Norway 67
    Bishop of 67
Nikolsdorf, Austria 182
Nordic Research Group for Foetal Loss in the
    Past 47n.61
Nordstrand, Charlotta Hanner 48n.61
Norfolk Horn, sheep breed 154
Nørgaard/Nørgård, Anna 102
Northern Ireland *see* Armagh, Deer Park
    Farms
Norway 1–3, 6–8, 19, 21, 24, 52, 55n.17, 62–69,
    72–73, 74, 85, 121, 135, 213
    Research Council of Norway 34n.17
    see also Anonymous *Historia Norwegiae*,
      Bergen, Borgund, Bryggen,
      Fristad, Hǫrðaland, Kapp Wijk,
      Kaupang, Nidaros, Oseberg,
      Oslofjord, Østeroy, Rogaland,
      Russekeila, Sande, Stiklestad,
      Svalbard, Tromsø, Trondheim,
      West Spitsbergen

Nutz, Beatrix   182

O'Donoghue, Heather   118–119
O'Neale, Turlough Lynagh, *Uí
      Néill*   131–132
O'Rourke, Dáire   77n.20
Offa, king of Mercia   149–150
Öhrling, Liselotte   xiii, 8, 200
Öhrman, Magdalena   95–96
Olaf Haraldsson, St, king of Norway   105
Olaf Hoskuldsson, 'the Peacock', in
      Laxdæla Saga and other Icelandic
      sagas   99n.31
Óláfr Skötkonung, Swedish king in *Gunnlaugs
      saga ormstungu*   122
Oláfsson, Guðmundur   51n.1
Old Icelandic/Old Norse language   1, 7, 9,
      26, 54–56, 98, 107, 110, 112–115, 118–119,
      123–125
Orkney, Scotland, formerly Norway   62, 121
      Orkney sheep   16, 21, 24, 28
      see also Scar
Oseberg, Norway, ship burial   34, 42, 110,
      165, 172, 182
Oslo, Norway, Viking Ship Museum   182
      Oslo stitch   207–208
Oslofjord, Norway   1
Østergård, Else   6, 148
Østeroy, Norway, Østeroy Museum   63
Outram, Alan K.   182
Owen-Crocker, Gale R.   xiii, 91n.1, 96, 112

Paisley, Scotland, museum   156
Paris, France, Musée du Louvre   70
Park, Juyeon   93
Peacock, Elizabeth E.   xiv, 6, 48n.61
Peacock, Elizabeth (1880–1969) textile
      designer, Festival of Britain, 'People
      of Britain'   148–149, 152
Pederson, Katherine Vestergaard   101
Persia   70
Peru   181
Plimoth Plantation, Plymouth, MA, USA   8
Pliny the Younger, Gaius Plinius Caecilius
      Secundus, Roman writer, 1st-century
      AD   72
Poland   62, *see also* Wolin
Polanyi, Michael, philosopher   170
Pomor people, hunters and fishermen of
      White Sea coast of Russia, 16th- to
      18th-century   42, 46

Preucel, Robert   51n.1
Price, Doug   66–67
Price, Neil   104
Pritchard, Frances   xiv, 7, 70–71, 140
Providence, Rhode Island, USA, Brown
      University   64
      Department of Earth and Environmental
         Planetary Sciences
         (DEEPS)   51n.1
      Department of Geochemistry
      Haffenreffer Museum of
         Anthropology   51n.1

Quernmore, Lancaster, England, log coffin
      burial   47

Ravenna, Italy, statue of St John the
      Baptist   70
Regia Anglorum (UK)   160
Reigate and Redhill School of Art, Surrey,
      England (1895–2003)   152
Rikhardsdottir, Sif   110, 115n.30, 121
Roberts, Howell Magnus   51n.1
Roberts, Morfudd   152n.21
Rogaland, Norway   51
Rome, Italy   72, 181
Roskilde, Denmark, Viking Ship
      Museum   151
Runesson, Anton   48n.61
Russekeila, Svalbard, Norway   42, 46–47
Russia   1, 16, *see also* Gnëzdovo, Kola
      Peninsula
Ryder, Michael   77

Saal, Alberto   51n.1
Sámi, nomadic people   2, 6–7, 92, 102–106
Sande farm, Norway   100, 104, 107
Saskatchewan river, Canada   181
Sauckel, Anita   109, 112
Saxo Grammaticus, Danish historian, 12th- to
      13th-century   84
Scandinavia   1–2, 16, 54, 69, 73, 76, 92, 95, 102,
      147n.1, 162, 181, 204, 211–212, *see also*
      Denmark, Norway, Sweden
Scar, Sanday, Orkney, Scotland, ship
      burial   3, 106
Scotland   3, 19, 23, 64, 74, 135
      Privy Council of Scotland   24
      see also Cnip/Kneep, Edinburgh, Eigg,
         Hebrides, Holyrood, Orkney,
         Scar, Shetland, Paisley, Unst

INDEX

Sepp, Kata   98–99, 103n.51
Shetland, Scotland   8, 16, 23, 26, 29, 62–63
  Shetland sheep   14, 16, 21, 22–24, 27–28
  Norn language   22
  see also Unst
Sidney, Sir Henry   131
Siftinga Sunnemøre Museum, Norway   51n.1
Sigtryggr Silkbeard, Hiberno – Norse king of
  Dublin   90
Sindbæk, Søren M.   4–5
Skálholt, Iceland, bishopric   58, 72
Slav region   83
Smith, Kevin P.   51n.1
Smith, Thomas R.   181
Snæsdóttir, Mjöll   51n.1
Snorri Sturluson, *Heimskringla*   52
Soay, sheep breed   16, 143
Society for Creative Anachronism/SCA   160
Speed, John, cartographer   133
Spenser, Edmund, *A View of the Present State
  of Ireland*   133
St Bee's Priory, Cumbria, England, lead coffin
  burial   47
Staffordshire, England, Hoard   149
Stallybrass, Peter   110, 119–120
Stanes, Elyse   96–97
Steiman, Charles   51n.1
Stickgold, Robert   195n.31, 196
Stiklestad, Norway, battle of   105
Stockholm, Sweden, Historiska
  Museet   174n.57
  University   48n.61
Stóraborg, Iceland   57–58
Straubhaar, Sandra Baliff   98, 113–115, 123
Sumeria, Mesopotamia, now Iraq, Sumerian
  culture   69–70
Sutton Hoo, Suffolk, England, ship
  burial   149–150
Svalbard, Norway   47, *see also* Russekeila
Sveinbjarnardóttir, Guðrún   51n.1
Sveinsson, Einar Ólafur   114
Svensson, Tom   102
Sweden   1–2, 85, 121, 135, 171, 199–200, 213, *see
  also* Åsle, Birka, Bocksten, Bohusläns,
  Bringetofta, Gällared, Gothenburg,
  Halland, Hammerum, Höllviken,
  Jönköping, Långön Island, Lödöse,
  Lund, Stockholm, Vivallen

Tamar valley, Cornwall, England,
  museum   156

Tamworth Castle, Staffordshire,
  England   149
Tegnhed, Stina   48n.62
Tetris, puzzle video game   195n.31
Þingeyrar, Iceland   58–59
Thor, Norse god   76
Þórðr in *Gísla saga súrssonar*   117, 119
Þórgrím in *Gísla saga súrssonar*   119
Þórgunna in *Eyrbyggja Saga*   99
Þórir Hundr in *Heimskringla*   105
Þorkell in *Gunnlaugs saga ormstungu*   123
Þorkell Skinnvefja in *Bárðar Saga
  Snæfellsáss*   103
Thursfield, Sarah   149
Tintern Abbey, Wales   67
Tolley, Clive   104
Tromsø, Norway, Museum   43n.46
Trondheim, Norway (formerly Nidaros)   54, 62
  Folkebibliotek (Public Library) site   55,
    67–68
  NTNU University Museum   51n.1
Tucson, AZ, Arizona State Museum, Arizona
  Openwork Cotton Shirt   193

United States of America (USA)   159, 175
  National Science Foundation   51n.1,
    56n.22
  see also Ann Arbor, Boston, Frankfort,
    Kentucky, Lancaster, Miami,
    Moorhead, Plimoth Plantation,
    Providence, Tucson
Unst, Shetland, Scotland   182

Vancouver, Canada, Simon Fraser University,
  IONA Islands of the North Atlantic
  conference   xv, 94n.10, 175
Vaudreuil, near Rouen, France   76
Venice, Italy, Gallerie dell'Accademia, Vittore
  Carpaccio, *Miracle of the Cross at the
  Ponte di Rialto/The Healing of the
  Madman*   191
Vinterverkstan, Swedish handicraft
  supplier   200
Vivallen, Ångermanland, Sweden   104

Wallace, Patrick F.   74n1, 75
  Viking Dublin   140
Wallop, Sir Henry   126–127
Walton [Rogers], Penelope   74n.1
  *Textiles, Cordage and Raw Fibre from
    16–22 Coppergate*   3, 150, 156

Waterford, Ireland 67
  'Waterford ruggs' 131, 133, 138
West Spitsbergen, Norway 46n.58
Wild, John Peter 35n.20
Williams, Dyfri 181
Wincott Heckett, Elizabeth 71–73, 141–142
Winnipeg, Canada 183
Wolin, Poland 71
Wu, Juanjuan 93

York, England 3, 85, 147, 163
  Coppergate, sock 8, 86
  Mickelgate Bar 181
  textiles 3, 78, 85, 150, 153, 163–165, 173, 177
  University 159n.9
  Viking festival 153
  York stitch 163

Zeigler, John 133, 144

MEDIEVAL AND RENAISSANCE CLOTHING AND TEXTILES

Previous volumes in this series:

I

The Troyes Mémoire: The Making of a Medieval Tapestry
Translated by Tina Kane

II

Medieval Dress and Textiles in Britain: A Multilingual Sourcebook
Edited by Louise M. Sylvester, Mark C. Chambers and Gale R. Owen-Crocker

III

Dressing the Scottish Court, 1543–1553:
Clothing in the Accounts of the Lord High Treasurer of Scotland
Melanie Schuessler Bond

IV

Refashioning Medieval and Early Modern Dress:
A Tribute to Robin Netherton
Edited by Gale R. Owen-Crocker and Maren Clegg Hyer

V

Textiles of Medieval Iberia: Cloth and Clothing in a Multi-Cultural Context
*Edited by Gale R. Owen-Crocker with María Barrigón,
Naḥum Ben-Yehuda and Joana Sequeira*

VI

The Dutch Hatmakers of Late Medieval and Tudor London:
with an edition of their bilingual Guild Ordinances
Shannon McSheffrey and Ad Putter